RISK *and* DECISION ANALYSIS

in Projects

Second Edition

RISK *and* DECISION ANALYSIS

in Projects

Second Edition

John Schuyler

PROJECT MANAGEMENT INSTITUTE

Library of Congress Cataloging-in-Publication Data

Schuyler, John R., 1950–
    Risk and decision analysis in projects / by John Schuyler.--2nd ed.
       p.   cm.
    Includes bibliographical references and index.
    ISBN 1-880410-28-1
    1. Decision making.   2. Uncertainty.   3. Risk management.   I. Title.

   HD30.23 .S545 2001
   658.4'03--dc21   2001019196
                                                 CIP

ISBN: 978-1-88041-028-8

Published by: Project Management Institute, Inc.
                             14 Campus Boulevard
                             Newtown Square, Pennsylvania 19073-3299 USA
                             Phone: 1-610-356-4600
                             Fax: 1-610-356-4647
                             E-mail customercare@pmi.org
                             Internet: www.PMI.org/Marketplace

PMI Publications welcomes corrections and comments on its books. Please feel free to send comments on typographical, formatting, or other errors. Simply make a copy of the relevant page of the book, mark the error, and send it to: Book Editor, PMI Publications, 14 Campus Boulevard, Newtown Square, PA 19073-3299 USA.

To inquire about discounts for resale or educational purposes, please contact the PMI Book Service Center.
PMI Book Service Center
P.O. Box 932683, Atlanta, GA 31193-2683 USA
Phone: 1-866-276-4764 (within the U. S. or Canada) or +1-770-280-4129 (globally)
Fax: +1-770-280-4113
E-mail: book.orders@pmi.org

The paper used in this book complies with the Permanent Paper Standard issued by the National Information Standards Organization (Z39.48—1984).

10   9

CONTENTS

This book uses EV to abbreviate expected value, the central concept in decision analysis. We hope this does not cause undue confusion with the earned value concept in project management.

LIST OF FIGURES

LIST OF TABLES

PREFACE

Is there anything more important to the success of a project than *making good decisions*? This management skill is certainly near the top of the list, yet few of us have had formal training in decision making. **Decision analysis** is a discipline that helps people choose wisely under conditions of uncertainty. This book introduces risk and decision analysis, with special attention to the decisions in project management.

We are seeing increasing interest in probabilistic techniques for all types of evaluations. Shorter business cycles and ever-greater competition are pressuring organizations for better resource management. Furthermore, every day each of us deals with—or at least worries about—risk. Fortunately, we are learning more about value creation and how to work with uncertainty. Recent evaluation and project management software provides help in assessing and managing threats and opportunities.

Project management and, especially, project risk management, are receiving great attention these days. Project owners are becoming more demanding of performance and less tolerant of surprises. Opportunities often accompany risk, and a value engineering-like approach can often deliver additional value.

The Project Management Institute (PMI®) realized "explosive growth" of about 350 percent during 1995–2000. As this edition was being written, PMI released *A Guide to the Project Management Body of Knowledge (PMBOK® Guide) – 2000 Edition*. The *Guide*'s Chapter 11, Project Risk Management, is the most changed.

PMI has available another risk management book: *Project and Program Risk Management: A Guide to Managing Project Risks and Opportunities*, edited by R. Max Wideman. His popular book provides a different, more managerial perspective from this book about the craft of project management and risks. I believe that the two books nicely complement each another.

Organization

We divided the book into three sections:

PART I—INTRODUCTION TO RISK AND DECISION ANALYSIS

This first half of the book introduces decision analysis, and discusses how it applies to project risk management. Chapter 2 outlines a general problem-solving process, and Chapter 8 describes project risk management.

PART II—MODELING AND INPUTS

Here we provide more details about project modeling, and discuss using probability distributions for uncertain inputs.

PART III—SPECIAL TOPICS

We finish by discussing some emerging techniques. These topics include critical chain project management, optimization, and expert systems. Chapter 16 is a brief tutorial about probability rules.

At the end of the book, we have appendices about decision analysis software and a table of methods for dealing with uncertainty. We hope you will find the Glossary and Index useful.

Acknowledgments

This book collects a series of eighteen articles from *PM Network*, PMI's professional monthly magazine. In mid-1992, I was invited to contribute an installment to a series on risk analysis edited by Richard "Dick" Westney, who initiated the idea. The one article gave way to three installments, which eventually led to the series. The first twelve articles appeared in the first month of every quarter, and the last six articles appeared in odd-numbered months during 2000.

I have been assisted by many people at PMI. Dr. Francis M. Webster, editor-in-chief (1987–1994) guided the first eight installments. Fran kept me focused on project management when I would occasionally revert to my roots, project evaluation. His passion for the project management discipline and his depth of knowledge made each piece robust and lucid.

James Pennypacker was PMI Publications' publisher fall 1994–1998. Jim skillfully oversaw installments nine through twelve, as well as the manuscript for this book, in 1996.

Sandy Jenkins, PMI Publishing's managing editor, encouraged and shepherded the *PM Network* articles numbers thirteen through eighteen during 2000.

I am especially indebted to the book editors, Mark Parker with the first edition and Toni Knott on this edition, who worked hard to polish my manuscript. For both editions, Michelle Owen redrew the illustrations and handled layout. Thanks Michelle, Toni, and Mark.

The *PM Network* series and the two book editions have been a pleasant endeavor. I have greatly enjoyed the association, professionalism, and contributions of the PMI staff. In addition, I'm pleased to be making a small contribution toward advancing project management.

Although the probability concepts are well established, our tools and knowledge of how to apply them continuously evolve. PMI Publishing and I will be grateful for your comments and suggestions, which will aid in a future revision of this book. You may send corrections to booked@pmi.org, and please send comments and suggestions to me:

John Schuyler
Aurora, Colorado
john@maxvalue.com

Amplifications and corrections to the book are posted online at
http://www.maxvalue.com/rdap2rev.htm

PART I

INTRODUCTION TO RISK AND DECISION ANALYSIS

Decision analysis is perhaps the most powerful management technique since the invention of the organization hierarchy. This first part introduces the methods and approach of applying decision analysis in project decisions.

CHAPTER 1

RISK AND DECISION ANALYSIS

Probability is the language of uncertainty. Fortunately, a few basic concepts in probability and statistics go a long way toward making better decisions. This chapter introduces some initial terminology and a few important concepts.

Introduction

Decision analysis (DA), sometimes called *risk analysis*, is the discipline for helping decision makers choose wisely under conditions of uncertainty. The techniques are applicable to all types of project decisions and valuations. Committing to fund a project does not end the decision making, for decisions continue to be made throughout the project life cycle. The quality of these decisions impacts cost, schedule, and performance.

This book explores the approach and principal techniques of DA. These methods explicitly recognize uncertainties in project forecasts. This analysis technology, on the leading edge in the 1970s and earlier, is becoming mainstream practice. The methodology is proven, accessible, and—I hope you will agree—easily understood.

Decision Problems

Most decision problems are about resource allocation: Where do we put our money, time, and other resources? DA involves concepts borrowed from probability theory, statistics, psychology, finance, and operations research. The formal discipline is called *decision science*, a subset of *operations research* (also called *management science*). *Operations Research/Management Science*

(*OR/MS* or *ORMS*) is the broad discipline of applying quantitative methods to problems of business and other organizations.

DA techniques are universal. They apply in any professional discipline and to problems in your personal life.

Although this book is oriented toward project management decisions, DA is a general problem-solving process and applies to three types of problems:

- Choosing between alternatives
  - ◆ Buy, make or build, or lease
  - ◆ Size or number of units of equipment to purchase
  - ◆ Best use or disposition of an asset.
- Appraising value
  - ◆ Project or venture value, or elements of projects or ventures
  - ◆ Estimating transaction or project proceeds.
- Determining the optimal values for decision variables
  - ◆ Bid amount to maximize the value of the bid opportunity
  - ◆ Optimal capacity or configuration of a facility or equipment.

All decisions seem to fall into one of these categories, and we evaluate each type in a similar manner. All we need is a way to measure value under uncertainty—the topic of Chapter 3.

Applying the DA approach requires:

- Capturing judgments about risks and uncertainty as probability distributions
- Having a single measure of value or the quality of the result
- Putting these together with expected value calculations.

DA provides the only logical, consistent way to incorporate judgments about risks and uncertainties into an analysis. When uncertainties are significant, these techniques are the best route toward credible project decisions.

Decision science emerged as a subcategory of management science during the 1960s. Yet still, evaluation practices and decision policy remain a **weak link** in many organizations (see Figure 1.1). This is despite great sophistication in the technical science and engineering disciplines. The purpose of this book is to strengthen that weak link.

Increasing business complexity, speed, and competition pressure us to improve decision making. People are maturing in traditional planning and evaluation practices, and dealing with uncertainty seems a logical improvement. *Sophisticated* decision making doesn't mean *more complicated*. We can solve many decision problems on the back of an envelope; however, low- and moderate-cost computer software is now available to implement the methods described in this book. Applying these techniques should lead to **faster, more confident decisions**.

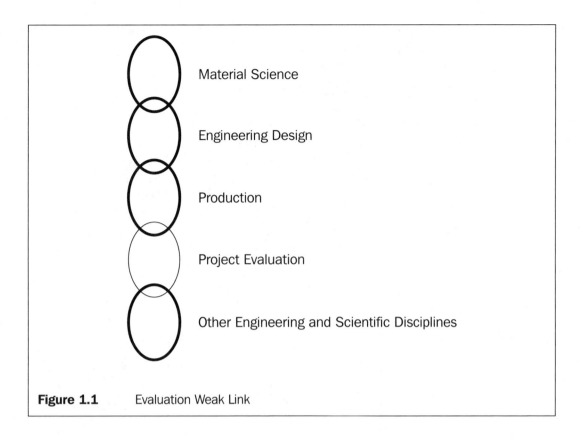

Figure 1.1   Evaluation Weak Link

Credible Analysis

Your job may involve estimating project or activity costs. How would you evaluate the quality of your estimates? Most forecast users recognize two principal, desirable characteristics in a credible analysis:

- **Objectivity**: Over a number of projects, estimates proving neither too high nor too low *on average*. Unbiased.
- **Precision**: Reasonable closeness between estimates and actual values— that is, minimal random "noise" in the estimates.

Forecast accuracy is a composite of low bias and high precision. *Objectivity*—lack of bias—tells us about the error of estimations compared to what actual values result. We demonstrate low bias by having an average forecast error of approximately zero. *Precision* tells us about the magnitude of the errors, and we desire small errors, of course.

In competitive situations, both bias and precision are important. For most internal purposes—where we're competing against nature, for example—objectivity is more important.

Applying the *expected value* (EV) concept enables more accurate forecasts and estimates. Understanding a few things about probability distributions will be helpful before introducing EV later in this chapter.

Before we leave the topic of credible analysis, we should recognize several additional important facets:

- The value measure in the model must correspond to the mission and objective(s) of the organization. A decision policy tells us how outcome value is measured. For example, how are we to make tradeoffs between cost, schedule, and performance? We discuss decision policy in Chapter 3.
- The model must faithfully represent the assumptions as presented.
- The analysis scope should encompass all the important effects of the decision alternatives. We are trying to estimate *incremental* value to the organization.
- Those persons preparing forecasts and evaluations should provide adequate disclosure and communication. Decision analyses are normally very transparent: The values and calculation details are readily available for inspection by a decision maker and other interested persons.

Risk and Uncertainty

Risk and uncertainty describe the possibility of different potential outcomes. Some systems feature inherent randomness, such as games of chance. In business, the risks and uncertainties reflect unknowns and variability in nature, materials, and human systems.

Risk is the quality of a system that relates to the possibility of different outcomes.

Informally, "risk" is used when there is a large, usually *unfavorable*, potential impact. Typically, the contingency event either happens or does not—for example, risk of failure.

Because there is no good antonym in English for a "good risk," many of us allow "risk" to encompass either undesirable or desirable outcomes, or both.

In project management, especially, we often classify risk events as either "threats" or "opportunities." This taxonomy, shown in Figure 1.2, is consistent with **SWOT analysis**, where a situation analysis focuses in turn on **S**trengths, **W**eaknesses, **O**pportunities, and **T**hreats. (This is a good process for creating decision-making opportunities.) This classification is useful in project risk management, where we want to reduce the probability and impact of a *threat* and increase the probability and impact of an *opportunity*.

For many people, *risk* is approximately synonymous with *uncertainty*. It is sometimes helpful to make a distinction.

Uncertainty refers to variability in some value. An informal distinction is that uncertainty applies to when the outcome is variable, such as a future commodity price. We know there is going to be a price; the uncertainty is how much.

❖ The definitions for *risk* and *uncertainty* are controversial. Few topics will generate as much debate as trying to achieve consensus definitions for these two common words. Some

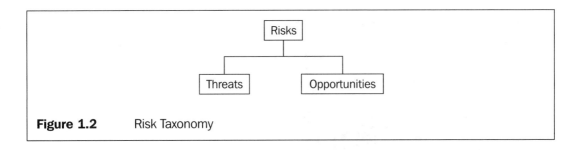

Figure 1.2 Risk Taxonomy

project management professionals are classifying *uncertainty* (i.e., a surprise or contingency) as the most general term. They then classify events with good outcomes as *opportunities* and those with bad outcomes as *risks* or *threats*. Another definition dimension, drawing argument, is whether we should classify risks and uncertainties as "known unknowns" or "unknown unknowns." I'll not argue the definitions here. Even if we disagree, there is little risk of serious miscommunication. I am merely offering definition suggestions according to what appears to be most common usage.

Frequency and Probability Distributions

Suppose that you and forty-nine other professionals estimate Project Cost. The collected values range from $26.7 million to $76.0 million. We can display the fifty estimates as a *frequency histogram*, as illustrated in Figure 1.3.

Here is the procedure for charting a frequency histogram. First divide the range of values into (typically) five to fifty intervals (segments, bins) of equal width. Next, count the number of values occurring within each interval. Now, draw a bar graph—one bar per interval—with the bar heights proportional to the number (or frequency) of occurrences within each interval. If you desire, label the y-axis with either numbers of values in the interval or percents of the total. Labeling the y-axis is optional, because anyone viewing such a chart expects that all of the data values are represented.

Suppose that, instead, we have 500 data points. More data and smaller value segment partitions provide the additional detail shown in Figure 1.4. We obtain a more accurate estimate of a central, average value as the number of data points increases.

If we obtain a great many data points and use smaller intervals, the frequency distribution converges into a smooth and continuous curve, a *probability density function* (p.d.f.), or, simply, a *probability distribution*.

A probability distribution can completely represent one's judgment about a chance event. If one or more inputs to an analysis are probability distributions, then project cost and other outputs will be probability distributions also.

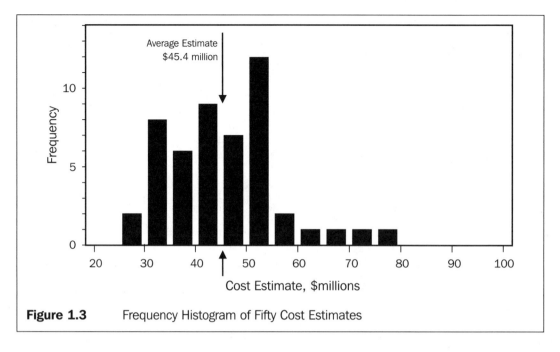

Figure 1.3   Frequency Histogram of Fifty Cost Estimates

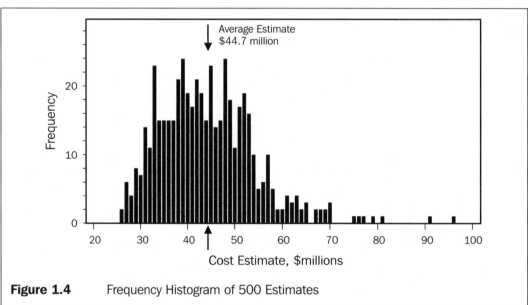

Figure 1.4   Frequency Histogram of 500 Estimates

A p.d.f. represents the population of all possible outcomes. Suppose that we want to judge the uncertainty in a new cost estimate coming from the same *population* as values obtained for Figures 1.3 and 1.4.

Figure 1.5 shows a probability distribution for the next sample for a Project Cost estimate. The units of the y-axis are not important; the y-axis is scaled so that the area under the curve equals 1. This figure shows the relative likelihood of estimate values along the x-axis. Fitting such a curve to

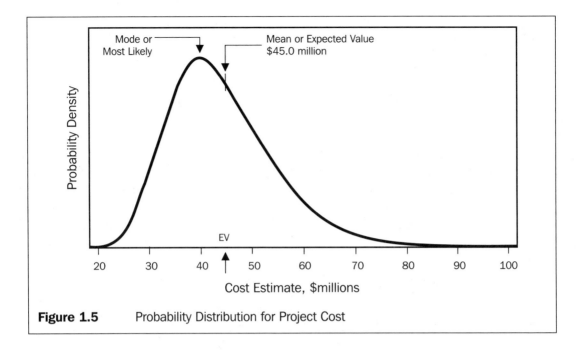

Figure 1.5   Probability Distribution for Project Cost

lots of representative data, this function would represent our best judgment of the distribution of cost estimates.

As such, the p.d.f. represents a judgment about uncertainty. In the case of Figure 1.5, it represents a judgment about new cost estimates. Unlike a frequency distribution, the p.d.f. is not representing data.

❖ Here, "density" describes the correspondence between area and probability. We will see that the EV calculation is analogous to a center-of-mass calculation with a two-dimensional mass of uniform density.

Popular Central Measures

There are two especially important statistics annotated in Figure 1.5:

■ The *most likely value* is about $40 million. Statisticians call this peak the *mode*. The mode is more probable than any other value, and we expect more data samples to be near this value than any other point. This statistic is useful in describing a distribution's shape, yet has little application in decision making.

■ The *expected value*, $45 million, is the probability-weighted average. Statisticians call this the *mean*, and use a Greek letter μ symbol. It represents the average of many values sampled from the population of project cost estimates represented by this probability distribution. If we know the probability distribution, then we know that the *EV* is the probability-weighted average of the distribution. This is the most important and most useful statistic: It is the best single measure of value under uncertainty.

❖ The "expected" term misleads many people. Expected value originated in a mathematics concept called *expectation theory*. The confusion arises because, in most cases, it is unlikely that we will realize the precise *EV*. In some situations, in fact, the *EV* is an impossible outcome value. Nonetheless, an *EV* is the best single-point estimate under uncertainty, as we'll discuss.

The mode and the mean are two "central measures" that indicate the "center" or position of the distribution curve on the x-axis. Central measures, variously, represent an "average" value. Because ***average*** is so often used (abused) in different ways, it has lost most of its meaning. Whenever someone says something like, "We used an average cost for this assumption," I feel the need to ask that person what he means by "average."

Cumulative Probability Density Curve

The p.d.f., shown in Figure 1.5, is easily converted into a ***cumulative (probability) density function*** (c.d.f.) curve. Figure 1.6 shows two versions of cumulative distributions. The solid curve sloping upward to the right is the c.d.f. To translate the p.d.f. distribution in Figure 1.5, sum the area under the curve, moving from left to right. This is equivalent to progressively integrating the p.d.f. Notice that the cumulative distribution ranges from 0 to 1 on the y-axis.

The dotted curve in Figure 1.6, sloping downward to the right, is the ***reverse cumulative distribution***.

Either cumulative curve contains exactly the same information as the p.d.f. The cumulative format allows us to read confidence levels and intervals directly. Here are example interpretations of the solid curve in Figure 1.6:

- Project Cost estimates are equally likely to be above or below $43.5 million. This centermost value, at 50 percent probability, is the ***median*** (annotated in Figure 1.6). This is another *central measure*, and widely used with demographics to indicate "average" values, such as house prices or salaries [1].
- About 74 percent of the Project Cost estimates are below $50 million. The 74 percent (less-than) *confidence limit* or *confidence level* is $50 million.
- About 80 percent of the Project Cost estimates are between $33 million and $57 million. This $33 to $57 million range represents an 80 percent ***confidence interval***.

The c.d.f. (solid curve in Figure 1.6) that we have been discussing is often called "the cumulative less-than distribution." Some people—most in fact—prefer to "flip over" this cumulative curve, rotating it around a horizontal axis. Then we have the *reverse cumulative distribution*, which is also called the "exceedance" or "greater-than" form of cumulative probability distribution (dotted curve in Figure 1.6). This format is especially popular when larger x-axis values are better, because management is accustomed to viewing "better" on graphs as being upward or rightward.

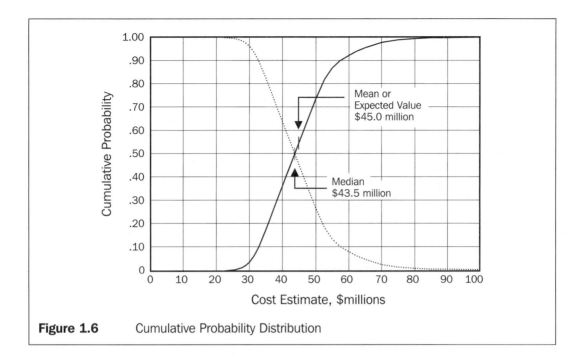

Figure 1.6   Cumulative Probability Distribution

Often, the inequality symbols "<" or "≤" or ">" or "≥" are used when labeling the cumulative functions. The use of the "=" part of the symbol is common, though this is optional and irrelevant with continuous distributions, because the probability of realizing the precise boundary value is virtually zero.

Figure 1.3 and Figure 1.4 illustrate sampled data. More commonly, one works instead with a *judgment* about a distribution for a cost of a *single project*, such as in Figure 1.5 and Figure 1.6. Suppose we characterize a population with a p.d.f. If we obtain many data from this population, the frequency distribution's shape converges to the p.d.f. This is perhaps the most important concept in statistics.

Discrete Events

Thus far, we have been examining ***continuous distributions***, where there is a continuum of possible outcomes.

In many situations, a risk is a binary event. Either something happens, or it does not. This is the simplest form of chance event. We have a ***discrete (probability) distribution*** when we have two to many (usually countable) possible specific outcomes.

Often we have a project contingency, an event that either happens or not. If this risk event occurs, then there is an *impact* on the project. Project risk management is mostly about considering discrete risk events and their impacts, and determining what actions are cost effective in mitigating such risks. We will discuss this process in Chapter 8 about project risk management.

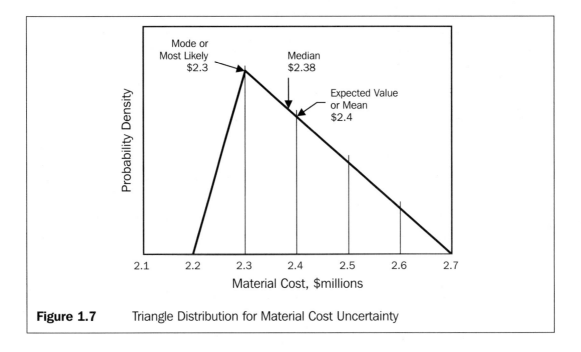

Figure 1.7   Triangle Distribution for Material Cost Uncertainty

Expected Value

Suppose in estimating Material Cost, an expert judges that the outcome could range from $2.2 million to $2.7 million, with a most likely value of $2.3 million. She further believes that the p.d.f. changes linearly between these points. We then have three points: low, most likely, and high values. These three parameters are sufficient to completely and uniquely describe the triangle distribution, illustrated in Figure 1.7.

This probability distribution, or its cumulative equivalent, completely expresses her material cost assessment. The judged distribution comes from subjective judgment, comparable historical data, modeling, or some combination. Regardless of how it comes about, a probability distribution fully discloses someone's judgment about the value of a project model input variable.

Converts to a Single Value

How should you respond if your boss or the client insists on a single-value estimate instead of a distribution? The **best single-point estimate is the expected value (EV)**, because *EV* is the objective (unbiased) value to represent a probability distribution. Of course, the model and judgments that go into it must be unbiased. For Material Cost, the case shown in Figure 1.7, $2.4 million would be the single-point estimate.

One would be confident that:

- Performing many similar projects (independent and no learning) would result in an average material cost of approximately $2.4 million.
- Over the long run, the average estimate error will approach zero.

Thus, *EV* is the only unbiased single-point forecast.

Note that forecasts that use the *most likely* (peak) or *median* (50 percent confidence) values would systematically understate Material Cost.

Calculating Expected Value

There are several ways to calculate the EV of a probability distribution. If we have the distribution expressed as a mathematical formula, one might be able to solve the integral equation:

$$EV = \int_{-\infty}^{+\infty} x \, \mathrm{f}(x) \, dx$$

where x is the value of the variable and f(x) is the p.d.f. of x.

Do not worry about the calculus. This equation is almost never one that we can solve with symbolic mathematics. We do not know how to integrate a project model. Moreover, it is very difficult to solve even simple mathematical operations with probability distributions.

❖ There are perhaps more equations in this chapter than in the entire rest of the book. Do not be alarmed. In almost every situation, we are calculating with simple equations, mostly just multiplying and adding. I have included formulas for those persons who may be interested.

Fortunately, we can solve for *EV*s. For a discrete distribution with *N* possible outcomes, the *EV* is the sum of the outcome values times their probabilities:

$$EV = \sum_{i=1}^{N} x_i \, \mathrm{P}(x_i)$$

where x_i are the outcome values, and P(x_i) are the probabilities of these outcomes.

Excel's SUMPRODUCT function is a convenient way to do this calculation, such as solving *EV*s in *payoff tables*. This formula is the fundamental calculation used in decision trees, which we will discuss in Chapter 5. Monte Carlo simulation, discussed in Chapter 7, is another popular calculation tool that uses a statistical sampling method to solve the EV integration.

EV calculations have two highly desirable properties when we are forecasting a cost or value:

- If we add an amount, *X*, to all outcomes, then the *EV* increases by *X*. For example, if a decision burdens a project with a cost *X* = $10k, and this affects all possible outcomes for this project, then the project's EV cost increases by $10k ("delta property").
- If we multiply all outcomes by a factor *Y*, then the *EV* changes by that factor. For example, suppose we split a project fifty/fifty with a partner. Then our share of EV cost, EV volume, and EV revenue is reduced by half ("distributive property").

We can obtain *EVs* for input distributions by numeric integration or graphical methods. We usually calculate the *EVs* of input variables, and use these for a **base case** analysis. This is not the base project plan, but merely one possible projection useful for discussion. Note that the *base case cost or value should not be used for decision making*, because its outcome is often substantially different from the EV result. Using EV inputs often does not provide an EV result. Chapter 13, Stochastic Variance, describes this phenomenon in detail. The main analytical benefit of using DA is **improved calculation accuracy** in valuing each alternative.

At first impression, it may appear that DA requires *more* work from the project or evaluation professional. Actually, DA can save time overall. There are several reasons for this:

- There is a *process* for the decision evaluation. This keeps the evaluation project team focused and directed.
- There is less work for additional what-if cases. Probability distributions already characterize the possibilities.
- The analysis incorporates the value function (decision policy). This measures the value of each outcome and alternative. The focus is on making progress toward the organization's objective, and any tradeoffs are explicitly valued in the decision policy.

Chapter 2 describes a ten-step DA process. I hope that you will find it common sense and in many ways similar to the problem-solving process that you already use.

Objective Project Estimates

One key to improving project estimates is ***performance feedback***. It is important to compare forecasts to what actually occurs. Project data that verify an objective estimating process will have these characteristics:

- The average estimate error approaches zero over many projects.
- This relationship (bullet above) holds for any classification subset of the data (e.g., stratified by project size or type).

Even if sufficient data are not available, we intend these features to be in an objective evaluation process. Let's see how this works with synthetic project data.

Consider the case of a company with original cost estimates and actual cost data on its last 100 projects or similar activities. Table 1.1 summarizes these data, with values for the first ten projects shown in detail.

The samples for actual costs, column 3 in Table 1.1, are from the population of projects, shown in Figure 1.8. The average Project Cost is $11.2 million, with most projects in the $500,000 to $30 million range.

Figure 1.9 is a graph comparing actual and estimate project data from column 5 in Table 1.1. This reveals the accuracy of the estimates. Accuracy, you may recall, is a combination of low bias and high precision.

					Dollar Amounts are $000s			
(1) Project Number	(2) Estimate	(3) Actual	(4) Error	(5) Actual Estimate	(6) Cumulative Error	(7) Average Estimate	(8) Average Actual	(9) Average Error
1	$4.12	$3.56	−$0.56	0.864	−$0.56	$4.12	$3.56	−$.561
2	3.27	3.12	−0.15	0.953	−0.71	3.70	3.34	−.357
3	3.54	4.30	0.76	1.215	0.05	3.64	3.66	0.016
4	4.91	2.86	−2.05	0.583	−2.00	3.96	3.46	.500
5	33.15	14.40	−18.75	0.434	−20.75	9.80	5.65	−4.150
6	3.39	2.42	−0.97	0.714	−21.72	8.73	5.11	−3.620
7	10.63	13.58	2.95	1.278	−18.76	9.00	6.32	−2.680
8	24.89	50.90	26.01	2.045	7.25	10.99	11.89	0.906
9	1.12	0.98	−0.14	0.873	7.11	9.89	10.68	0.790
10	9.74	14.76	5.02	1.515	12.12	9.88	11.09	1.212
20	3.09	3.40	0.31	1.102	33.88	12.82	14.51	1.694
30	5.26	8.38	3.12	1.594	73.11	13.69	16.13	2.437
40	5.80	3.67	2.13	0.632	88.47	12.97	15.19	2.212
50	3.57	2.97	0.60	0.831	76.74	12.27	13.81	1.535
60	3.43	3.53	0.10	1.029	59.32	12.31	13.30	0.989
70	3.30	3.10	0.21	0.937	25.12	12.26	12.62	0.359
80	15.69	12.89	2.80	0.822	6.36	15.68	15.76	0.079
90	12.62	14.34	1.72	1.136	15.81	14.56	14.74	0.176
100	20.49	17.32	3.17	0.845	9.49	13.78	13.87	0.095
200	4.36	6.54	2.18	1.501	−5.22	12.36	12.33	−.026
300	0.77	0.56	0.21	0.727	69.80	12.55	12.78	0.233
400	16.69	20.94	4.25	1.255	41.05	12.35	12.45	0.103
500	1.05	0.99	0.06	0.944	64.76	11.99	12.12	0.130
600	19.92	12.64	7.28	0.635	−33.44	11.67	11.62	−.056
700	21.27	18.64	2.63	0.877	−87.23	11.86	11.73	−.125
800	7.54	7.05	0.48	0.936	−130.74	11.44	11.27	−.163
900	12.91	10.21	2.70	0.791	−121.76	11.25	11.11	−.135
1,000	2.96	5.55	2.59	1.873	−131.14	11.31	11.18	−.131
2,000	3.95	3.01	0.94	0.762	−399.43	10.89	10.69	−.200
3,000	4.69	3.07	1.62	0.655	−625.64	10.99	10.78	−.209
4,000	2.32	2.01	0.31	0.868	−773.02	11.11	10.92	−.193
5,000	10.19	5.24	4.95	0.514	−695.35	11.14	11.00	−.139
6,000	2.40	1.94	0.46	0.809	−862.71	11.24	11.09	−.144
7,000	2.21	2.38	0.16	1.074	−890.67	11.13	11.01	−.127
8,000	4.64	6.14	1.50	1.324	−921.08	11.23	11.11	−.115
9,000	17.13	24.29	7.16	1.418	−1001.93	11.15	11.04	−.111
10,000	14.91	7.96	6.95	0.534	−1126.07	11.12	11.01	−.113

Table 1.1   Project Estimate and Actual Costs

For illustration, Figure 1.10 presents the same data as a cumulative frequency distribution. It has exactly the same information content as Figure 1.9. As discussed earlier, sometimes we prefer a cumulative distribution format that directly represents confidence levels. For example:

- There is about a 60 percent confidence that the actual result will be within the range of 0.75 to 1.20 times the estimate.

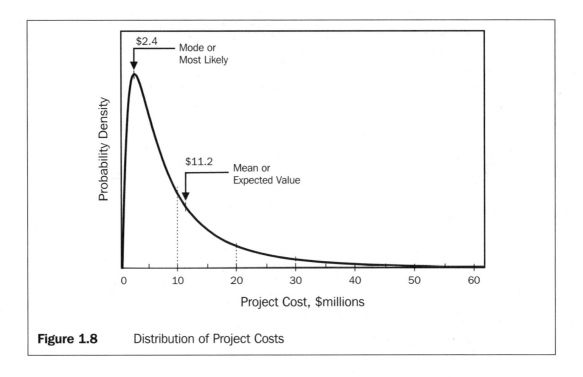

Figure 1.8   Distribution of Project Costs

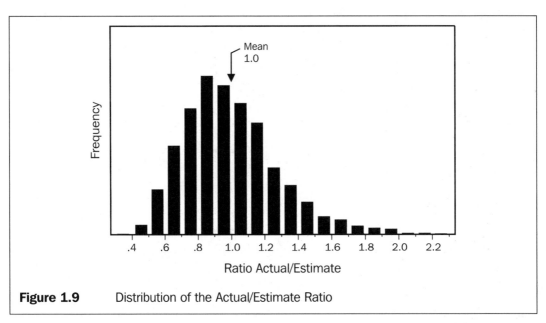

Figure 1.9   Distribution of the Actual/Estimate Ratio

❖ From Figure 1.10, we see that the probability of Actual/Estimate (*A/E*) being less than 0.75 is about 20 percent, and the probability of *A/E* being less than 1.2 is about 80 percent. The width of this range is a measure of the evaluation precision. Alternatively, we could use the *standard deviation* or another statistic.

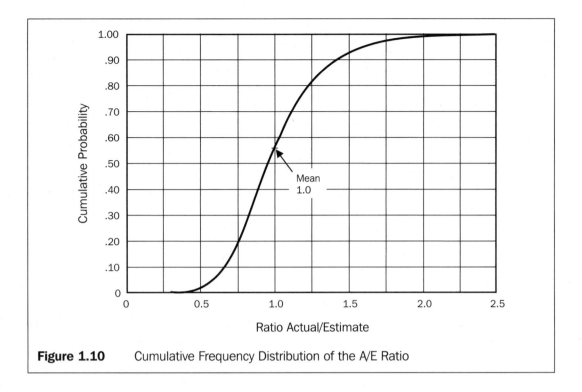

Figure 1.10   Cumulative Frequency Distribution of the A/E Ratio

■ There is a 56 percent chance that the actual result will be lower than the estimate.

Figures 1.11a and 1.11b show the average error plotted as a time series. Figure 1.11b shows a great volume of synthetic data on a log scale generated by the demonstration simulation.

Table 1.1 and Figure 1.9 and Figure 1.10 are feedback tools for monitoring and improving project estimates. Since the A/E ratio is nearly 1 in these figures, these estimates appear to be unbiased. With perfectly objective analyses, the ratio will approach 1 as the number of evaluations becomes very large. Whether or not we have sufficient data to demonstrate, this is a characteristic of **objective evaluations**—that is, those without appreciable bias.

Even with objective evaluations, Cumulative Error, column 6 in Table 1.1, will usually diverge in either direction. This is contrary to what many expect, and is caused by chance deviations. With objective analysis, however, the **average error is diluted** as the number of observations (projects) in the sample increases, shown in the last column in Table 1.1, by the decreasing Average Error.

Summary: Expected Value, the Best Estimator

Probability is the language of uncertainty. A probability distribution is a graph or mathematical expression that completely represents the likelihood

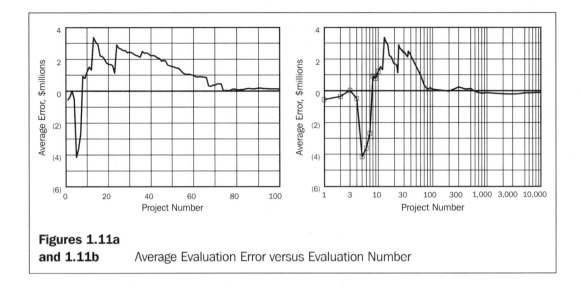

**Figures 1.11a
and 1.11b**   Average Evaluation Error versus Evaluation Number

of different possible outcomes. Quantifying a judgment doesn't necessarily mean that it is more accurate. However, a numeric representation is at least unambiguous. Also, conveniently, quantified risks and uncertainties can be employed in useful calculations.

Sometimes, distributions for the alternatives are difficult to compare. The EV calculation collapses a distribution into a single value number for comparison.

For logical, consistent decision making, we want to know the *EV* of each alternative. Perception of value depends upon the preferences of the decision maker; we discuss decision policy in Chapter 3. Next, in Chapter 2, we discuss a near-universal approach to problem solving, with particular emphasis on concepts from DA.

APPENDIX 1A

MOMENT METHODS

This section describes some other useful statistics. You may skip this section if you are not inclined to read more about statistics.

We have discussed the most popular and most useful statistic, EV. The second most important statistic is the *standard deviation*. The standard deviation, which is a measure of uncertainty, is symbolized by the Greek letter sigma (σ).

Standard deviation is the square root of another statistic called the *variance*. Variance (σ^2) is the EV of the squared difference between possible outcomes and the mean.

$$\sigma^2 = \sum_{i=1}^{N} P(x_i)(x_i - \mu)^2 = E\left[(x_i - \mu)^2\right]$$

where $E()$ is a common representation for the EV of whatever is inside the parentheses.

For a typical continuous probability distribution, about two-thirds of the probability is in a 2σ interval within the highest portion of the probability distribution. Figure 1A.1 shows four distribution shapes, each with a standard deviation of ten units. Notice that the four distributions appear to have comparable widths.

We can sometimes work with statistics of probability distributions. The "parameter method" and the "method of moments" are two alternative names given to these evaluation techniques. *Parameter* refers to statistics about the location and shape of probability distributions. *Moment* refers to the calculation of the statistics. Usually, only the first two moments are used [2].

❖ The *EV* is the first moment about the origin for a p.d.f. Outcome (x-axis) values are weighted with the probability of occurrence (y-axis). A mechanical analogy is the moment arms in calculating torque [3]. The *variance* is the second moment about the mean, a calculation similar to the moment of inertia.

Popular Equations

The fundamental equations in moment methods are based upon adding means and variances. When adding distributions, means (μ's or *EV*s) always add:

$$\mu_{\text{Total}} = \mu_A + \mu_B + \mu_C + \dots$$

The sum of normal distributions is a normal distribution. If there are many additive distributions of similar magnitude, then the sum will be approximately normal regardless of the shape of the individual distributions (from the central limit theorem). This sometimes guides us to when a normal distribution is the best distribution shape. Chapter 10 discusses the most popular distribution types.

When we add normal and independent distributions, the variances (σ^2) also add:

$$\sigma^2_{\text{Total}} = \sigma^2_A + \sigma^2_B + \sigma^2_C + \dots$$

Equations for adding means and variances form the basis for traditional PERT calculations and many simple calculations in quality control.

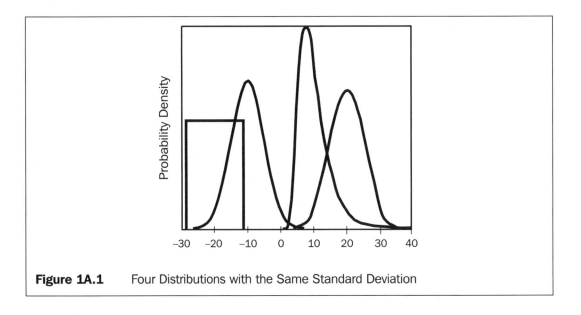

Figure 1A.1   Four Distributions with the Same Standard Deviation

For example, engineers often assume component dimensions are normally distributed and independent. We can then add means and variances to get the total dimension mean and variance for an assembly.

Correlation

Correlation between two variables means that one variable somehow affects or is affected by another. *Association* is another name for this relationship. Independence is an antonym.

A positive correlation between X and Y means that an increase in X is generally associated with an increase in Y. This concept is important to the discussion that follows.

Somewhat more complex, the variances of two added, nonindependent, normal distributions is calculated by:

$$\sigma^2_{A+B} = \sigma^2_A + \sigma^2_B + 2\rho_{AB}\sigma_A\sigma_B = \sigma^2_A + \sigma^2_B + \sigma_{AB}$$

where ρ_{AB} (AB correlation coefficient, Greek letter rho) is the linear *correlation coefficient* between elements A and B. The correlation coefficient ranges from –1 (perfect negative correlation) to +1 (perfect positive correlation). If $\rho_{AB} = 0$, then A and B are independent. This is calculated in Excel with the CORREL function.

The *covariance* term in the earlier formula is calculated:

$$\sigma_{AB} = E\left[(A - \mu_A)(B - \mu_A)\right] = E(AB) - \mu_A\mu_B$$

which, for a discrete distribution in two variables (such as represented in a *joint probability table*), x_i and y_i is:

$$\sigma_{xy} = \sum_{i=1}^{N} P(x_i \cdot y_i)(x_i - \mu_x)(y_i - \mu_y)$$

The *correlation coefficient* used popularly in simulation is:

$$\rho_{AB} = \frac{\sigma_{AB}}{\sigma_A \sigma_B}$$

❖ We often see an "r-squared" statistic (r^2, sometimes capitalized R^2, *coefficient of determination*) in reports about regression models. They refer to the same statistic, only with sample data. R^2 explains the portion of the variance in actual data explained by the (usually regression) model.

This appendix describes some statistics calculations that appear in the literature. Moment methods are sometimes useful in simple cases, and they can be useful in first approximations. However, the more rigorous calculations described in subsequent chapters are important for confidence in the evaluation calculations (except fuzzy logic in Chapter 17).

We will revisit correlation coefficients, though without the equations, in Chapter 12, Relating Risks.

Endnotes

1. There are other central measures. The geometric mean (GM) is especially useful with inflation and other measures involving ratios. The GM is the nth root of the product of n values. There is also a harmonic mean that has applications in electronics and fluid flow.

2. Moment calculations are common in engineering, such as when determining a moment of inertia. The mean is the first moment about the origin. The variance is the second moment about the mean. Skewness is the third moment about the mean divided by σ^3, and kurtosis is the fourth moment about the mean divided by σ^4.

3. The weighted center of a probability distribution is the balance point about which the torque (sum of the first moments) is zero. Thus, the *EV* is the probability graph's center of gravity projected to the x-axis. If you cut out a p.d.f. printed on card stock, this figure balances on the x-axis at the *EV*.

CHAPTER 2

DECISION ANALYSIS PROCESS

In most work, we expect professionals to use consistent, proven processes. A sales consultant friend of mine, Don Aspromonte, uses dentistry as an example. When you go to a dentist for some work, such as filling a tooth, you expect him to know exactly how to do the job. He has successfully filled many cavities with excellent results. As he approaches your tooth, he isn't asking, "What method should I try today?" Rather, he will apply a tried and proven process.

Ten Steps toward Better Decisions

Decision analysis is a *process* for solving problems. While most decisions are unique, the general process can be the same. Figure 2.1 outlines a ten-step sequence for decision making. The following subsections describe each step in more detail.

1. Proactively Identify Decision Opportunities

Most of us are so busy that we seldom go looking for problems. However, there may be better opportunities to add value than what we have planned.

Be proactive in creating or identifying decision-making opportunities. Brainstorming techniques are helpful.

A **SWOT analysis** is a good source of ideas: performing a situation analysis; identifying **S**trengths, **W**eaknesses, **O**pportunities, and **T**hreats. Follow this with planning your strategies and tactics.

2. Define the Problem

Ask exactly what is the problem we want to solve. Are we addressing a root problem or merely a symptom?

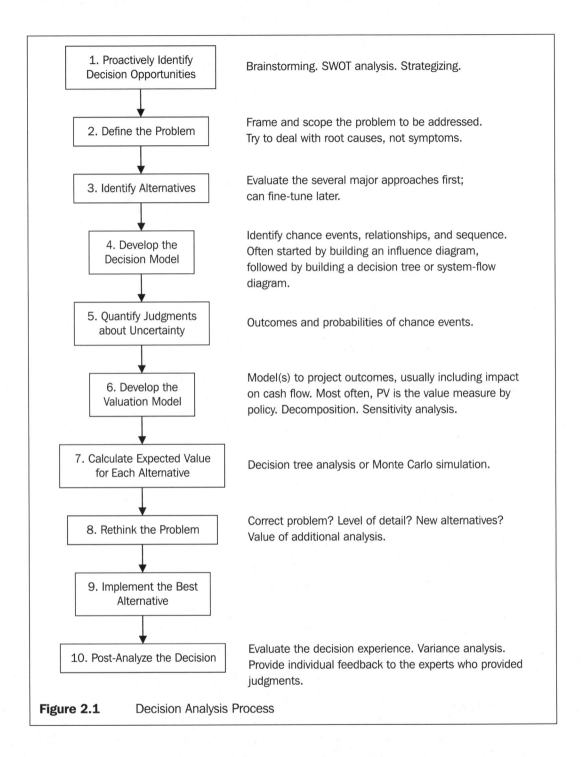

1. Proactively Identify Decision Opportunities	Brainstorming. SWOT analysis. Strategizing.
2. Define the Problem	Frame and scope the problem to be addressed. Try to deal with root causes, not symptoms.
3. Identify Alternatives	Evaluate the several major approaches first; can fine-tune later.
4. Develop the Decision Model	Identify chance events, relationships, and sequence. Often started by building an influence diagram, followed by building a decision tree or system-flow diagram.
5. Quantify Judgments about Uncertainty	Outcomes and probabilities of chance events.
6. Develop the Valuation Model	Model(s) to project outcomes, usually including impact on cash flow. Most often, PV is the value measure by policy. Decomposition. Sensitivity analysis.
7. Calculate Expected Value for Each Alternative	Decision tree analysis or Monte Carlo simulation.
8. Rethink the Problem	Correct problem? Level of detail? New alternatives? Value of additional analysis.
9. Implement the Best Alternative	
10. Post-Analyze the Decision	Evaluate the decision experience. Variance analysis. Provide individual feedback to the experts who provided judgments.

Figure 2.1   Decision Analysis Process

People often talk about **framing** a problem—that is, defining the boundaries. What is the context of the decision in terms of corporate mission, goals, and strategy? What are the **constraints**, and how firm or real are they?

❖ Many other authors include a step something like, "Identify the relevant criteria" in the decision process. I think decision policy should be known and stable and not reexamined with each new decision.

Does this decision affect other decisions? Are there any synergies? Sometimes we need to expand the scope of the evaluation model to encompass effects of this decision on other projects and operations.

Step 2, if not Step 1, is a good time to involve the decision maker(s) and **stakeholders**. Communication with and the support of these people are important to project success. Further, they may have ideas and important information to contribute.

3. Identify Alternatives

Good decision-making opportunities (Step 1) and good alternatives are more important than the actual evaluation methods. Ensure that plenty of time and attention are devoted to this step. Be creative.

For a complex problem, such as designing a facility, there are often **several stages of design decisions**. Perhaps you should determine the best technology and location first; then fine-tune the configuration.

4. Develop the Decision Model

Develop a map, **diagram**, or outline of the decision problem. This should include the alternatives and possible outcomes of each. Decision trees and influence diagrams are good techniques, because they provide an illustration of the problem. In some cases, flow diagrams or scripting may be more convenient.

Identify the **decision and chance events**, their relationships and sequence.

5. Quantify Judgments about Uncertainty

From Step 4, we know what chance events are included in the model. Usually, we enlist the most knowledgeable available person to judge a chance event (as a **probability distribution**). We also need the expert's judgment about any relationships (correlations) with other variables in the model.

Sometimes a chance event is difficult to judge directly. Decomposing the system further and building a **submodel** may be a good way to develop a distribution for a variable in the top-level decision model.

Sometimes there may be **multiple experts**, or at least opinions, involved with a chance variable. It is the decision maker's responsibility to designate those to provide the judgments going into the model. This includes any opinion-weighting or tie-breaking rules.

6. Develop the Valuation Model

We need a means to determine a **value for every possible outcome**, combinations of decision and chance variable outcomes. The core of the model—and the most work if it is a special evaluation—is usually a deterministic operations and cashflow model. Commonly in business, the model projects incremental net cash flow and **present value**. What scale you use comes from your decision policy. Utility scales are useful for risk-averse organizations and for those with multiple criteria.

If using multiple criteria, your decision policy should describe the multi-criteria value function. For every project scenario, we want a single number to measure the quality of the outcome.

The valuation model links to the decision model, and vice versa. The valuation model must generate a value for every possible scenario generated by the decision model. That is, every combination of decision and chance event outcomes is a unique scenario, and the decision model tells the cashflow model what are the decision and chance variable values of the scenario.

If you have an existing template or economic model, we can often do this deterministic modeling step very quickly. For new problem types, creating the model might require considerable time and effort. **Decomposition** and **sensitivity analysis** are important modeling techniques. Work to keep the model as simple as possible for the purpose at hand. We seldom need to optimize every possibility. Discard (prune) alternatives as soon as you determine that they are inferior. For unimportant chance events, set these to single values or combine the effects with other variables.

Remember, we only need to do analysis to the point where we know the best alternative. For optimization or valuation problems, ensure that additional analysis work costs less that the incremental benefit.

7. Calculate Expected Value for Each Alternative

Decision tree analysis and **Monte Carlo simulation** are the workhorses of decision analysis. There is a calculation method for influence diagrams, closely aligned with decision trees. Payoff tables and other methods are suitable for some simple situations.

It is often expedient to use multiple expected value-solving methods in the same evaluation—for example, using trees for what trees do best and simulation for what simulation does best.

8. Rethink the Problem

Are you solving the **right problem**? Do the decision and cashflow models have the appropriate level of detail? Does this need to be solved now? Or at all?

While this ten-step process may look linear, often there is necessary **rework** because of new information or a new insight about the problem. You may need to loop back to an earlier step to include a new alternative or risk.

What is the value of additional analysis? Are there cost-effective sources of information that would better define some chance events? Are there ways to add control to the strategies, mitigating threats and enhancing opportunities?

9. Implement the Best Alternative

We should consider who will implement the decision in our evaluation. Ideally, the person responsible for implementing the decision has also been involved in the evaluation process.

Project feasibility analysis involves some **early project planning**. This carries forward into project implementation and detailed planning.

Monitor the risks and assumptions throughout the project life cycle. Anticipate where there may be decision points to reallocate resources. Continue looking for decision-making opportunities. Decision analysis methods are useful also for the many decisions a project manager faces.

10. Post-Analyze the Decision

Perhaps the most important single way to improve the quality of decision making in your organization is a **post-implementation review** [1]. Plan and budget to get the project team members together again to review the decision process. What did you learn? Did the decision model prove adequate? Were the outcomes of chance events in the middle regions of the distributions? **Feedback** is most effective when it is personal to the experts who provided inputs to the evaluation.

A **variance analysis** may be a useful tool. Analyze the factors and contributions to the difference (variance) between forecast and actual outcome.

The **learning organization** is a popular concept in modern management. What are the **lessons learned** that you want to preserve to share with others in the organization? Models, templates, data sources, and such might prove useful to later teams. Placing a copy of the decision analysis document might provide inspiration to others pursuing similar evaluations.

The post-implementation review is not a "search for the guilty." I suggest not inviting managers outside the project evaluation team. The primary purpose is to help team members recognize and learn from the experience.

The decision analysis process works best when everyone is motivated to provide his best, unbiased efforts. Nothing causes people to become conservative faster than a fear of punishment. We want to **reward people for making good decisions**—not for experiencing good outcomes.

Who Does All This Work?

You and your colleagues do! Except perhaps for Step 6, developing the deterministic valuation model, all of this work is best performed by people close to the problem. They are typically engineers, scientists, and others who understand the technology, problem, and project.

Usually, the technical problems are also people problems. The project evaluation team must often sell the recommendation to not only decision makers, but to other stakeholders as well. Involve these people early and throughout the process.

This ten-step evaluation process should **save you time**. There should be little or no need for separate "what-if" analyses; the decision model has already considered the possibilities.

I hope you will find this general problem-solving process useful in keeping the project team focused and directed to the evaluation task at hand.

Endnotes

1. The post-implementation review is the topic of Lessons Learned Through Process Thinking and Review by George Pitagorsky (2000).

CHAPTER 3

DECISION POLICY

*With an appropriate choice of a value measure, the **expected value** becomes a foundation for logical, consistent decisions under uncertainty. An example problem illustrates two tools for calculating expected value: a payoff table and a decision tree.*

Intuition Is a Poor Method

Because human intuition is typically so poor at processing probabilities and dealing with details, important evaluations under uncertainty will benefit from the decision analysis approach. We all rely daily upon our intuition, and the purpose here is not to replace intuition. Rather, the *quantitative methods will bolster our intuition*.

Chapter 1 introduces probability distributions and the expected value concept. We saw that *expected value (EV)* is the only unbiased predictor and the best single-value estimate for forecasting. Again, *EV* is the probability-weighted average of all possible outcomes represented in a probability distribution.

Many organizations continue using decision practices that are decades out of date. Partially responsible are misconceptions in project evaluation in many of the textbooks about capital-investment analysis. Most traditional decision criteria do not work well with uncertainty—which is most of the time. As with any discipline, it is important to understand the theory and to apply best practices. I hope this chapter will guide you in crafting or reaffirming a logical decision policy.

Decision Maker's Preferences

Decision analysts customarily refer to a ***decision maker*** (DM) when describing the person with this role in the decision-making process. In an

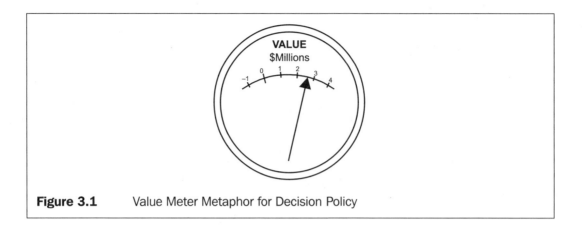

Figure 3.1   Value Meter Metaphor for Decision Policy

organizational context, the DM acts—or at least should act—according to the organization's mission and objective(s). When appropriate, there may be multiple objectives, and typically these are aligned with different stakeholder group interests.

In addition to calculations with probabilities, the decision analysis approach needs a way to measure outcome value. Value is in the context of the organization's objective(s). *Preferences* are the dimensions of value. They are the DM's attitudes toward different characteristics of decision problems based upon beliefs and values.

> It's essential to have a grip, a clear understanding, of what your values
> and priorities are. Without a clear set of values, one decision is as good
> as another.
>
> Kotkin 2000

The decision analysis approach is straightforward. Consider a value meter, illustrated in Figure 3.1. An analogy is a voltmeter. (Decision trees, as we will soon see, look much like electronic circuit diagrams.) Which alternative—the path we choose on a decision diagram—has the highest value? The value meter has a scale calibrated in dollars, another currency, or even some arbitrary scale that we design. In making decisions, we want to find the alternative with the greatest value reading. Recognizing uncertainty (continuing the metaphor, somewhat like a.c. voltage), we will choose the alternative with the highest *EV*. All three analysis problem types, identified in Chapter 1, can be solved by having a way to assess value: ranking alternatives, appraising value, and optimizing decision variables.

Most decision analysts find it convenient to segregate preferences into three categories: objective(s), time value, and risk attitude. We can deal with each preference separately, providing a more logical and consistent basis for evaluation analysis. We examine these three dimensions of decision policy in the following sections.

Attitude toward Different Objectives

What is the mission? What is the organization's reason for existing?

Creating wealth is the customary purpose of business. The usual driving objective is maximizing the monetary value of the enterprise (or total return to stockholders).

Other considerations that ultimately affect cash flow and enter the evaluation include:

- Operating legally
- Doing business in socially acceptable ways
    - providing a quality product or service
    - creating and protecting jobs
    - contributing to the community
    - recognizing the interests of employees, suppliers, and customers

while not

- trashing the environment
- exploiting any group of people
- Doing business with countries, companies, and people whom we like.

I cannot overemphasize the importance of being clear about the organization's mission and purpose. This is the basis for valuing the outcomes of decisions. Decision policy should specify how we measure "goodness" or progress toward the organization's objective.

For example, providing great customer service is an important theme in many companies. Yet, is this an objective? Since stockholders own the business, most people—certainly most investors—agree that "maximizing shareholder value" is the logical and legitimate objective.

In my opinion, being a good **corporate citizen** is consistent with optimizing shareholder value. Let's continue with the customer-service example. Poor customer service destroys the brand. Also, excessive customer service would be at the expense of shareholders. Determining the right customer-service level is an optimization problem. Investments in health, safety, and the environment are other examples with a similar solution approach.

Enduring corporations have a core purpose beyond just making money: something to inspire the troops and customers [1]. Where creating monetary wealth is the most important objective, decision policy is often based upon money. At least, money is a convenient measurement unit. A good technique for recognizing nonmonetary considerations in the analysis is to translate them into money equivalents. Otherwise, multi-objective decisions are more difficult, because it is less clear how to measure value. We will discuss multi-criteria decision-making methods later in this chapter.

Attitude toward Time Value

When we measure the outcome in monetary units, the impact of a decision is the effect on the organization's future net cash flow. Most everyone prefers to receive money sooner rather than later. Conversely, we prefer to postpone payment obligations. We call this preference, "time value of money."

Present value (PV) discounting is the generally accepted method to recognize time preference for money. Discounting makes most sense in the context of money, but costs and benefits measured in nonmonetary units can be time-discounted as well.

The customary equation is:

$$PV = \frac{CF}{(1+i)^t} = CF(1+i)^{-t}$$

where

> PV = present value at a reference time, typically the effective date of the next decision;
>
> CF = a net cashflow amount, positive or negative, realized at a future time;
>
> t = number of compounding periods. This is the time, usually in years, between the effective, or as-of, date, and when the future cashflow (CF) amount is realized; and
>
> i = the PV discount(ing) rate, usually expressed as a rate per year. This is similar to an annual interest rate, hence the symbol, i.

This equation always works. CF is typically projected and discounted period by period, and t is the time from the as-of date to the middle of the projection period. We call this ***midperiod discounting***. Beware that Microsoft Excel and functions in most other analysis tools typically assume—wrongly for most evaluations—that the t's should be integers.

The discount rate, i, represents the DM's attitude toward the time value of money. I recommend that a company choose i such that PV objectively measures increase to company value by doing the project, as viewed from an average stockholder's perspective.

Almost all companies use a fixed PV discount rate, i, in their decision policy. That is, the rate chosen applies to all future periods. However, it is appropriate to use different rates for different years, based on expectations about changing inflation and/or capital market conditions.

If the value measure is something other than money, the discount rate rationale is murky. How would you represent time-value for outcomes measured in human lives? Or old growth trees? Analysts usually apply the same formula, though the discount rate reasoning is difficult.

EV *PV* is the value measure broadly recommended for widely held corporations seeking to maximize monetary value. This measure is so important that it has its own name: ***expected monetary value*** (*EMV*).

❖ Do not increase the discount rate for risk! In decision analysis, we recognize risks with probabilities. Most companies are double-risking their projects when they use stochastic analysis. Awareness of this issue is what I consider the most important single insight that I've gained in twenty-five years of evaluation experience [2].

Cashflow Analysis Guidelines

PV and net present value (*NPV* or *PV*) are generally synonymous. CFs and *PV*s are usually net-of-investment expenditures, except when calculating a benefit/cost ratio. Many people involved with project evaluation make serious errors in PV calculations. Here are several guidelines for proper **discounted cashflow** (DCF) analysis.

Design the CF projection to be cash receipts net of investment and cash costs. We want to forecast the incremental CF effect on the company from doing the project (or whatever alternative is being considered). Often, we compare doing a project against a "do-nothing" or "current plan" alternative, set to zero value for reference. Be careful that overhead costs are legitimately incremental.

Set the PV discount rate to the company's marginal, after-tax cost of capital. This is necessary for objectively measuring incremental company value. A firm's chief financial officer should be able to provide this rate. Be careful that the discount rate does not include a build-up for project risk! Analysts often assume a risk premium in the discount rate, and this results in double risking when probabilities are applied. In decision analysis, we handle risks explicitly and separately with probabilities. Also, ensure that the discount rate is consistent with whether or not the forecast model incorporates inflation. In most cases, including financing is unnecessary because of the typical cost of capital reference for determining the discount rate.

Be careful about timing. Discount CFs to a single date, usually the next decision or investment point. Be sure your calculation tool properly recognizes the timing of CFs. Midperiod discounting is the most widely accepted timing approach, where a period's entire CF amount is assumed realized at the center of the respective forecast period.

Ignore sunk costs. Previous investment expenses or other prior CFs should be ignored for analyzing for today's decision. Do a "point-forward analysis." Recognize prior investments only when those amounts are part of future net CF calculations, such as the effects of contract terms and taxes.

Attitude toward Risk

You may skip this section if you are comfortable with measuring value as money, and if you are unemotional about the money amounts.

Risk attitude, or risk preference, is a fascinating aspect of decision analysis. Unaided intuition, for most people, leads us to make inconsistent tradeoffs between value and risk. That is, **most people, unknowingly, make choices that are inconsistent with their long-term objectives**. We do better in project evaluations, decisions, and negotiations by understanding the concept of risk preference. This is the purpose of risk policy.

The uninitiated typically exhibit **excessive conservatism**. For example, consider the manager of a large project who foregoes a chance to invest $1 million to gain a 50 percent chance at saving $10 million in project PV cost. That is, there are equal chances between a $1 million loss and a $9 million *PV* net gain. This behavior may seem rational if the manager or project has a modest budget. "Risk $1 million with a 90 percent chance of failure?!"

A more proper perspective, however, is to consider decision outcomes relative to the size of the entire organization's capital. For the example, the *EMV* for this decision is:

$$EMV = -\$1 \text{ million} + [.5 \,(\$10 \text{ million}) + .5 \,(\$0)]$$
$$= .5 \,(-\$1 \text{ million}) + .5 \,(+\$9 \text{ million})$$
$$= \$4 \text{ million.}$$

For our example, a risk-neutral decision maker would be indifferent between having $4 million cash in hand or having this project opportunity. Risk-neutral means being objective about money; that is, the scale of the outcomes does not matter. This means being an EMV decision maker.

The EMV decision criterion is widely used in decision analysis, either as a decision criterion by itself or as a reference to the "objective" value.

How much risk aversion is appropriate for a corporation? The ideal perspective, though perhaps impractical, is to compare the possible project outcomes to the collective net worth of the stockholders. For the second term, one approach is to assess a typical stockholder's net worth and multiply this times the number of stockholders. Very risky projects would have little effect on individual investors. For large, widely held companies, a nearly risk-neutral decision policy is perhaps best. Even for conservative individuals, **most persons should be nearly risk-neutral for modest day-to-day decisions**.

Upon realizing the implications of conservative selections, most people begin to make future decisions more objectively. An investment like the earlier example will reduce the project's cost by $4 million on average. This is clearly a good decision in a portfolio of many similarly sized decisions. When the project's value—or, better, the company's value—is large in comparison to the outcomes of a particular decision, the project manager generally will be better off using a neutral attitude toward risk when evaluating alternatives.

However, if one *does* want to have a conservative risk policy as a part of the decision policy, there is a straightforward way to do this. We determine a **utility function**, unique to the DM or organization, that relates "value" (i.e., utility) to wealth. It defines how the DM feels about money. This function also portrays a DM's **risk policy**. The utility function transformation provides a guide in how to make tradeoffs between objective value and risk. In calculations, we translate outcome value (usually *PV*) into utility units. The usual methods apply for calculating expected (value) utility. Then, the *expected utility decision rule* is to choose the alternative with the highest expected utility (*EU*). The next chapter details this topic.

Decision Policy Summary

Consistent decisions in an organization require a clear decision policy. Setting the guideline is straightforward, yet most organizations fail to do this. The result is sub-optimal decision making across the organization. Some parts of the organization are rejecting opportunities that would be approved elsewhere.

Most companies use DCF analysis for project evaluations. Dollars or other currency units measure value. PV discounting reflects attitude about the time value of money.

If desired, a utility function expresses a conservative risk policy. Many people may have never seen or heard of the technique. Instead, they subjectively make tradeoffs between risk and value. And, typically, people do this poorly. Fortunately, adjusting for risk aversion is not important for most decisions. If the outcomes are small in comparison to project value, then risk aversion should have little effect on decision making. For most purposes, *EMV* adequately measures value.

This leads us to the ***EMV decision rule***—a complete decision-policy statement suitable for most projects:

Choose the decision alternative having the greatest EMV.

If there is insufficient money, a common *ranking criterion is risked discounted return on investment (DROI)*:

$$DROI = \frac{EMV}{E(PV\ Investment)}$$

DROI prioritizes what investments to make first. The denominator is usually money (expected value PV investment) but can be any acting constraint.

This ranking criterion is an effective heuristic (rule of thumb) applicable to simple resource-constraint situations.

If the organization needs a conservative risk policy, we use a **EU decision rule** instead (described briefly in this chapter and in more detail in Chapter 4):

Choose the alternative having the greatest expected (value) utility.

For day-to-day decisions, these rules are equivalent. The rest of this book, except Chapter 4, applies the EMV decision rule.

Crane Size Decision

The problem-solving approach in this example is typical, and illustrates use of the EMV decision rule. In this example, the decision is what Size Crane to order for a specific task. We will solve this using two different presentation and calculation methods: a payoff table and a decision tree.

The project manager is planning Activity 15, which requires use of a crane. Table 3.1 shows the crane-size alternatives and possible outcomes, valued in activity Completion Days. A Medium Crane and a Large Crane are available by rental. The medium-sized crane is adequate in performing Activity 15. A large crane, however, would accomplish the activity faster. The decision pending is: Which Size Crane is the best alternative?

If the project goes according to the **baseline plan**, Activity 15 is *not* on the *critical path* ("not critical") and does not delay the overall completion time. (Critical path is discussed in Chapter 9 and Chapter 14.) A conventional project analysis sees no benefit of greater crane capacity on the project completion time. In fact, the Large Crane is inferior because of its higher cost.

However, a stochastic (probabilistic) project model shows the potential for Activity 15 (A15) to be on the experienced critical path. Suppose that the probability that A15 will be critical is .30 (30 percent, the *criticality index*) with the Medium Crane. That is, there is a .70 chance that A15 will not be critical. Table 3.1 represents best judgments about completion days, regardless of whether A15 is critical.

Initial costs to bring in the crane are $10,000 for the Medium Crane and $15,000 for the Large Crane. Daily crew costs are $1,500 and $2,000, respectively.

In a typical project model, we can make this approximation:

■ If the activity is critical (on the critical path), it delays the project by the full time to complete the activity.
■ If the activity is not critical, it has no effect on the project completion time.

Time to Complete	Medium Crane		Large Crane	
	Probability	Days	Probability	Days
Quick	0.3	16	0.3	12
Average	0.5	18	0.5	14
Slow	0.2	23	0.2	18

Table 3.1   Delay Days Given Activity 15 Are Critical

We will assume this holds for this example analysis. However, be aware that there are often situations when we will change an activity's criticality if we shorten its duration enough so that another path becomes critical.

We will also assume that the Time to Complete A15, with either crane, is independent of whether A15 is on the critical path. This, too, is not always a safe assumption, and sometimes the full model is necessary for proper calculations. Fortunately, for most day-to-day decisions, a simplified analysis is quite appropriate.

Early project completion adds $17,000 per day to the value of the asset. Symmetrically, each day's delay reduces the asset value by $17,000. In the Crane Size decision, this matters only if Activity 15 is on the critical path. Per Day Daily Cost is either $17,000 or zero, depending upon whether Activity A15 is critical.

In evaluating the Crane Size alternatives, we are concerned only with incremental project cost for each alternative:

$$\begin{pmatrix} \text{Total} \\ \text{Cost} \end{pmatrix} = \begin{pmatrix} \text{Initial} \\ \text{Crane} \\ \text{Cost} \end{pmatrix} + \begin{pmatrix} \text{Daily} \\ \text{Crane} \\ \text{Cost} \end{pmatrix} + \begin{pmatrix} \text{Delay} \\ \text{Cost} \end{pmatrix}$$

$$= \begin{pmatrix} \text{Initial} \\ \text{Crane} \\ \text{Cost} \end{pmatrix} + \left[\begin{pmatrix} \text{Per Day} \\ \text{Crane} \\ \text{Cost} \end{pmatrix} + \begin{pmatrix} \text{Per Day} \\ \text{Delay} \\ \text{Cost} \end{pmatrix} \right] \times \begin{pmatrix} \text{Days to} \\ \text{Complete} \\ \text{A15} \end{pmatrix}$$

In this calculation, the Delay Cost is always positive. If we wanted to show the benefit of early completion, we might subtract the baseline Days to Complete from the Days to Complete in computing Delay Cost. Regardless, the difference in EV cost is the basis for making the decision.

Payoff Table

Which Crane Size should the project manager choose? Payoff tables, such as that illustrated in Table 3.2, are a popular way to show the possibilities and perform the EV calculations.

			Amounts are in $thousands		
Scenario		Medium Crane		Large Crane	
Time to Complete	Probability	Total Cost	Probability × Cost	Total Cost	Probability × Cost
Not Critical and Quick	.7 × .3	$34.0	$7.14	$39.0	$8.19
Not Critical and Average	.7 × .5	$37.0	$12.95	$43.0	$15.05
Not Critical and Slow	.7 × .2	$44.5	$6.23	$51.0	$7.14
Critical and Quick	.3 × .3	$306.0	$27.54	$243.0	$21.87
Critical and Average	.3 × .5	$343.0	$78.99	$281.0	$42.15
Critical and Slow	.3 × .2	$435.5	$26.13	$357.0	$21.42
Expected Value Cost			$131.44		115.82

Table 3.2   Payoff Table for Crane Size Selection

One dimension of Table 3.2 shows the chance event outcomes. I use rows in this case for each *joint-event* combination of [Critical or Not] × [Time to Complete A15].

The other table dimension—columns in this example—represent decision alternatives. Value amounts inside the table are the "payoffs," hence, the name. I also include columns to show the components of the EV calculation, though these columns are often omitted.

Payoff tables are sometimes an excellent way to present a simple decision situation. Most people use computer spreadsheets for the layout and calculations.

Decision Trees

Decision tree analysis is a standard calculation method in decision analysis. Decision trees can accommodate more complex problems than payoff tables. Trees are often non-symmetric and have subsequent decision points, which are difficult features to represent in a table.

The tree diagram is the decision model and serves as a template for calculating expected values. Decision trees are flexible in expressing the logic of a complex decision. Chapter 5 and Chapter 6 feature decision tree analysis.

Squares represent decision points, and circles represent chance events. Figure 3.2 shows a decision tree analysis for the Crane Size problem. We can solve small problems easily without special software. Decision trees can quickly become enormous (hundreds or thousands of branches), and decision tree software is immensely helpful. An example decision tree program is DATA (Decision Analysis by TreeAge), and Figure 3.3 is a screen showing the solved tree.

For most people, combining values and probabilities is difficult with unaided intuition. The Crane Size decision shows the power of simple decision analysis when intuition and conventional analysis fall short.

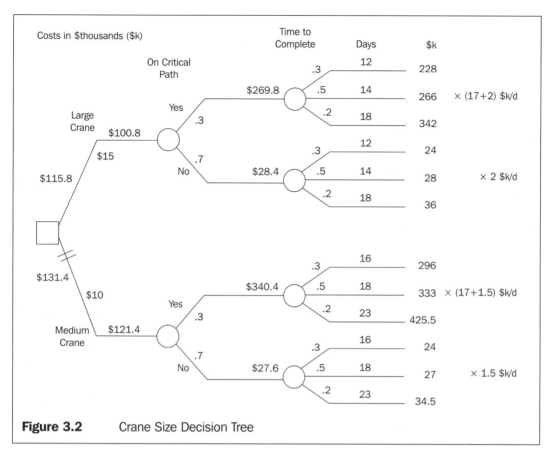

Figure 3.2   Crane Size Decision Tree

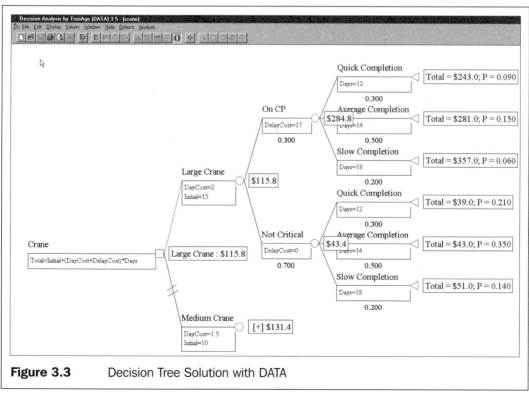

Figure 3.3   Decision Tree Solution with DATA

Methods Summary

We have now seen two decision model formats: a payoff table and a decision tree. The payoff table works adequately in simple decision models involving a single decision point, several alternatives, and several discrete outcomes. Usually, the chance events in these tables apply symmetrically to every alternative.

Decision trees are better able to represent sequences of chance events and subsequent decision points. A problem's structure is often different for each alternative, and decision trees handle this easily.

Monte Carlo simulation, described in Chapter 7 and elsewhere, is another important EV calculation method that is better suited to some problem types.

Endnotes

1. Good reading about a company's core purpose is *Built to Last: Successful Habits of Visionary Companies*, by James C. Collins and Jerry I. Porras (1997).
2. I have detailed the rationale for determining a PV discount rate in Rational Is Practical: Better Evaluations through the Logic of Shareholder Value, *Proceedings*, 1995 Society of Petroleum Engineers' Hydrocarbon Economics and Evaluation Symposium.

CHAPTER 4

UTILITY AND MULTI-CRITERIA DECISIONS

This chapter is for people and organizations that are not content to value decision outcomes in terms of money or money-equivalence. Even if monetary wealth is the objective, a decision maker may want a conservative risk policy.

Exceptions to Expected Monetary Value Decision Policy

Most businesses base their decisions upon monetary value—at least that is the primary consideration. The **cost/benefit/risk analysis** focuses on the calculation of expected monetary value (*EMV*). Recall that *EMV* is expected value (EV) of the present value (PV) net cash flow. (The PV formula is in Chapter 3.) Maximizing *EMV* is a suitable decision policy for most business situations.

However, not all circumstances are appropriate for *EMV*-maximizing. The primary exceptions are:

- When there is not enough money, or other resource, to do all of the worthwhile projects or actions (then most organizations use a ranking criterion, such as *discounted return on investment* described in Chapter 3, or *return on investment*, described in Appendix 8B).

- When possible outcome values are relatively large, and the decision maker is conservative.

- When money is not an appropriate measure. Or, when it's not the sole measure of value, and nonmoney considerations cannot be converted easily into monetary equivalents.

This chapter shows how utility theory provides a logical, consistent way to deal with these last two situations.

Conservative Risk Attitude

Logical decision making is based upon appraisal. We appraise or value the alternatives and implement the best one. In evaluating a particular alternative, we calculate or judge the value for each possible outcome. We then weigh these possible outcomes with their probabilities of occurrence. The probability-weighted average value is the *EV*.

In decision analysis, we use probabilities to represent judgments about uncertainty. In a credible analysis, all of the analysis inputs should be judged as objectively as possible. Properly done, the analysis results in an unbiased distribution of project value (or cost). Assume that monetary value, *PV*, is the measure of value. The *PV* outcome distribution shows the range of possible outcomes and each outcome's likelihood of occurrence. The *risk-neutral* decision maker need only know the EV *PV*, which is the expected monetary value *EMV*, for each alternative, in order to choose the best one. The EMV decision rule would be the organization's decision policy.

Example of Risk Aversion

What does it mean to be "risk neutral" or "conservative?" Suppose your company is having an expensive component manufactured. You are negotiating a cost-plus fabrication contract with the supplying manufacturer. Discussions have been candid, and both parties are sharing all data, especially cost details. There is a large fabrication contingency that potentially will quadruple the component's fabrication work and cost. Thus, manufacturing cost is a major uncertainty. With a cost-plus contract, you, the buyer, bear the cost risk. Assume that other factors, such as performance and schedule, are fixed.

Under the cost-plus contract, the possible cost outcomes to your company, the buyer, and the probabilities are:

Best Outcome = $1 million cost, p = .90
Worst Outcome = $4 million cost, p = .10.

Then:

EV cost = .9($1 million) + .1($4 million) = $1.3 million.

(Throughout our discussion, you may rescale the amounts to make the outcomes more closely match the magnitude of important costs typically encountered in your business.)

You are about to close the deal when the supplier surprises you by suggesting that she is willing to change to a fixed-cost contract. She asks, "What fixed price would you be willing to pay instead [1]?"

The equivalent fixed price—to you—depends on your company's attitude toward risk:

- If the company is *risk-neutral*, it would be *indifferent* toward either paying a fixed $1.3 million or accepting the cost-plus contract outcomes and risks.

- If the company is willing to pay somewhat more than the $1.3 million EV cost, it is conservative or *risk-averse*. Willingness to pay a *risk premium* is common decision behavior. For example, a conservative buyer might agree to a higher price—say, $1.5 million.

- If the risky, cost-plus contract is preferred to a fixed $1.3 million price, the company is *risk-seeking* in this situation. This is unusual behavior, except when there is entertainment value in gambling or when striving to reach a goal. Everyone pays more than the EV payoff when playing casino games or buying lottery tickets.

Conservative Behavior

Conservative behavior is widespread—almost universal. Should this be an important part of decision policy? Yes, if it is important.

For small decisions, decision makers can afford to be risk-neutral. When the outcomes become large compared to the reference net worth, often decision makers will make substantial value adjustments for risk attitude.

- For large, publicly held corporations and governments, risks are shared by many investors. For these entities, many of us believe that the EMV decision rule is appropriate.

- For individuals and small, closely held companies, a conservative risk policy is more suitable. Still, small day-to-day decisions will be almost exactly the same as with the EMV decision rule. However, decisions with large potential gains or losses may require conservatism. Utility theory describes how to modify an EMV decision analysis for a conservative risk attitude.

Utility is a measure of value reflecting the preferences of the decision maker, based upon beliefs and values. The EV concept still applies for decision making under uncertainty; outcome value, however, is measured in utility units instead of *PV*. The decision rule is to choose the alternative having the highest expected (value) utility (*EU*).

Utility Function for Risk Policy

In this section, we are using utility theory only for expressing risk attitude. Later, we will discuss how utility theory applies also to multi-criteria decisions.

Assume that maximizing monetary value is the objective. The *objective* value measure, then, would be *PV* using an appropriate discount rate. In the probabilistic sense, the objective measure is *EMV*.

Risk aversion is exhibited in what economists call the **law of diminishing marginal utility**. As an example, for most persons, winning a $1 million prize would be a tremendously exciting event. If one already has $10 million, however, the added $1 million would be hardly noticed. Incremental positive amounts add incrementally less value as wealth is accumulated.

Thus, for conservative persons, value is *not* a linear function of *PV*; twice the positive *PV* does not represent twice as much value. We could graph a function relating to how we perceive value versus the actual monetary value. This graph is a **utility function**. Economist and decision theorists use the word *utility* synonymously with *value*. Utility units are often called *utils*.

Figure 4.1 shows an example utility function. It translates *objective* value, *PV* (x-axis), into *perceived* value, utility (y-axis). The y-axis scale is arbitrary, including choice of origin. Utility curves that are concaved downward represent conservative risk attitudes.

The upward-sloping straight line in Figure 4.1 represents the utility function of a risk-neutral decision maker, where value is proportional to *PV*. This is a risk-neutral decision policy, i.e., an EMV decision maker.

Many decision analysts scale the y-axis so that the worst possible outcome has utility = 0, and the best possible outcome has utility = 1. The curve, regardless of shape or scale, is usually deduced from the decision maker's answers to a series of hypothetical decision problems.

I prefer the smooth exponential shape. Rather than arbitrarily defining the scale, I prefer to scale the y-axis in somewhat tangible units: **risk-neutral (RN) dollars**. This makes the utility measure more meaningful:

–RN$1 million cost is one million times worse than a $1 cost.
+RN$1 million benefit is one million times better than a $1 benefit.

Note that for positive *PV*s (benefits), incremental utility value decreases as *PV*s get larger. Conversely, costs or losses are amplified for negative *PV*s.

For small decisions, near zero *PV*, the straight line and the curve are nearly coincident. The result is that a value determined by *EMV* is nearly identical with the value obtained when recognizing risk-aversion.

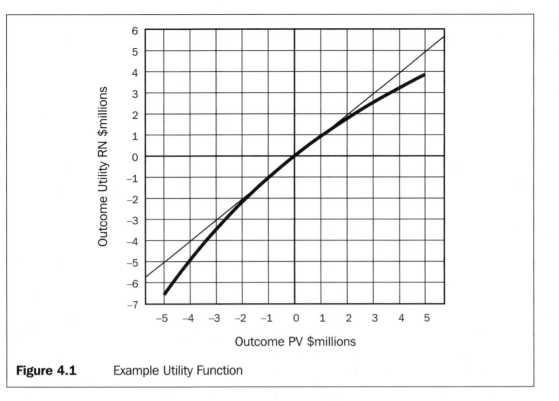

Figure 4.1   Example Utility Function

❖ In principle, we could use a graph such as that in Figure 4.1 to convert money to utility units. However, the calculation precision and convenience is better if we have a formula for the curve shape. I use and recommend this *exponential utility function* formula:

$$U(x) = r\,(1 - e^{-x/r})$$

> (in units of "RN$")
> where x is the outcome value in PV$
> r is the risk tolerance coefficient in $

The EV of U(x) is called *EU*.

The inverse function for obtaining the *certainty equivalent* (*CE*) is:

$$CE = -r\ln\left(1 - \frac{EU}{r}\right)$$

> where *EU* is the EV utility.

In Figure 4.1, r = $10 million.

Certainty Equivalent

A simple example will show how we use the utility function to help make decisions. Figure 4.2 shows an *EMV*-based *decision tree* for the contract example. The *objective* cost forecast and assessment is the EV of the possible

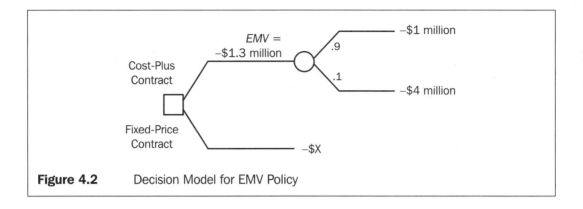

Figure 4.2   Decision Model for EMV Policy

outcomes. The cost-plus contract alternative at $1.3 million and the fixed-price contract alternatives have equal value to a *risk neutral* decision maker.

Recognizing a conservative risk policy requires a slight adjustment to the method. Assume that the company's *risk policy* is the *utility function* we saw in Figure 4.1. Some theorists suggest that this curve is appropriate to a company with a net worth of about $60 million. The degree of risk aversion is usually proportional to the size of the company. The risk tolerance coefficient is typically one-fifth or one-sixth of the organization's net worth.

❖ The organization's net worth and the one-fifth or one-sixth factor produce a risk tolerance coefficient (r) that is too low for widely held, public corporations, in my opinion. A higher r is more suited because many diversified stockholders share the risks.

We want to determine the fixed-price contract equivalent to the cost-plus contract uncertainty. First, calculate the *EU* of the cost-plus contract. From the utility function of Figure 4.1 or its equation:

U(–$1 million) = RN$1.0517 million
U(–$4 million) = RN$4.9182 million.

Calculating *EU* (actually EV utility):

EU = .9(–1.0517) + .1(–4.9182)
= –RN$1.4384 million.

❖ I'm showing the additional decimal places to demonstrate the calculation method, rather than to imply that we have great precision in these numbers.

EU is suited for comparing alternatives that all have uncertainties. Here, however, we are comparing an uncertain alternative to a fixed-dollar outcome. *We cannot compare dollars and utility* because of different units.

What we need to know is what guaranteed cost, $X, is equivalent to the uncertain cost-plus alternative. $X represents what we call the **certainty equivalent** (CE).

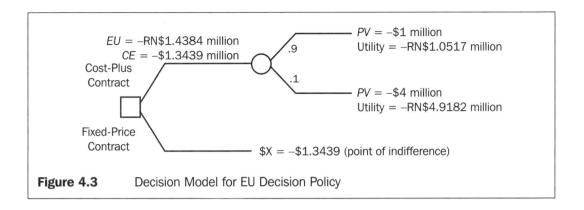

Figure 4.3   Decision Model for EU Decision Policy

We use the utility function to translate *EU* into *CE*. Figure 4.1 (or the inverse transform equation) shows that *EU* = –RN$1.4384 corresponds to a *PV* of $1.3439 million, the *CE*. Thus, for this company, a $1.3439 million fixed-price contract is equivalent to the uncertain cost-plus contract.

Figure 4.3 shows a decision tree solution solved with the **EU decision policy**. The approximately $44,000 (= $1.3439 – 1.3000 million) difference between *CE* and *EMV* is called the ***risk premium***. This premium is the additional amount the company is willing to pay, or sacrifice, to avoid risk. Note that *CE* and *EMV* are nearly the same in this case, even though the *PV* range is 30 percent of the scale. The risk premium is only 3.4 percent of the *EMV*.

Applying the Risk Policy

In decision analysis, we value the alternatives with either their *EUs* or *CEs*. The EMV decision policy is a special case: *CE* = *EMV* when the utility curve is a straight line, meaning that r = ∞. Either the *EU* or *CE* criterion results in the same decisions. However, if any alternative is a fixed-dollar amount, then conversion to *CEs* is necessary. When evaluating alternatives with utility, I like to calculate every node's *EMV*, *EU*, and *CE* when back-solving decision trees. If there are costs placed along tree branches, these costs may then be subtracted from the *CEs* as the tree is back-solved.

Interesting situations arise, sometimes, when the highest *EMV* alternative is not the same as the highest *EU* (or *CE*) alternative. That is the point of having a risk policy: to show which risk versus value tradeoffs are appropriate.

An interesting application arises in a problem of **optimizing participation fraction** or "working interest" in a project. If the project has a positive *EMV*, the EMV decision rule says, "Take it all." (We are assuming, here, that not investing is the alternative and has a $0 value.) However, if the potential downside is serious, it may be advisable to share the risk with one or

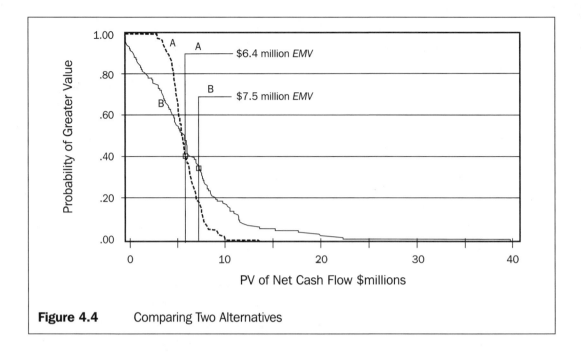

Figure 4.4   Comparing Two Alternatives

more partners. If the project has a positive *EMV*, then some fraction ownership is always desirable. However, you may not want it all.

What is the optimal interest you would want in a project?

A utility function representing risk attitude is the logical way to solve this problem. By iteration, deduce the shape of the function of *EU* (or *CE*) versus participation fraction. Choose the participation interest that maximizes *EU*. Keeping 100 percent of the project is often desirable. However, if the project cost is high and there is sufficient risk, a fractional share of the project will maximize utility.

When running a *Monte Carlo simulation* (simulation; we'll discuss how in Chapter 7), we calculate the outcome *PV*, then convert it to utility units in every trial. *EU* is the average of this utility-measured outcome.

When using simulation, it is customary to provide the decision maker with risk-versus-value profile curves. These are typically reverse cumulative frequency distributions for *PV*, and are the natural presentation format for simulation results. Most decision tree software provides similar, although sometimes more stairstep-looking, graphs. Figure 4.4 shows example reverse cumulative distribution curves produced by simulation.

If the curves cross, *and* when the best-*EMV* alternative is riskier (wider), having a risk policy is useful. This is the typical and unfortunate reality: Alternatives with better *EMVs* are usually associated with greater risk, as illustrated in Figure 4.4. Alternative B has a higher *EMV*, and has greater uncertainty. Which alternative has the best risk-versus-value profile? That depends upon the decision maker, who may visually compare the curves, allowing his intuition to make the decision. The more consistent—and recommended—way is to convert each curve into its *EU* (or *CE*); then choose the best alternative based upon the EU decision rule.

The utility function is a ***succinct, complete risk policy*** for an organization or individual decision maker. This is a powerful concept for a conservative company that wants to delegate decision making downward. It enables decision makers at all levels in the organization to make consistent risk-versus-value tradeoffs.

Decision analysis keeps separate: objective, time value of money, risk attitude, and judgments about uncertainty. This decomposition facilitates more logical and more consistent evaluations.

Multi-Criteria Decisions

Multi-criteria decision making (MCDM) is an approach for problems where value is multi-dimensioned. Usually these arise because of multiple objectives or goals. A city government, for example, faces tradeoffs across many dimensions such as schools, roads, and police protection. It can apply MCDM to solve such problems in a reasonably consistent way.

There are three principal ways to deal with MCDM problems:

- Recast the problem solely as an economic issue, and maximize *EMV, EU*, or *CE*.
- Convert nonmoney considerations into monetary equivalents, then maximize *EMV, EU*, or *CE*.
- Use a multi-criteria value function (which can have risk aversion embedded), and maximize *EU*.

Monetary Value Objective Approach

In project management, goals commonly relate to cost, time, and performance. How are we to make tradeoffs between these three dimensions? Understanding and quantifying tradeoffs is difficult unless a value model is used.

Suppose a project plan is in trouble. The main alternatives are:

- Spend an additional $1 million to complete on time.
- Finish three months late but within budget.

Which alternative is better?

Figure 4.5 maps project outcome value according to two dimensions, cost and schedule, for illustration. We measure project outcome value in PV dollars. (While the uncertainties are unresolved, however, we would be measuring project value as *EMV*.)

The project feasibility model determines the shape and position of the iso-value contours. In this case, the contour undulations reflect the seasonality of the business. Interpolating between the curves:

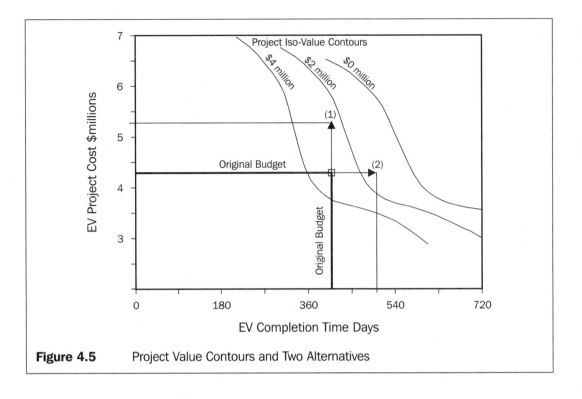

Figure 4.5   Project Value Contours and Two Alternatives

Alternative 1: Cost overrun   *EMV* = $2.4 million.
Alternative 2: Late   *EMV* = $1.5 million.

Both alternatives have unattractive outcomes compared to the original feasibility study. If maximizing *EMV* is the corporate decision policy, then Alternative 1 is the clear and logical choice. The *contours* (or the equivalent value formula) *represent decision policy.*

Monetary-Equivalents Approach

Dollars are a convenient and standard measure for comparing decision alternatives, especially in business. Increasingly, even government and not-for-profit organizations are making decisions based primarily upon monetary value.

Sometimes, developing a comprehensive value model is impractical or inappropriate. However, costs or monetary value often represent 80 percent or more of the decision basis. Minor additional considerations can be included in the analysis by factoring in monetary-equivalent values for the side factors.

Consider the situation of a national oil company that located a new refinery. One site was near an urban area that already had most of the needed infrastructure and good availability of labor. An alternative was to locate the refinery in an impoverished, rural area where jobs were greatly needed. Most of the decision was driven by the refinery's value in the nation's

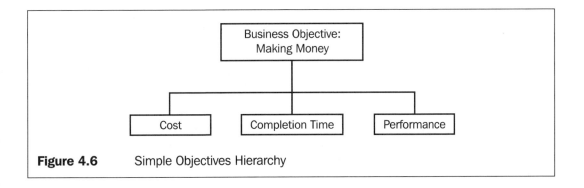

Figure 4.6   Simple Objectives Hierarchy

economy. However, because the company was government-owned, it was important to consider and balance other secondary objectives, such as improving employment opportunities.

All that we need for the substitution approach are ways to translate non-monetary criteria into money equivalents. For example, it may cost $5,000 to create a new job in the local economy. Economists can assess the value, cost, and timing of job creation, and we can then add cost equivalents into the cashflow projections. Then we can make the decision based upon *EMV* or *CE*, calculated in the usual way.

Multi-Criteria Value Functions

For true MCDM problems, the principles of decision analysis still apply. A key challenge is devising a way to measure value. Often, multiple objectives are involved, usually the result of having multiple stakeholder groups. Different stakeholders, of course, have different preferences.

EMV-maximizing businesses also use MCDM on occasion. It is sometimes impractical to develop a model to characterize different alternatives' impacts on corporate value, such as hiring decisions and employee evaluations. Although possible, it is usually cumbersome to attribute incremental cash flow to an employee because cashflow benefits are too hard to quantify.

In project management, most decisions are made considering impacts on **cost**, **schedule**, and **performance**. These form a hierarchy, as shown in Figure 4.6. This example structure has only two levels, but sometimes objectives hierarchies have several more levels.

A popular way of constructing the hierarchy is the ***analytic hierarchy process*** (*AHP*) [2]. This technique uses subjective, pairwise comparisons to determine the numeric weights of decision criteria and criteria scores for candidate alternatives. A mathematical technique translates a matrix of comparisons into composite criteria weights and alternative scores. Regardless of whether a hierarchy structure is used, MCDM uses a value function that combines various attributes (measured by decision criteria) of the problem.

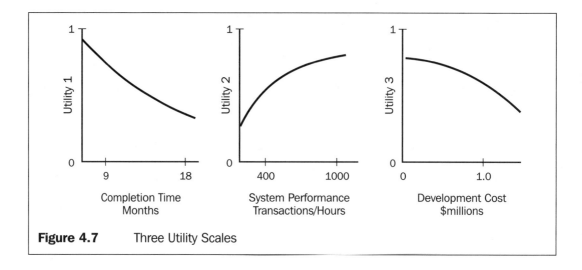

Figure 4.7   Three Utility Scales

Consider a software project manager who is evaluating staffing options in terms of cost, schedule, and performance. Because she wants to be systematic in her thinking, she develops a utility scale for each dimension, as shown in Figure 4.7. The y-axis of each scale represents goodness or *utility value* in the context of the respective attribute. She scales the x-axes according to the range of possibilities. The utility scales are arbitrary, and coefficients a, b, and c are just scaling factors weighing each component.

The utility y-axes have arbitrary scales. Ideally, each utility function is unique to a subobjective. Regardless of the shape, utility functions can also incorporate the decision maker's attitude toward risk.

Once the manager has the relevant quantitative attribute value measures, she can weight each attribute. The combination is a single *objective function*, often in the simple form:

$Utility = wt_1 \times Utility_1 + wt_2 \times Utility_2 + wt_3 \times Utility_3.$

The utility scales are arbitrary. The decision maker chooses utility curve shapes and weights (wt_i) so that the value behaves according to her intuition about the problem. Because of simplicity's appeal, most people use a linear additive formula like this for the value equation. Sometimes organizations craft more complex formulas with multiplicative or exponential terms.

❖ Arbitrarily, one might have component utilities use zero-to-one scales and have the weighting fractions total one; this ensures that the composite utility value function lies within a zero-to-one range.

Note that this valuation approach is *highly subjective*. The strength of MCDM, however, is in providing a structure that addresses all important factors and helps keep the process somewhat logical and complete.

Having a way to measure value enables a project manager to make consistent decisions throughout the project. To recognize uncertainty, we weigh outcome values with probabilities in the usual EV calculations. The decision rule is to pick the alternative having the greatest *EU*.

❖ Note that it doesn't make much sense to attempt calculating a *CE* in MCDM. If the decision maker is comfortable using monetary equivalents, she is better off converting the metrics directly into monetary equivalents.

Monte Carlo Solution

We will see how we can solve a MCDM problem with simulation. Consider our manager deciding whether to staff her software project for normal or fast-track development. The difference between strategies is the number of programmers/analysts assigned to the project.

A project model captures the project team's understanding of the development process and the team dynamics. We would have input variables in areas of application complexity, coding productivity, changing requirements, design performance, and amount of rework.

We run the simulation project model for each staffing alternative. Each trial produces a Completion Time, System Performance, and Development Cost. We convert each dimension into value components with the respective utility functions, as in Figure 4.7. We then, for each trial, combine the component utility values, weighted according to the value function.

The simulation model produced the following analysis results:

Normal Staffing:	*EU* = 0.723.
Fast-Track Staffing:	*EU* = 0.693.

Based on *EU*, the project manager logically chooses Normal Staffing. Figure 4.8 shows the three criteria distributions, and Figure 4.9 shows the composite value distribution with *EU*s indicated. The *EU*s are sufficient to make a decision. The graphs provide supplemental information for the manager to check and enhance her intuition about the project.

Three Pillars of Decision Analysis

Let me restate and amplify something important in Chapter 1. Decision analysis has three key characteristics:

1. Judgments as Probabilities. Usually we ask the most knowledgeable people available to express their expert judgments about risks and uncertainties as probability distributions.

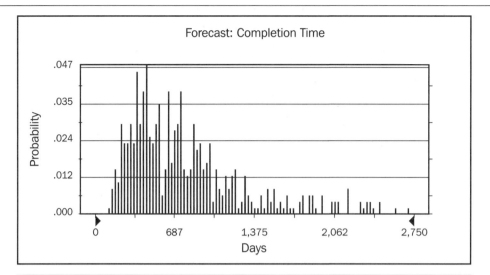

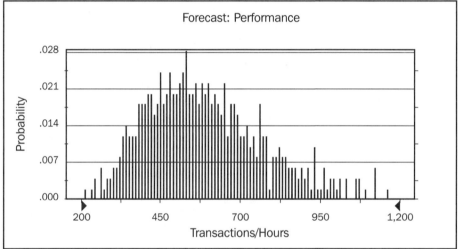

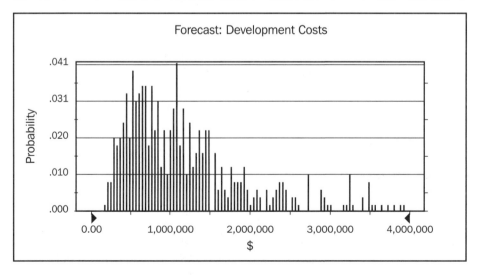

Figure 4.8   Decision Criteria Distributions

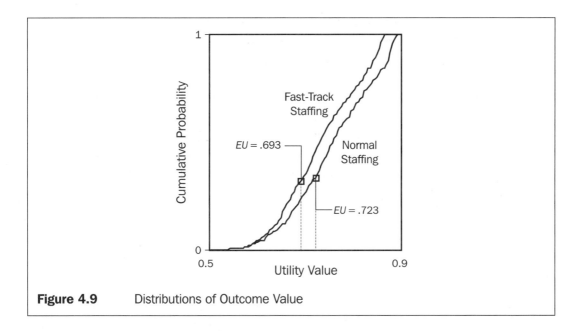

Figure 4.9   Distributions of Outcome Value

2. Single Value Measure. The company or decision maker has a way of measuring outcome value as a single parameter. This is the "value function" or "objective function" that we seek to optimize. For example, many for-profit companies use PV of net cash flow, *PV*, for this purpose. This value function may be composed of several criteria that represent measures for each of several objectives.

3. Expected Value. The EV calculation is the basis for calculating value under uncertainty. We condense the distribution of possible outcome values into a single measure—*EV*, the probability-weighted average—for valuing alternatives.

Any of these requirements can be barriers to wholly accepting decision analysis. Some people are uncomfortable about quantifying risk (#1). Others may be unconvinced regarding the applicability of the EV concept (#3), because of not having a "many-repeating-experiments" condition, for example.

In my experience, the value function (#2) is the cause of most situations where decision analysis is not wholly satisfactory. That is why we have devoted this and the previous chapter to decision policy. In project management, we need a quantitative way of relating cost, schedule, and performance so that we know how to make tradeoffs in one dimension against the others.

Even more troublesome are decisions involving health, safety, and the environment. Almost always, we can improve safety, reduce emissions, and improve service and product quality by spending more money. However, for example, how do we trade off human lives versus money? For some people, one solution to this dilemma is to consider EV lives in terms of other people's lives. Where in our organization can we apply money to save lives?

And at what cost? If we look to the most efficient place in our company to put additional money into safety (assuming we already operate a generally safe workplace), this best opportunity provides a benchmark (as EV cost per EV life) for the marginal cost of saving lives.

You can always perform stochastic calculations by putting judgments about risks and uncertainties into models (#1). Decision policy tells us how to value the potential outcomes (#2). And, evaluations (of reliability, benefit, and so on) under uncertainty are greatly eased with the EV calculations (#3). Making logical, consistent choices under uncertainty requires all three characteristics in your evaluation and decision-making process.

Decision Policy Summary

Project decisions are complicated when there are several objectives or sub-objectives. I have described three approaches for structuring decision policy in such cases. The starting point is always: Be clear about the objectives. Decisions are easier if there is *focus on a single objective*. Consider these example single objectives:

- For corporations: Maximize shareholder value.
- For governments: Maximize the quality of life for citizens.
- For professional associations: Maximize the organization's value to members.
- For individuals: Maximize personal happiness over a lifetime.

Measuring value toward the objective may have several components. Multiple criteria are sometimes used because it is inconvenient, or impossible, to fully develop the project model to assess value. Then we have a MCDM problem, and we should craft a value function to measure what is important.

Decision policy conflicts arise, most often, because of multiple objectives. Management should be clear about whose interests are being represented and what is being optimized.

All approaches examined in this chapter employ a means to arrive at a *single* value measure for possible outcomes. Decision analysis explicitly recognizes risks with probabilities, which are used to weight possible outcomes. After applying probabilities, *we arrive at a single value for each alternative*. Using probabilities in this way is much better than recognizing "risk" as simply one more criterion.

Endnotes

1. For the fixed-cost equivalent in the contract discussion, we are concerned only with the *CE*. *Game theory* would have us posture the optimal strategic response to the vendor's question.

2. The popular AHP technique is discussed by its inventor in Saaty 1994, and somewhat less enthusiastically in Zehedi 1989, both in *Interfaces*.

   Interfaces is the leading journal reporting operations research (management science) applications. The articles are about applications of quantitative methods, including decision analysis, and exclude most theoretical details. *Interfaces* is available in most university libraries or from INFORMS—the Institute for Operations Research and the Management Sciences, 290 Westminster Street, Providence, RI 02903.

CHAPTER 5

DECISION TREES

A decision model represents our understanding of an evaluation situation. This chapter describes what many consider the most powerful modeling and calculation technique in decision analysis.

Decision Trees

A decision tree is a graphical representation of *expected value* (EV) calculations. The tree consists of decision, chance, and terminal nodes connected by branches. This acts as a *blackboard* to develop and document our understanding of the problem, and facilitates team collaboration and communication.

Conceptually, *any* decision, no matter how complex, can be analyzed with a decision tree analysis. Other alternatives, especially Monte Carlo simulation, have advantages and disadvantages for certain problems. Decision tree analysis is especially suited for everyday problems when one wants to pick the best alternative quickly and proceed.

Node Types

There are three types of *nodes* in a decision tree:

- *Decision nodes*, represented by squares, are variables or actions that the decision maker controls.
- *Chance event nodes*, represented by circles, are variables or events that cannot be controlled by the decision maker.
- *Terminal* or *end nodes*, represented in a decision tree diagram by unconnected branches, are endpoints where outcome values are attached.

By convention, the tree is drawn chronologically from left to right and branches out, like a tree lying on its side. Decision tree analysis language includes colorful biological analogies. The starting (usually) decision node is called the *root*, and the radial lines are called *branches* (sometimes *twigs*). The terminal nodes are sometimes called *leaves*, and an overly complex tree bears the label, a *bushy mess*.

Tree Annotations

We label the decision tree diagram with these numbers:

- *Probabilities* for each outcome branch emanating from chance nodes.
- *Outcome values*, representing present values (*PVs*) of the resulting cash-flow stream, discounted to the date of the root decision. Sometimes, we may choose to place benefits and costs along branches as they are realized. More commonly, terminal node values represent the entire outcome.
- Node *expected values*, calculated during the process of solving the tree. When solving with a utility function as risk policy, I like to show expected monetary value (*EMV*), expected (value) utility (*EU*), and certainty equivalent (*CE*) for each node.

Tree Calculations

Solving a decision tree is a simple back-calculation process. This is sometimes called *back-solving* or *folding back* the tree. Starting from the terminal nodes at the right, moving left, we solve for the value of each node and label it with its *EV*. These *EVs* are *EMVs* or EV costs when we measure value in dollars or other currency.

Here are the **three simple rules** for solving a tree:

- At a chance node, calculate its *EMV* (or EV cost) from the probabilities and values of its branches. This becomes the value of the node and the branch leading to it.
- Replace a decision node with the value of its best alternative. We are applying the EMV decision rule.
- If a cost value lies along a branch, recognize that cost in passing from right to left. That is, subtract a cost when solving a tree to maximize *EMV*. Treat the rest of the cost as a "toll" to be paid when traversing the tree. (Sometimes a tree is designed to solve for EV costs, in which case, a cost along a branch is added.)

Wastewater Plant Example

In this case, we assume that your company is developing a new gold mine that will be operated by another company.

Development is nearing completion when your team discovers that water discharge contaminant levels are above those seen in the original survey samples. A regulatory agency now mandates an improved treatment facility

Probability	Other Activities Complete
.30	in three months
.40	in four months
.30	in five months
1.00	

Table 5.1   Completion Time for All Activities except Wastewater Plant

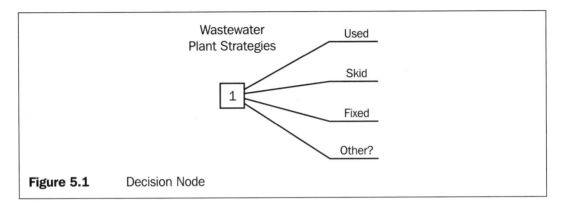

Figure 5.1   Decision Node

to recover heavy metals from the mine discharge. This extended pollutant-recovery capability was not designed into the nearly completed mine facility.

The best general solution is to construct or bring in a wastewater treatment module (referred to as the Plant in the following tables and figures). In addition to the investment and operating costs of the Plant, adding this capability has the potential to delay mine start-up.

Data Assumptions

There are uncertainties affecting the mine project completion time. For all other activities except the wastewater system, the engineers judge the completion time in three scenarios, as shown in Table 5.1.

Assume that extending construction activities to meet a later start-up date will not affect costs. Further, completion times are independent of the wastewater treatment system.

Three plant alternatives are being considered:

- **Used**: Buy a used, skid-mounted wastewater plant.
- **Skid**: Buy a new, skid-mounted plant.
- **Fixed**: Buy a new, fixed plant.

Figure 5.1 shows how the root decision node will appear, adding a branch for another alternative to be evaluated later. The square in the figure represents the decision point, and branches coming out of the right side are alternatives. For illustration in this chapter, the nodes have reference numbers inside, though this is not customary.

Used	{.3, 3; .35, 4; .35, 12 months}	
Skid	{.2, 4; .6, 5; .2, 6 months}	
Fixed	{.2, 5; .5, 6; .3, 8 months}	

Table 5.2 Time to Acquire and Install Wastewater Plant

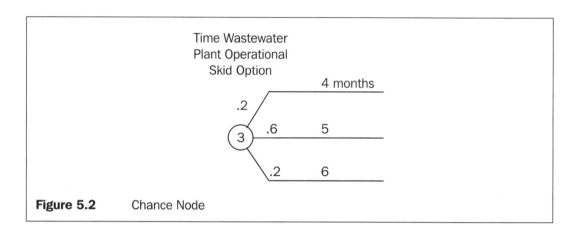

Figure 5.2 Chance Node

Although costing more initially, the Skid plant costs less to operate and is faster to install, plus it is likely to have greater salvage value at mine abandonment than a Used plant. A Fixed plant costs less to buy and operate than a skid-mounted plant, but requires more time to install. Clearly, trade-offs will be necessary in making the decision.

The engineers use three weighted scenarios in each case as the form to judge times to implement each plant-acquisition option. Engineers for the plant vendors and the project team jointly make these assessments, as three-level discrete distributions, as shown in Table 5.2.

These pairs of numbers represent outcome values (second in each pair) with their associated probabilities (first value, a decimal, in each pair). This *lottery notation* is a way of expressing a discrete chance event. The other mine activities are *independent* of the wastewater plant. Figure 5.2 illustrates what a Time Plant Operational chance node looks like for the Skid option. The branches coming off at the right at the node represent the possible outcomes. Note that the branch probabilities at any chance node always sum to 1.

An important consideration is the cost of delaying the mine start-up. In this case, the **opportunity loss** is the foregone asset value, due to increased development costs and delaying mine production. Assume that, from the project feasibility model, the project team determines that delays to mine start-up are valued at $150,000 per month (pre-tax) cost. Early completions have the opposite effect. The mine is projected to operate for six years. Other information about the options is shown in Table 5.3. These values are known well enough that single-point estimates can be used.

All costs are pre-tax $thousands			
Expenditure	**Used**	**Skid**	**Fixed**
Acquisition + Installation	$650	$1,480	$1,150
Salvage Value	$0	$600	$200
Operating Costs Per Month	$8.0	$6.3	$5.0

Table 5.3   Plant Cost Information

Over half the work of a typical custom evaluation involves developing a **project cashflow model**. The model provides the outcome value for each scenario: combination of decisions and chance-event outcomes. The model underlying the outcome values shown in Figure 5.3 includes, in addition to the assumptions in Tables 5.1–5.3, such items as inflation, cost of capital, depreciation, and taxes.

Try Your Intuition

Now you have seen all of the input data. Can you judge the best alternative by intuition? Try estimating EV cost for each option. What is the difference in EV cost between the first choice and the next best alternative?

For most of us, even this small problem is much too complex to internalize in our heads. The plant choice is not obvious because each alternative has advantages:

- **Used**: Lowest initial cost.
- **Skid**: Fastest and lowest-risk acquisition time, medium operating costs, highest salvage value.
- **Fixed**: Lowest operating costs, medium investment.

No single alternative dominates across all attributes. Most of us need an analytic tool to have confidence in our selection.

Evaluating Options

The *appraisal approach* of decision analysis is a logical way to evaluate the three plant-acquisition alternatives. Figure 5.3 shows the complete decision tree model: terminal nodes (right column) show outcomes if the respective tree path is realized; the outcome value is PV costs. Again, these terminal values are from a cashflow projection model. Since all monetary values are costs, one may work with EV costs instead of *EMVs*; minimizing EV cost is exactly equivalent to maximizing *EMV*.

The root node is the Type Plant Decision. There are two chance events affecting outcome value: Time Plant Operational *and* Time Other Activities Complete. The latest event controls when the mine development project is complete. In labeling the tree, we annotate these chance-event outcomes

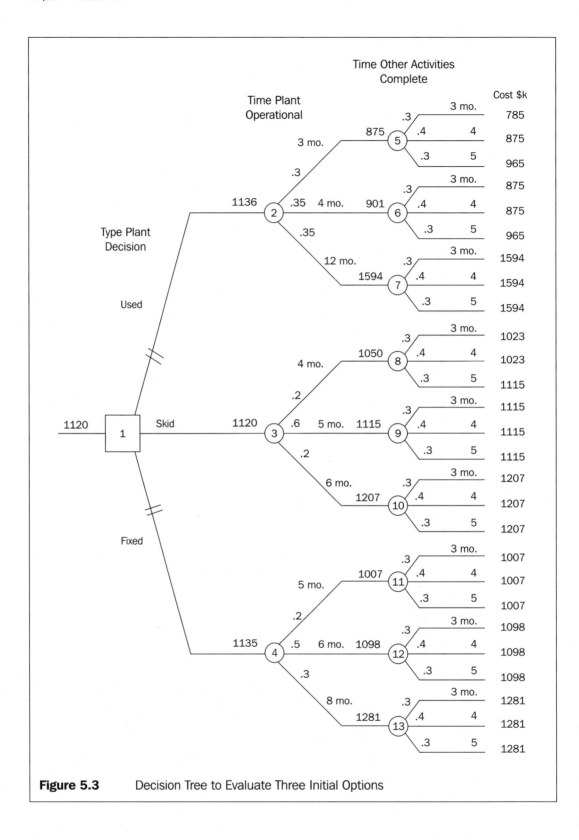

Figure 5.3   Decision Tree to Evaluate Three Initial Options

EV(5) = .3(785) + .4(875) + .3(965) = $875k
EV(6) = .3(875) + .4(875) + .3(965) = 901k
EV(7) = .3(1594) + .4(1594) + .3(1594) = 1594k
EV(8) = .3(1023) + .4(1023) + .3(1115) = 1050k
EV(9) = .3(1115) + .4(1115) + .3(1115) = 1115k
EV(10) = .3(1207) + .4(1207) + .3(1207) = 1207k
EV(11) = .3(1007) + .4(1007) + .3(1007) = 1007k
EV(12) = .3(1098) + .4(1098) + .3(1098) = 1098k
EV(13) = .3(1281) + .4(1281) + .3(1281) = 1281k
EV(2) = .3 EV(5) + .35 EV(6) + .35 EV(7) = .3(875) + .35(901) + .35(1594) = $1136k
EV(3) = .2 EV(8) + .6 EV(9) + .2 EV(10) = .2(1050) + .6(1115) + .2(1207) = $1120k
EV(4) = .2 EV(11) + .5 EV(12) + .3 EV(13) = .2(1007) + .5(1098) + .3(1281) = $1135k

And applying the expected value decision rule:

EV(1) = Minimum{EV(2), EV(3), EV(4)} = Minimum{1136, 1120, 1135} = $1120k

Values are to the nearest $thousand, although calculations were done with greater precision.

Table 5.4   Calculations in Back-Solving the Tree

with labels (months to complete) and the probability of the respective outcome. When solving the tree, we label each chance and decision node with its EV cost.

We back-solve the decision tree to evaluate the three alternatives. Normally, the nodes do not have numbers, though I numbered them here to illustrate the calculations. Table 5.4 shows the sequence and components of node EV cost calculations.

Note that there are fewer calculations at each column of nodes in progressing from right to left through the tree. For large trees, the progressive thinning of branches provides considerable **calculation efficiency** (as compared to a payoff-table approach). Acquiring a Skid plant ($1,120,000) appears the best of the three alternatives, although its superiority is slight ($16,000). The "cut" marks on branches indicate inferior alternatives that have been "pruned."

Tree Software

We can draw small decision trees on the back of an envelope and solve them with a hand calculator. A mostly manual solution is practical for trees of up to, say, 100 branches. By "manual," I include the use of a hand calculator. If we will be solving a tree more than once, including revisions to the numbers, a computer will help. I often build a Microsoft® Excel template for small- and medium-sized trees. One can even use Excel's Draw functions to illustrate the tree structure.

For people who frequently develop decision trees and for someone needing to develop a large tree, I recommend obtaining and learning decision tree software. The two programs that I use and teach with are DATA™ by TreeAge Software, Inc., and PrecisionTree™ by Palisade Corporation. More information is in Appendix B, Decision Analysis Software.

Decision Tree Summary

Decision tree analysis is a convenient way to analyze project decisions having one or several important uncertainties. We use probability distributions to encode judgments about risk and uncertainty. For all but the simplest of problems, decision tree models greatly bolster our intuition.

A single value measure, gauging benefits or progress toward the organization's objective, is a central idea in decision analysis. Money is a convenient measurement scale for most purposes. The Wastewater Plant example combines cost, schedule, and performance criteria into a single monetary value measure, EV cost:

> *Schedule* was translated into cost equivalents by recognizing the asset value lost due to project delay.

> **Performance** was recognized by different plant operating costs during the mine life.

Many practitioners believe that insights gained into decision problems are more important than the numerical results. Further comfort comes from credible quantitative-analysis results.

CHAPTER 6

VALUE OF INFORMATION

Creating good decision alternatives [1] is one of the most important project management functions. Often, there are opportunities to do additional analysis or to otherwise get more information before making a resource commitment. This chapter shows how to solve value of information problems, where there is an option to obtain more information.

Revisiting the Wastewater Plant Problem

In the Wastewater Plant example in Chapter 5, we evaluate the plan alternatives with decision tree analysis. The expected value (EV) costs are remarkably similar, ranging from $1.120 to $1.136 million. Figure 6.1 shows the decision model in a "shorthand" format: Implicitly, a copy of every following node is attached to the end of each branch of the preceding node. There are two chance events affecting the cost outcome: Time Plant Operational and Time Other Mine Activities Complete. Whichever chance event is *latest* controls when the mine commences production.

The decision policy I recommend is to choose the alternative having the lowest EV cost. This is the expected monetary value decision rule, only we are minimizing costs. **Schedule** and **performance** criteria are incorporated explicitly into the analysis as **cost equivalents**, based upon their impact on mine value.

Value of Information

More information, *even if imperfect*, is generally useful in revising prior assessments. Here are example sources of additional information:

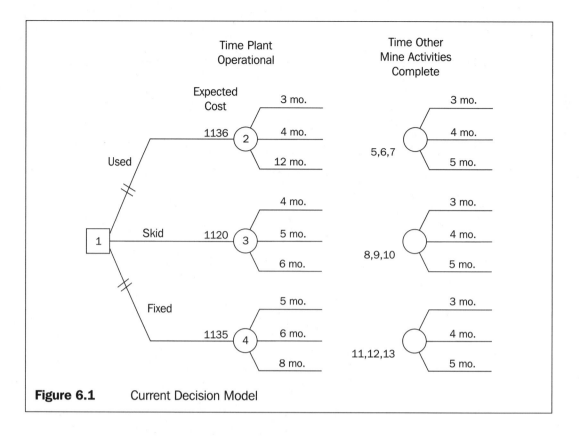

Figure 6.1 Current Decision Model

- Prototyping, market studies, and similar directed research
- Obtaining and analyzing more data
- Modeling in greater detail
- Spending additional effort in eliciting expert judgments about model input variables.

Time permitting, it might always appear that additional data and analysis are always desirable. However, we should weigh the cost, any delay, and other possible impacts against the *value added*.

What is the value of additional information? We determine this by adding an information alternative to the decision tree. A new chance node in the tree represents the possibilities of information-gathering results. We will use the information to revise project assessments or, more often, ***prior probability assessments***.

The equation to determine the value of additional information is:

(value of additional information) =
(value of new decision tree) – (value of old decision tree).

In this calculation, the convention is to temporarily ignore the cost of acquiring the additional information. We compare the value of information to the cost of obtaining the information. If the cost is less than the value, then it is better to acquire the information.

Project delays, often adding to costs, can also be temporarily ignored by assuming that delay is a component of the cost of information. Be certain that the evaluation properly compares the new versus the old tree, both incorporating cost and delay of obtaining more information.

A similar concept is *value of control*. In a decision analysis, "control" means controlling or influencing the outcome of chance events. Examples include:

- Acquiring services or products through turnkey contracts that fix costs
- Limiting losses with insurance
- Protecting commodity prices by forward-selling production
- Specifying higher-grade materials to reduce chance of failure
- Using conservative operating practices
- Investing in backups, redundancy, and flexibility.

Valuing additional control is similar to valuing additional information: compare the new control alternative with the previous best alternative. Control, like information, is most often imperfect.

Note that the analysis does not change the risks. However, information and control concepts often lead to adopting new alternatives with more-desirable risk characteristics.

Plant Information Alternative

Now consider a new information alternative for the Wastewater Plant: evaluating the Used Plant first. We can spend approximately one month testing and evaluating the used plant to determine when it could be operational. The evaluation will not change the actual lead-time if we select Used Plant; the used plant would need inspection anyway. The value of the information is in providing a basis to *reassess* the Used Plant lead-time probabilities.

Lead-times for other alternatives would be the same from the date of commitment. For example, if we spend one month evaluating the Used Plant and then make a decision to purchase a new one, then the New Wastewater Plant acquisition is delayed one month.

The initial cost of evaluating the Used Plant alternative is $30,000 (pretax) and is not refundable. This includes a deposit plus the evaluation cost, and would apply to the installation expense if we chose this alternative.

Figure 6.2 shows the expanded decision model. The decision tree shorthand illustrates the structure in compact form. The nodes are numbered to match the example calculations to the figures.

Revising Probabilities

The used plant evaluation and testing provide information useful for revising the prior probability assessments in the Time Plant Operational

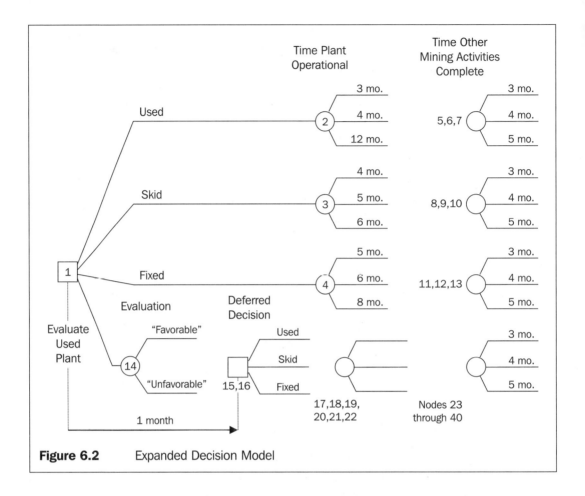

Figure 6.2   Expanded Decision Model

nodes. Note that the evaluation node in this section of the tree is followed by the investment decision. This is necessary to represent how and whether the new information adds value. If we already know the plant alternative, further information gathering and analysis are pointless.

Additional information adds value to the project *only* if it has the *potential to change what you are going to do.*

For simplicity, I classified the evaluation results into just two outcomes: "Favorable" and "Unfavorable." Project engineers judge the *quality* of this imperfect information, as shown in Figure 6.3. These nodes are not numbered, as this tree is a *side calculation* intermediate step.

The probabilities at the second column of nodes in Figure 6.3 are judgments about the quality of the information. The first node is the prior probability assessments about the event that matters, with today's information. Figure 6.3 has nodes in inverse sequence from the decision model. However, eliciting the judgments in this manner separates them, so that the expert(s) need consider only one event at a time.

For the decision model (see Figure 6.2 and Figure 6.4), we need to reverse the sequence of the nodes in Figure 6.3. My custom is to place double

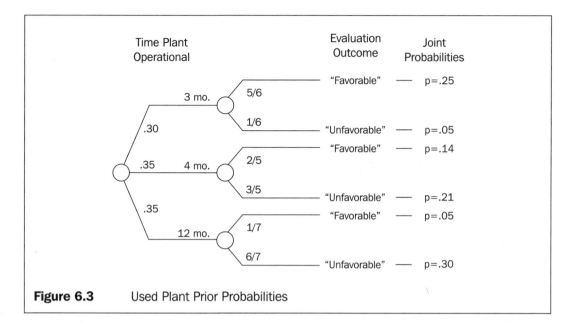

Figure 6.3   Used Plant Prior Probabilities

quotes about the information event outcome labels to help distinguish the information event (Evaluation Outcome) from the event of interest (Time Plant Operational). The expert assessed probabilities for the evaluation outcomes *conditioned* upon the Time Plant Operational event outcomes. Representing conditional probabilities is a convenient and powerful feature of decision trees.

The order of nodes in Figure 6.3 is the logical way to express the assessments and relationships between the two events. The cause-and-effect relationship is from left to right. However, the sequence is in reverse order from what we need to solve our real-world problem. The actual sequence would be according to the project:

- Get the evaluation result.
- Make the plant decision.
- Experience how long it takes to complete the plant.

We need to reverse or *invert the nodes* from the sequence in which the probabilities are assessed. We do this with a straightforward technique called **Bayesian revision** (using Bayes' theorem; see Appendix 6A, Bayesian Analysis). We revise the prior probabilities about Time Plant Operational based upon Evaluation Outcome. Table 6.1 and Figure 6.4 show the original and revised probabilities for each Time Plant Operational case, based upon the evaluation outcome.

Evaluating the New Alternative

Figure 6.4 shows the decision model extended for the Evaluate Used Plant alternative. The terminal or end values on the right of the diagram are

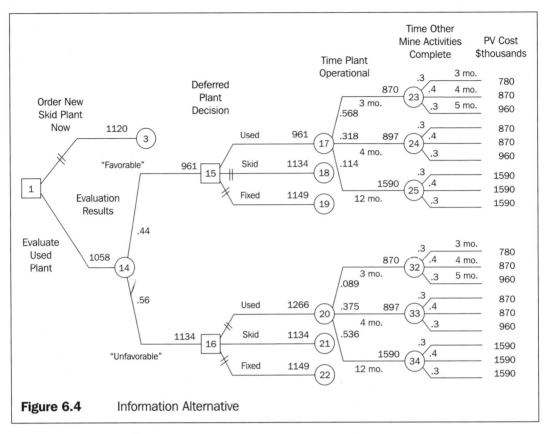

Figure 6.4   Information Alternative

Test and Evaluation Outcome

Probabilities and Times to Install for Three Cases

Current Information
Original Probabilities: {.300, 3; .350, 4; .350, 12 months}

"Favorable" Evaluation, Probability = .44
Revised Probabilities: {.568, 3; .318, 4; .114, 12 months}

"Unfavorable" Evaluation, Probability = .56
Revised Probabilities: {.089, 3; .375, 4; .536, 12 months}

Table 6.1   Probabilities for Used Plant

---

present value (PV) costs for the respective paths through the tree, and include any penalty for a delayed mine opening.

Figure 6.5 details the calculations for the EV cost of the delayed Skid alternative, given the Evaluate Used Plant choice. This value changed from $1.120 million to $1.134 million because of the added evaluation cost (about $18,000 after taxes) less the present value-timing adjustment (about $4,000) of delayed investment.

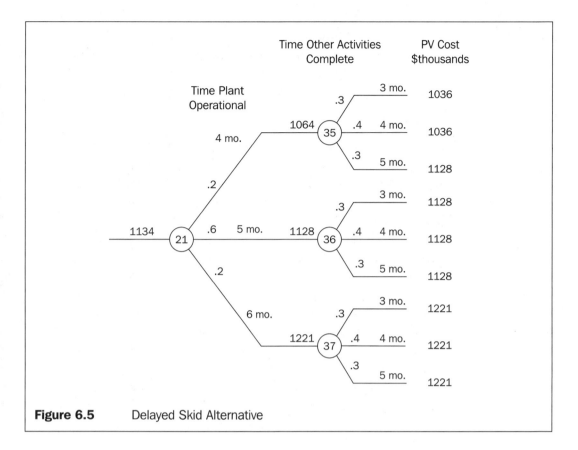

Figure 6.5   Delayed Skid Alternative

Again, new information adds value only if it has the potential to change a decision. In this example, the project manager should choose to install the Used Plant instead of the Skid Plant, if the evaluation result is "Favorable." If the evaluation result is "Unfavorable," then install the Skid Plant as planned.

The Evaluate Used Plant option is the best alternative. Spending pre-tax $30,000 on inspection adds a net $62,000 (= $1.120 – $1.058 million) of after-tax value to the project.

The decision tree was back-solved to compute the EV cost for each alternative. Starting at the right, each chance node is replaced (and annotated) with its EV cost. We replace every decision node with the value of its best alternative. Here are several example calculations, starting at the upper right of Figure 6.4 and working backwards:

EV(23) = $870,000 = .3(780) + .4(870) + .3(960)
EV(17) = $961,000 = .568(870) + .318(897) + .114(1590)
EV(15) = $961,000 = minimum of (961,1134,1149)
EV(14) = $1,058,000 = .44(961) + .56(1134).

Value of Information Summary

Many projects have a sequence of decision points. Analyzing these *options* is extremely important in an evaluation. Decision trees are especially useful for analyzing situations with decision points after additional information will become known.

We continually have decision opportunities. We cannot put many into a decision tree, though it is important to represent the key decisions. One option, that adds value to a project, is the ability to terminate a project that is performing poorly. Appendix 6B discusses project "kill" decisions.

We extended the Wastewater Plant decision tree analysis to value a new alternative to get more information. Many projects have opportunities to improve value through such additional data gathering and analysis. In most cases, it is convenient to structure the decision model using the new information to revise prior probabilities. Alternatively, we can revise assessments for event-outcome values. This usually involves modeling the system to understand and quantify the relationship between the information event (symptom) and the chance event of interest. Occasionally, we may want to model changes in *both* chance-event probabilities and chance-event outcome values.

Fairly complex problems can be handled in an orderly way with decision tree analysis. For some problems, the tree can become exceedingly large. The preeminent calculation alternative for such cases is Monte Carlo simulation, discussed next in Chapter 7.

APPENDIX 6A

BAYESIAN ANALYSIS

Bayes' theorem is credited to **Rev. Thomas Bayes**, an 18th century British clergyman. Bayes' formula is the most common way to revise probabilities based upon new information. Bayes' theorem is most often stated as:

$$P(e_i|A) = \frac{P(A|e_i)P(e_i)}{\sum_{j=1}^{N} P(A|e_j)P(e_j)}$$

where

e_i = outcome *i* of the chance event of interest

N = number of possible outcomes for e_i

A = attribute of new (imperfect) information, the outcome of an information event (symptom).

While the formula is more ominous than difficult, a more convenient solution technique is to construct and inspect a *joint probability table*. Table 6A.1 contains the full information content of Figure 6.3.

The values inside Table 6A.1 are the ***joint probabilities***, i.e., probabilities for the compound events comprised of combinations of Evaluation Outcome and Months to Complete Skid Plant. The values in the table margins have the extraordinary name, ***marginal probabilities***. Note that the right-column marginal probabilities are the same prior probabilities for Time Plant Operational as in Figure 6.3.

We can read (with some practice) probabilities for the inverted tree, as shown in Figure 6A.1, directly from Table 6A.1, by inspection. For example, let's assume that we have a "Favorable" Evaluation Outcome. There is a .44 chance of this occurring (the marginal probability, total of left column). The "Favorable" outcome restricts us to the left side of the table, which has three possibilities for Months to Complete Skid Plant: {3, 4, or 12}. The probabilities of the Months to Complete Skid Plant outcomes are in proportion to {.25, .14, or .05}. However, these values (joint probabilities) do not sum to 1. They must be ***normalized*** in order to total 1. We accomplish this by dividing each number in the left column inside Table 6A.1 by the column total. The normalized numbers then represent the revised probabilities conditional on the "Favorable" Evaluation Outcome, as shown in Figure 6A.1.

Still unclear? If you are confused about Bayes' rule, you are not alone. Although straightforward once understood, Bayesian revision usually requires a more careful explanation plus a couple of hours' practice before a person is comfortable with the process.

		Evaluation Outcome		
		"Favorable"	"Unfavorable"	
Months to Complete Skid Plant	3	0.25	0.05	0.30
	4	0.14	0.21	0.35
	12	0.05	0.3	0.35
		0.44	0.56	1.00

Table 6A.1 Joint Probability Table

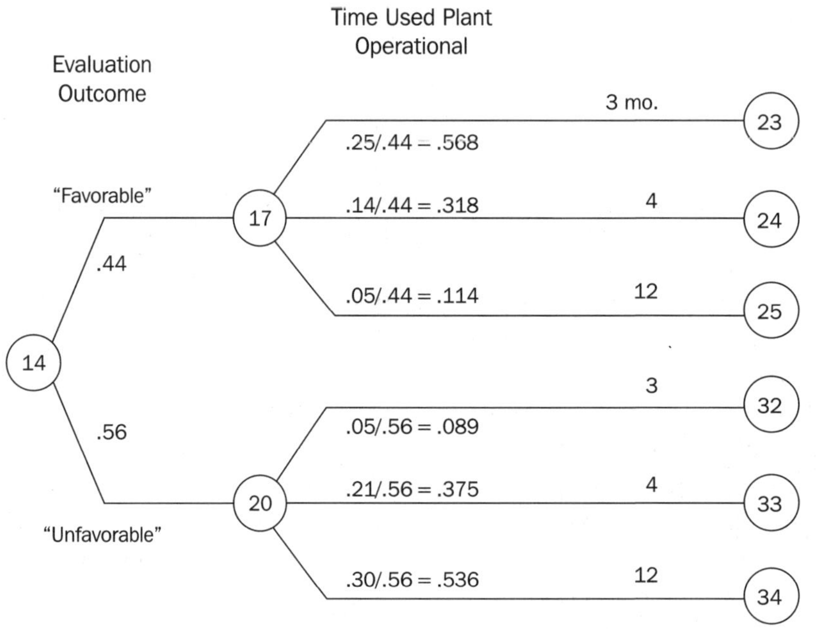

Figure 6A.1 Inverted Probability Tree

APPENDIX 6B

KILLING THE PROJECT IN TIME

Things happen [2]. Some projects will never reach the customer. When necessary, let's hope that the project "kill" decision is deliberate and made in time. New information during the project helps us to determine when dramatic intervention may be necessary.

Early Warnings

Experienced project managers recognize trouble. Some clouds on the horizon include:

- Poor productivity: habitually late targets; many activities exceeding estimates, and none reported earlier (suggesting activity teams might be wasting slack); unfavorable variances; rework; missed performance tests
- Tension, stress, and burnout among team members; requests for transfers out
- Waning enthusiasm (perhaps because the need for the project deliverable is diminishing, change in the company strategy, problem is proving more difficult)
- Worsening communications: difficulty in scheduling meetings; late when returning phone calls; responding slowly to requests for information
- Improving communications: requests for meetings and information; heightened formalism about change requests and approvals; adding someone to review the project.

A persistence of sick project symptoms indicates a need for intervention. When things start to go wrong, often many things go wrong together. The appropriate and extreme change might be terminating the project.

Gateways

Research projects often have a formal series of "gateways" or stopping points. Perhaps best known is the process for a new drug, from conception to market. Each successful drug goes through a series of stages of development, testing, and approval. (A fast-tracking strategy may shorten or bypass certain steps.) Each milestone is a decision point, primarily to continue or drop.

In the decision tree model, Figure 6B.1, we represent decision points as squares when the decision is not automatic, with the alternatives coming off the right side. A decision tree is a graphical representation of the problem, and provides a template to calculate the *EV* for each alternative. The normal decision policy is to choose the alternative with the highest *EV*.

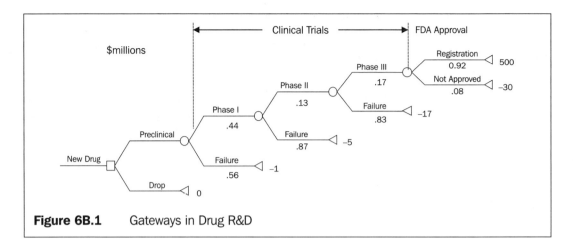

Figure 6B.1   Gateways in Drug R&D

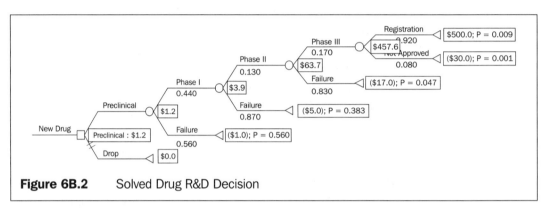

Figure 6B.2   Solved Drug R&D Decision

Figure 6B.2 shows the solution tree drawn and evaluated using the DATA decision tree program [3]. The node *EV*s are in boxes to the right of each node. At the explicit decision node (square), two "cut" marks indicate the "pruned" inferior Drop branch.

In tree diagrams, circles represent chance variables—that is, risks and uncertainties. In the pharmaceutical model, I can represent gateway decisions as chance variables because success at any stage obviously means that we go forward (on the upward branch at a chance node). The cumulative outcome value and joint probability are shown at each terminal node (triangles at end nodes).

Point-Forward Analysis

In evaluating a decision, our attention should be forward-looking. I am assuming here that the decision maker wants to do what is right for shareholders and is not posturing to optimize his career. Despite whatever has happened in the past, the decision best serving the organization is the alternative having the best *EV*, calculated from possible future outcomes.

Humans sometimes have difficulty in only looking forward. Animals are better at quickly cutting their losses. We humans often behave in ways that exhibit the *fallacy of sunk costs*. This is when our decision is influenced by sunk investment—money we've already spent. Sometimes a project has so much investment inertia that we continue pouring in money. We may be "putting good money after bad." Rather than continuing to invest—hoping that we'll get lucky—it may be time to stop the hemorrhaging.

We've been taught expressions, such as, "That's spilled milk" and "water under the bridge." The maxims are good ones: Look forward. Remember the fallacy of sunk costs the next time you feel committed to finishing that expensive meal when you are full, or when you have an hour invested in a movie that you are not enjoying.

Options Add Value

A lengthy project typically has milestones. Figure 6B.2 shows *planned* decision points. However, there are many others, a continuum really, where we can reexamine the project's viability at any point.

The best presentation of a decision analysis is the distribution of possible outcomes. A manager may say, "These extreme outcomes aren't possible. I would never let the situation get this bad before doing something."

We know that we have many opportunities to reallocate resources during a project, even perhaps killing the project. The evaluation model should include the most important of these decisions. Incorporating the decisions into the model, and the resulting calculations, more faithfully represents the true project value.

Decision points—*options* in the language of finance—add value to a project. In finance, risk is the friend of an option holder, because it is the uncertainty that creates the value of the option.

Feel Good about Your Decision

A *good decision* is one that is consistent with the decision policy of the organization and all of the information available at the time. Here are some key points about decision making:

- Good decisions are correlated to good outcomes. That is the justification for doing a decision analysis.
- Good decisions do not ensure success, though they often improve the likelihood of success.
- A success is not always the result of a good decision. However, a pattern of good decisions over the long run will increase the likelihood of success.

We want to reward people for making good decisions. This is an un-common perspective. In most participative organizations, the organization feels better having participants share in the project outcome, good or bad.

However, in the context of a *portfolio* of decision opportunities, making individual choices to maximize individual project success impairs long-run value. Killing projects, downsizing, divesting businesses, and such are typ-ically unpopular decisions. Think big picture and long run. This occasion-ally means a timely decision to kill a project, when that choice is the EV-maximizing alternative. We should appreciate decision makers who make good decisions under emotionally difficult circumstances.

By definition, we cannot control chance events. However, we should sleep well at night knowing that we have done the best with what we know.

Endnotes

1. An excellent source of inspiration in creating and evaluating alternatives is Keeney 1992. Keeney's book is about multi-criteria decision making, which we discuss at the end of Chapter 4.
2. Adapted from Center for Business Practices 2001.
3. Figures 6B.1 and 6B.2 were generated using the DATA decision tree program by TreeAge Software, Inc., and are used with permission.

CHAPTER 7

MONTE CARLO SIMULATION

Monte Carlo simulation is perhaps the most popular of the various management science techniques. The simple, elegant method provides a means to solve equations with probability distributions.

Approximating Expected Value

Decision trees solve for the *expected values* (*EVs*) of decision alternatives. Conceptually, we can solve any decision problem with a decision tree. For some problems, however, a combinatorial explosion of branches makes calculations cumbersome or impractical.

Monte Carlo simulation (simulation) uses a random sampling process to approximate *EVs*. This technique easily deals with many possible outcomes, and has other important advantages over decision tree analysis.

Wastewater Plant Revisited

We will continue the discussion about the Wastewater Plant example from Chapter 5 and Chapter 6. Figure 7.1 and Table 7.1 summarize the decision tree model. We have considered four alternatives for acquiring a government-mandated wastewater treatment facility that was not part of the original project.

The chief uncertainties in this problem are the time to implement the plant choice and the longest completion time of all other mine-development activities. Fixed assumptions include mine life, plant operating costs, salvage values, and delay cost (per month impact on mine value of delaying or accelerating startup).

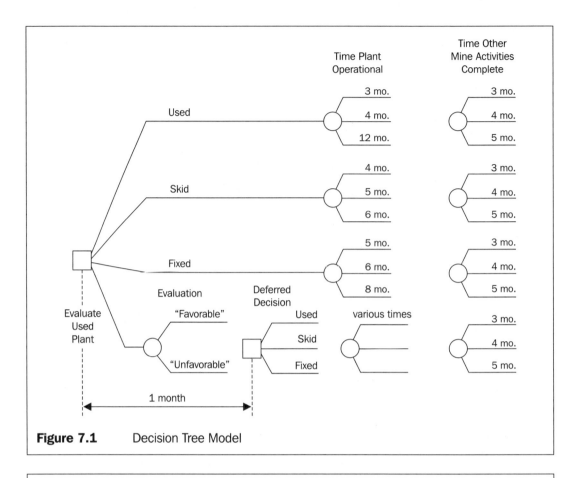

Figure 7.1   Decision Tree Model

Short Name	Alternative
Used	Acquire a used, skid-mounted wastewater plant ($650k initial outlay).
Skid	Acquire a new, skid-mounted plant ($1480k initial outlay).
Fixed	Acquire a new, fixed plant ($1150k initial outlay).
Evaluate	Take one month ($30k expense) to evaluate the condition and time needed to ready the used, skid-mounted plant, *then* decide which plant to acquire.

Table 7.1   Wastewater Plant Alternatives

Difficulties in Extending the Tree Analysis

Decision tree analysis provides a logical, credible basis for the wastewater plant decision. Some problems are quite cumbersome to solve as decision trees, and simulation provides another approach better suited to some problems.

Consider the three plant type alternatives. There are twenty-seven possible outcomes:

3 decision alternatives
× 3 Time Plant Operational outcomes
× 3 Time Other Mine Development Activities Complete outcomes
———
27

The paths in the Evaluate Used Plant alternative (lower) part of the tree add another fifty-four possible outcomes. Adding a few more uncertainties can lead to thousands of decision tree paths to evaluate. As we add decision and chance nodes, decision trees often grow exponentially.

Decision trees also require that we represent uncertainties as discrete probability distributions. For example, we characterized the outcomes for Time Other Mine Activities Complete as being exactly three, four, or five months. We considered only three completion time scenarios. In reality, the possibilities are infinite, and we could measure time in weeks, days, or even shorter periods. A continuous distribution represents a better view of this variable. However, decision trees accept only discrete-chance events, and we must convert any truly continuous events into discrete approximations. Additional outcome branches on the chance nodes would provide finer resolution, but exacerbate the combinatorial explosion. A decision tree can easily become a *bushy mess*.

Monte Carlo Technique

Simulation does not suffer the difficulties mentioned earlier. While not a panacea, it has advantages in certain situations. It allows a richer, more detailed representation, which can sometimes be important. In competitive bidding, for example, even small differences can affect who wins the contest.

Conceptually, either decision tree analysis or simulation can solve any evaluation problem. There are advantages and disadvantages to each technique. The choice depends upon the problem, tools at hand, and personal preference.

We credit legendary mathematician **John von Neumann** (originally Johann, 1903–1957) with popularizing the Monte Carlo technique, while participating in the design of the atomic bomb. He recognized that a relatively simple sampling technique could solve certain mathematical problems that are otherwise impossible. Among the applications is solving for *EV*, the probability-weighted average of a probability distribution. A valuable side-benefit is that we easily obtain approximate outcome *probability distribution shapes*.

Simulation depends upon two essential elements:

■ A model that projects project outcome and outcome value.
■ A technique that repeatedly generates scenarios, driven by randomly sampling input probability distributions.

The details follow.

Inputs as Distributions

Probability distributions express expert opinions about uncertainties. An expert's forecast for time to complete an activity is better as a distribution than as a single-value estimate. The distribution completely represents the expert's opinion about the outcome range and the relative likelihood of values within that range.

The foundation for simulation is a *random sampling process*. We generate many possible project scenarios (trials). Then, we examine the distributions of trial outcome values. Trials, in sufficient number, preserve the characteristics of the original probability distributions and approximate the solution distributions.

The simulation process is appealing because it is easily understood and not a black-box solution. We can inspect any trial result to determine what combination of input values led to this outcome scenario projection. A simulation model is a straightforward extension to the customary, single-valued *deterministic* model (so-called because every input is singly *determined*). This is why simulation persists as perhaps the most popular technique in operations research/management science.

❖ The word *simulation* is a very general term, used whether or not the model involves probabilities. In decision analysis, we are always talking about stochastic (probabilistic) models, so that *simulation* in this book is always referring to a model solved with the Monte Carlo method.

Every trial pass through the model generates a plausible scenario. Extreme cases can be examined to see what conditions gave rise to these *outlier* results. Examining outliers is a powerful method of validating the model.

Figure 7.2 shows, conceptually, how we extend a conventional, deterministic model for a simulation analysis. The deterministic model sometimes needs little modification to prepare for simulation. We only need changes necessary to ensure that the model's calculations are valid over all possible ranges and combinations of input values.

If one or more inputs to the model are probability distributions, then the outputs will be probability distributions also. Instead of a single outcome value, such as a present value (*PV*), simulation yields a distribution for value. We can generate projections for *timespread variables*, such as *net cash flow*, and display them as EV and confidence curves.

Simulation Process

An iterative loop surrounds the deterministic project model and controls the process—generating many plausible "trial" solutions. Figure 7.3 is a flow diagram of a simulation. Most of the action is at the left, where the system performs many *trials*. Each trial is a pass through the steps at the left, and generates a possible case for the behavior of the project. The program

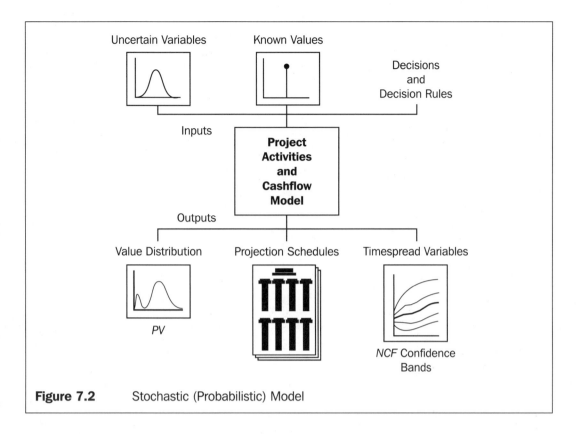

Figure 7.2 Stochastic (Probabilistic) Model

generates many cases until a predetermined number of trials, or until a *stopping rule* condition, is satisfied. Typically, several hundred trials are necessary to obtain enough data for reasonable precision in the *EV* calculation.

Here is a typical sequence of steps in the simulation process:

1. Sample probability distributions representing the several random, or stochastic, variables.
2. Substitute the trial values of the random variables into the deterministic model. Re-solve the model, obtaining project results and outcome values.
3. Store preselected outcome values, e.g., time and cost to complete, in a data file.
4. Return to Step 1 and repeat until the number of trials is sufficient to provide the required level of precision.
5. Analyze the stored results.

When the trials are complete, we analyze the generated synthetic data. Averaging trial values approximates *EVs*. Frequency distributions and timespread variable confidence bands are easy to obtain—for example, the *PV* distribution shown in the lower left of Figure 7.3.

Averaging the *PV* outcomes *approximates* the expected monetary value (*EMV*). The precision of the *EV* and probability distribution shape approximations improves as we increase the number of trials.

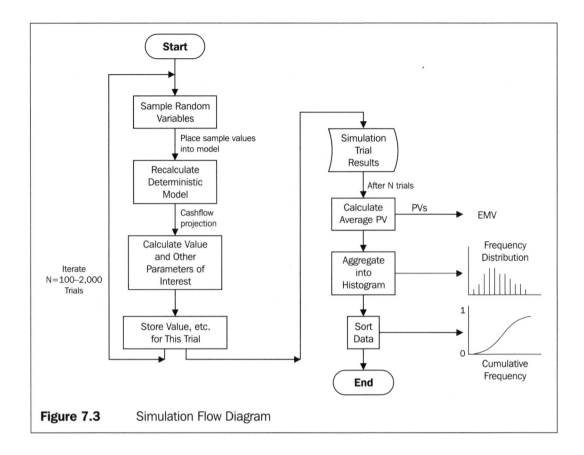

Figure 7.3   Simulation Flow Diagram

The *EMV* may be sufficient information for decision making. However, in the spirit of full and clear communication, it is good practice to include the *PV* distribution in the analysis presentation. Different distribution formats are available:

- Aggregating *PV*s into groups by size and displaying the values as a *frequency histogram* provides the approximate shape of the *PV* probability (density) function.
- Sorting *PV*s by magnitude and displaying *PV* as a function of rank yields the *cumulative frequency distribution*.

These frequency distributions approximate the shape of the solution probability distributions.

How Random Sampling Works

We obtain sample, or trial, values for chance variables by a simple process. In simulation, we often call these ***random variables***, because a random number generator drives the sampling process. Synonyms include *chance variable* and *stochastic variable*. We will look at conventional Monte Carlo sampling for continuous and discrete events.

Time to Complete Other Activities	Probability
3 months	.30
4 months	.40
5 months	.30

Table 7.2   Three-Level Input Distribution

Discrete Distribution

In the decision tree analysis, we needed to abstract Time to Complete Other Activities into a discrete distribution. Table 7.2 shows my three-level distribution. [There are many combinations of branch outcome values and probabilities that will provide the same target mean (μ) and standard deviation (σ).] With simulation, we can avoid this discrete abstraction: we can represent the full range of possible outcomes of any uncertainty. However, for illustration, let's look at how we could sample the discrete Time to Complete Other Activities distribution in a simulation.

A random number function provides a *random sampling* parameter between zero and one. Most *random number generators*, such as the **RAND ()** function in Excel, provide a uniform distribution with equally-likely values in the range, zero to one.

To set up the discrete distribution for sampling, divide the zero-to-one interval into segments whose widths correspond to the probabilities of different outcomes, as illustrated in Figure 7.4.

Each partition's width corresponds to the probability of the corresponding outcome. The example logic works like this:

RN = random number
If RN < .3, then
    Time to Complete Other Activities = 3 months
else if RN < .7, then
    Time to Complete Other Activities = 4 months
else
    Time to Complete Other Activities = 5 months.

When using Monte Carlo simulation, we seldom would use a discrete approximation for a continuous event. "Risks," however, are often binary: either the risk event happens or not. This is easy to simulate with logic such as:

Probability of Weather Delay = .24
RN = random number
If RN < Probability of Weather Delay, then
    Weather Delay = True.

If true, then we could apply a time, cost, or other impact in the form of a continuous distribution, as explained next.

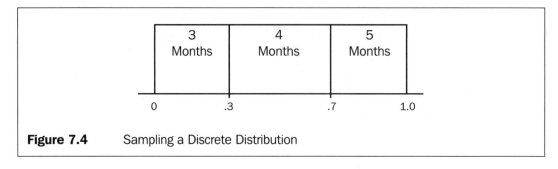

Figure 7.4   Sampling a Discrete Distribution

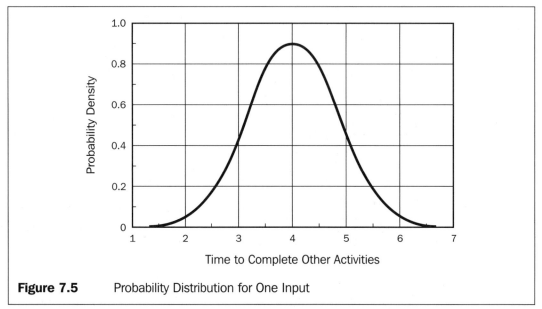

Figure 7.5   Probability Distribution for One Input

Continuous Distribution

After an expert takes time to judge Time to Complete Other Activities, she would normally express her opinion as a probability distribution. Consider the probability density function in Figure 7.5. This is a *normal (Gaussian) distribution* shape, with $\mu = 4$ months and $\sigma = .775$ month. This distribution is this expert's *forecast* for this variable.

In the decision tree analysis, Time to Complete Other Activities was abstracted into the three-value discrete distribution, shown in Table 7.2. With simulation, we do not need to convert the form of the original distribution if it was a continuous distribution. In simulation, we can represent the full range of possible outcomes.

Simulation software often allows directly entering the probability density distribution as an input assumption. Do not worry about the actual calculation method. Conceptually, the sampling process uses the cumulative form of the distribution.

We want to convert the density curve of Figure 7.5 into the cumulative curve of Figure 7.6 [1]. The conversion is straightforward. The probability

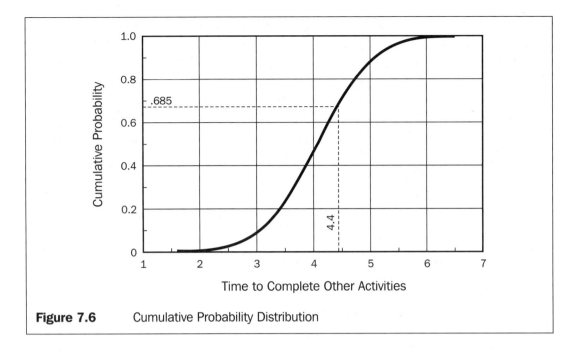

Figure 7.6   Cumulative Probability Distribution

density distribution has a *normalization requirement* that the area under the curve equals 1. We obtain the cumulative distribution by adding the area (i.e., integrating) under the probability density function from left to right.

Both Figure 7.5 and Figure 7.6 fully represent someone's judgment about the uncertainty, Time to Complete Other Activities. The cumulative form is more convenient for our present purpose. For any Time to Complete, *t*, on the x-axis, the curve intercept is the probability that the outcome will be less than *t*.

Refer to Figure 7.6 for this explanation of how (traditional) Monte Carlo sampling works for a continuous distribution [2]. On a single pass through the simulation model, we want to determine a trial value for this activity completion time. Most random number generators produce a number corresponding to a zero-to-one uniform distribution. This is the sampling parameter and, conveniently, maps to the cumulative probability axis. To obtain a *trial value* for this variable:

1. Enter the y-axis at the sampling parameter (random number).
2. Move rightward to the cumulative curve.
3. Move down to the corresponding value on the x-axis. This x-axis value is the *trial value* for this variable.

Suppose the random number generator provides a value of .685. As indicated in Figure 7.6, this corresponds to 4.4 weeks on the x-axis. We substitute this trial value into the deterministic project model. We next obtain trial values for the other random variables in similar fashion, using a different random number for each variable. We then solve the model for a trial projection. This is but one particular scenario in the simulation run.

Note that if we sample an input distribution many times and graph the values in a frequency histogram, then the shape will approximate the original probability distribution. The key to simulation is that this random sampling process preserves the character of the original distributions. The match improves with more trials and finer histogram divisions.

If we sample a distribution many times and average the result, the average approximates *EV*. The mathematically inclined may recall the integral equation that random sampling solves:

$$EV = \int_{-\infty}^{+\infty} x \, f(x) \, dx$$

where x is the outcome value, and $f(x)$ is the probability density function. The simulation process performs the integration for us—approximately. We need simulation because for most evaluation problems of interest, the integration defies direct mathematical solution. We do not have a simple equation form for the solution $f(x)$; it is distributed through the fabric of our model. Thus, Monte Carlo simulation is solving a very difficult, if not impossible, calculus problem for us!

Wastewater Plant Simulation

Figure 7.7 shows a revised decision model for the Wastewater Plant decision of the gold mine development project. We now use continuous probability distributions when we can, to represent the possibilities more completely. Being able to use continuous distributions is an important advantage that simulation has over decision trees.

The Evaluate Used alternative in Figure 7.7 involves inspecting and testing the used unit. In the decision tree analysis, the evaluation outcome was either "Favorable" or "Unfavorable." These outcomes are correlated with the time to complete the used unit through a joint probability table. On the basis of the evaluation outcome, the probabilities for the different times to complete outcomes were revised by applying Bayes' rule.

Simulation allows a richer representation. While we can discretely model Bayes-like dependencies easily, we can use a more real-to-life description. In the simulation, we obtain an estimate for Time to Complete Used Plant. The uncertainty of this *imperfect information* is represented by a separate Estimate Error distribution. Here is the way I model the estimation result:

(Estimated Time to Install) =
(True Time to Install New Plant) × (Estimate Error Function).

We can incorporate virtually any number of chance events into a simulation model. This is unlike decision trees, which can quickly become too large to solve. Table 7.3 documents the probability distributions in the Wastewater Plant model.

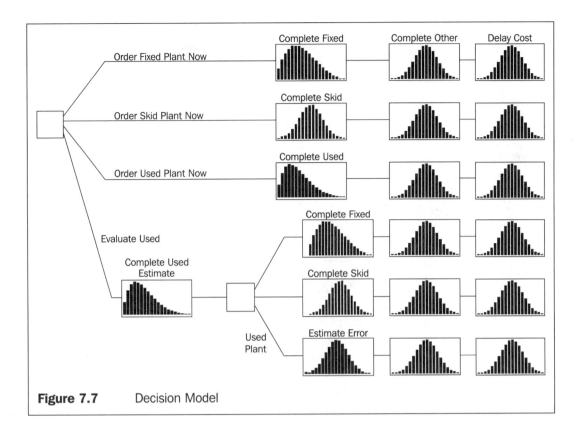

Figure 7.7   Decision Model

To further embellish the Wastewater Plant example, I added another chance event, a Delay Cost variable. This is the per-month financial impact of delayed (or accelerated) mine start-up. (In previous decision tree models, this had been a fixed-impact, pre-tax $150k/per month.)

Figure 7.7 shows the various distributions used in the simulation model. Note that the discrete distributions used earlier are now represented by either *normal* or *beta* distributions. The normal distribution has two parameters (μ and σ). Beta distributions are simple functions that can resemble many shapes (by adjusting two shape parameters, a scaling coefficient, and an offset), ranging from a symmetric, normal distribution-looking distribution to highly skewed (asymmetric) distributions. Here, beta distributions provide asymmetric bell-shaped distributions with *positive skewness* (longest tail on the positive side). Chapter 10 describes these and other popular distribution shapes.

Results

Table 7.4 shows the results of a 500-trial simulation run. The numbers, while close to those obtained from the decision tree analysis, are somewhat different due to the increased detail of the continuous distributions and the added Delay Cost variable. The Used Later cost is lower than the Used Now

Input Variable	Discrete Distributions (Decision Trees)	Continuous Distributions (Simulation)	Units
Time to Complete Other Activities	{.3,3;.4,4;.3,5}	Normal(4,.775)	Months
Time to Complete Skid Unit	{.2,4;.6,5;.2,6}	Normal(5,.632)	Months
Time to Complete Fixed Unit	{.2,5;.5,6;.3,8}	3.067 + 10 × Beta(2,4)	Months
Time to Complete Used Unit	{.3,3;.35,4;.35,12}	1 + 27.5 × Beta(2,8)	Months
Used Unit Estimation Error		Normal(1,.3)	Estimate Factor
Delay Cost		Normal(150,22.5)	$Thousand/Month

Table 7.3   Input Distributions

Alternative	Expected Value Costs $thousands
Fixed Now	1130
Skid Now	1120
Used Now	1141
Fixed Later	1143
Skid Later	1136
Used Later	1137
Evaluate	1024

Table 7.4   EV Costs

cost because, in this model, the testing and inspecting cost ($30,000, including deposit) is expensed rather than capitalized for taxes. This cost, however, reduces the investment required if this Used alternative is chosen after inspection.

Without the Evaluate Used option, the decision would be made today by comparing the distributions for the three base plant alternatives. Figure 7.8 presents the cumulative distribution curves [3] for these options. The Skid alternative has a slight advantage in having the lowest EV cost. The skid plant also is the least risky (risk evidenced by the width of the distribution). The *stair steps* are caused by using monthly time periods in the cashflow projection model.

It is also an option to inspect the used plant before committing to a choice. After taking one month to do this evaluation, the project manager will again compare the plant alternatives. Now the Fixed and Skid alternatives would be delayed one month, slightly increasing their EV costs. The Used alternative is also reassessed, based upon the evaluation information. The decision policy would be to choose the alternative having the lowest EV cost. Figure 7.9 compares the Evaluate Used alternative with the Skid alter-

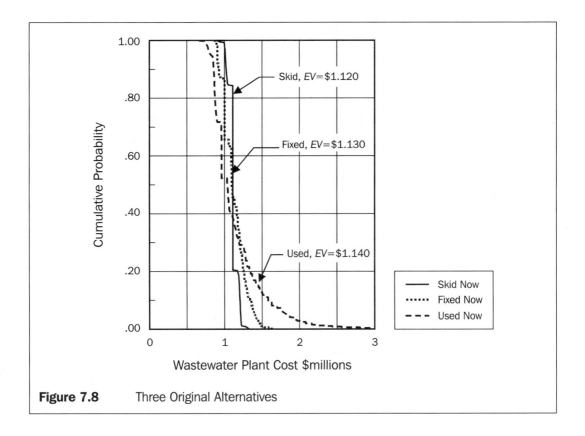

Figure 7.8   Three Original Alternatives

native. Pursuing the information alternative, Evaluate Used, adds $96,000 of value to the project.

Simulation in Practice

Simulation is excellent for calculating distribution curves for various outcome parameters of interest. Figure 7.10 shows a histogram of simulation results for the improvement offered by the Evaluate Used alternative. Superimposed on the figure is the cumulative distribution. Random sampling and the accumulation buckets typically result in an irregular distribution shape. Although the histogram appears lumpy, this has little impact on the EV calculation. The cumulative curve appears smoother, because it avoids the time bucket effect and dilutes any random sampling errors. Cumulative curves are most popular, in general, for comparing the risk-versus-value profiles of the different alternatives. The simulation model in this analysis uses discrete, monthly time periods. This contributed to the discontinuities in the resulting distributions. Without too much effort, we could modify the model to use weeks, days, hours, and so on, to meet the precision requirements of the study.

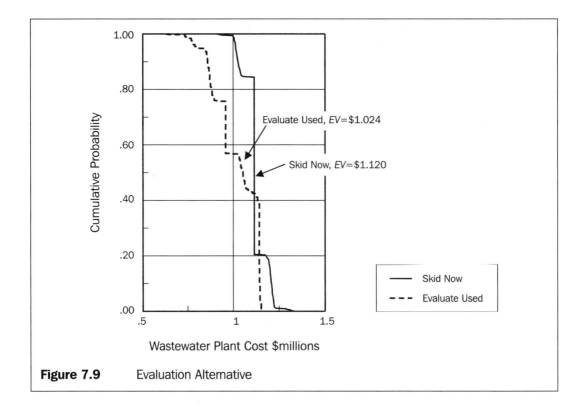

Figure 7.9   Evaluation Alternative

To minimize computer running time while increasing detail, there are sampling techniques generally described as "design of experiments" (mentioned briefly in Appendix A, Summary of Methods). A closely allied technique called Latin Hypercube Sampling (LHS) has become very popular in recent years. This is a hybrid between *uniform sampling* and traditional *Monte Carlo sampling*. LHS reduces the number of simulation trials by as much as 90 percent to obtain a desired precision.

Software

I think we can declare that Microsoft won the spreadsheet war. Most people are using Microsoft® Excel in developing custom business models. This applies to project models as well, unless using project scheduling software such as Microsoft Project.

Excel is a great analysis tool for small- to medium-sized models. Personally, I prefer a procedural programming language for the big jobs, though other analysts are comfortable creating enormous spreadsheet models. Payoff tables are straightforward, and I use Excel for these. Excel already has functions for sampling normal and binomial distributions, and I will not be surprised if a future release includes simulation capabilities. The data-analysis functions are already available, though not as convenient as these next add-in tools.

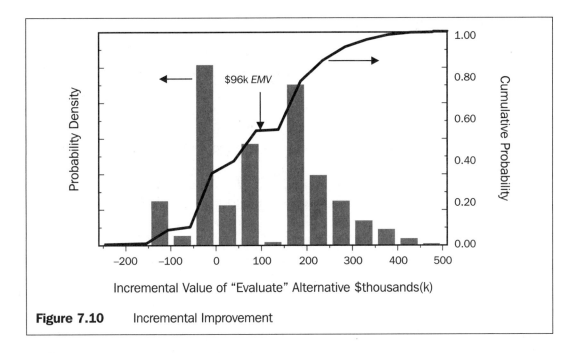

Figure 7.10   Incremental Improvement

In recent years, two add-in products have dominated the market for Monte Carlo simulation in spreadsheets: @RISK® by Palisade Corporation and Crystal Ball® by Decisioneering, Inc. Both companies have aggressively matched most features of the other's products, and the software users are the beneficiaries. These tools have different heritages and somewhat different design approaches. Nonetheless, each program has most of the other's capabilities. In my opinion, these are both excellent tools. Depending upon particular needs, however, some people may find one program better than the other. Appendix B, Decision Analysis Software, has vendor information, including Web sites with demonstration downloads.

@RISK versions are available also for Lotus® 1-2-3® and for Microsoft® Project. There are at least two competing simulation add-ins for Project, a testament to both the popularity of Microsoft Project and increasing recognition of Monte Carlo simulation in the project management community.

Optimization, Chapter 15's topic, is particularly difficult with uncertainty. We need simulation because probability distributions are difficult, if not impossible, to combine mathematically. This requires typically from 100 to 1,000 times more computer time than solving a deterministic project model. Decisioneering has a companion program to Crystal Ball, OptQuest®, that optimizes decision variables. RISKOptimizer® is Palisade's solution. For the really big jobs, both companies offer versions that distribute the simulation across a PC network.

Comparing Simulation to Trees

Monte Carlo simulation is a complementary calculation alternative to decision tree analysis. Each technique has its advantages and disadvantages. The nature of the problem at hand, available tools, and personal preference determine the choice of method. *Simulation is usually preferred* in situations:

- Having many significant uncertainties and contingencies
- Involving a portfolio (e.g., strategic decisions involving a portfolio of projects)
- Where outcome probability distributions are desired, providing additional insights and for comparing risk-versus-value profiles
- Involving complex decision policy (i.e., one not maximizing *EV*).
  In contrast, *decision trees are usually preferred* for situations:
- Involving a sequence of decisions (e.g., value of information problems); usually, these involve Bayes' theorem calculations to revise prior probabilities
- Where there are low-probability events
- Where a simple decision model will suffice (often, decision analysts start with a decision tree model and then move to simulation when the model becomes more complex).

Simulation and decision trees are the principal computation techniques in decision analysis. Both methods solve for *EVs*, though they do so in very different ways.

Appendix A, Summary of Methods, includes a table that matches evaluation problem features to the better EV calculation tool.

Endnotes

1. This figure shows a Cell Assumption window from Crystal Ball® by Decisioneering, Inc. Used with permission. See Appendix B, Decision Analysis Software, for vendor information.
2. This is conventional Monte Carlo sampling for independent variables. There are other Monte Carlo simulation sampling methods available, notably Latin hypercube sampling.
3. Technically, the outcomes of a simulation are frequency distributions. *Frequency* refers to sample data—in this case, synthetic data from simulation trials. A frequency distribution converges to the true probability density distribution if collected in many fine bins and after sufficient trials.

CHAPTER 8

PROJECT RISK MANAGEMENT— BY THE NUMBERS

Project risk management is about optimizing value. Decision analysis is the discipline for making decisions under uncertainty and provides a logical, consistent process for project management decisions.

The Business Perspective

A Guide to the Project Management Body of Knowledge (PMBOK® Guide) – 2000 Edition defines project risk management (PRM) as "the systematic process of identifying, analyzing, and responding to project risk." In decision analysis, our understanding of a system is structured and quantified. Probability is the language of uncertainty, and experts express their judgments about risks and uncertainties as probabilities and probability distributions. In this discussion, I will emphasize quantification and value-based decision making beyond what the *PMBOK® Guide* suggests.

In Chapter 3, I stressed that most organizations whose objective is to maximize shareholder value are well suited to an expected monetary value (EMV) decision policy. Project decision policy is most effective when we combine the usual triple objectives of time, cost, and performance into a single value measure. *EMV* is the expected value (EV) of the present value (*PV*) of net cash flow. The project cash flow can be either actual cash or cashflow equivalents:

$EMV = \text{EV}(PV).$

Organizations with multiple objectives and others with multiple decision criteria can also apply decision analysis methods, as described in Chapter 4.

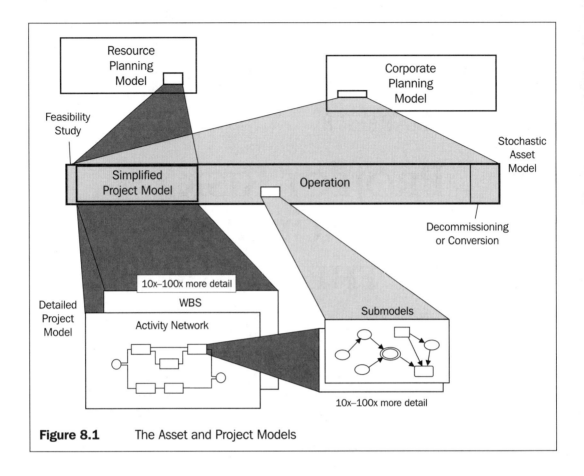

Figure 8.1   The Asset and Project Models

Then, the logical decision policy consists of measuring value (utility) with a multi-criteria value function and maximizing EV utility (expected utility, *EU*).

Model Scope

Most projects develop or build some form of asset. The asset life-cycle model represents how business value depends upon the completion date and changes in the asset's functionality or performance. Figure 8.1 illustrates relationships between the asset model and the project model. Both may incorporate the results of detailed submodels developed to understand particular processes, subprojects, or system components.

The asset model, itself, may be part of a higher-level corporate or resource-planning model. The asset model should always be a stochastic model—that is, incorporating probability distributions—because every project has uncertainties. The asset model relates such elements as:

- Cost, time, and performance
- Value of early completion
- Impact of parameters, such as scope changes
- Project projections, including criticality indexes.

2.1	Project Phases and the Project Life Cycle
4.1	Project Plan Development
5.2	Scope Planning
6	Time Management (project modeling)
7	Cost Management
8.1.2.1	Benefit/Cost Analysis
10.3.2	Tools and Techniques for Performance Reporting (variance analysis; earned value)
11	**Project Risk Management**
12.1.2	Tools and Techniques for Procurement Planning (contract type selection)
12.4	Source Selection

Table 8.1   Project Activities for Using Decision Analysis

The detailed project model is typically deterministic, that is, without distributions. If less than, say, fifty activities, we might incorporate distributions into the detailed project model. The amount of detail appropriate, in either an asset or a project model, depends upon the situation and the capabilities of the analysis team. Models with hundreds or thousands of probability distributions would overwhelm most of us. Expert system assistants (Chapter 17) will enable us to develop, maintain, and apply larger models.

As Figure 8.1 illustrates, I'm advocating (a) a stochastic asset model with a lesser-detailed project model inside, and (b) a deterministic project model for detailed planning (not evaluation) and control. We can do most risk-response evaluations on the side as simple decision analyses.

PRM benefits from focusing on the key drivers, risk mitigation actions, and the effects of uncertainty. In contrast, project execution and control benefit from planning in great detail. Thus, the asset life-cycle model typically contains a simplified project submodel, developed initially before the detailed project model. The full project model contains typically ten to 100 times more detail as the asset model, in terms of resolution.

In modeling the project, do not neglect end of life. The asset may have a successor use or be saleable. We might decide to build-on into a next version or renovate to extend the planned life. Some assets will have significant decommissioning or abandonment costs.

PMBOK® Guide Sections

The Project Management Institute (PMI) released the *PMBOK® Guide* - 2000 Edition in December 2000, as I was writing this section. Most changed is the *Guide*'s Chapter 11, Project Risk Management.

Decision analysis is useful throughout the project life cycle. The *Guide*'s chapter on risk management is the most obvious area for application. Table 8.1 identifies additional areas of project management, identified with *PMBOK® Guide* sections, that benefit from decision analysis.

❖ I am in general agreement with the *PMBOK® Guide* - 2000 Edition. My Appendix 8D, Comparison with the *PMBOK® Guide* - 2000 Edition, describes several exceptions between PMI's official pronouncement and the process that I describe.

In a streamlined risk-management process, described next, I use the same *PMBOK® Guide* function numbers and names, with two noted exceptions.

Pre-Project Risk Management

Risk management begins in the feasibility study. A stochastic (probabilistic) model of the asset life cycle provides the basis for justifying the project. This includes a preliminary and coarse project model for calculating distributions for time and cost to do the project. The structure of the summary project model developed at this stage has a preliminary work breakdown structure (WBS) or other activity network representation. Include major discrete contingencies. Probability distributions, of course, express judgments about uncertain input variables.

We should maintain this asset model throughout the life cycle. Update this model as new information becomes available. As illustrated in Figure 8.1, there are two project models in different detail. Check the project model and asset model after revisions to ensure consistency.

Important risks provide opportunities for improving the project. What alternatives exist to improve the project's risk-versus-value profile?

During the Project

The numbering on the following risk management functions matches the *PMBOK® Guide*.

11.1—Risk Management Planning

In the early stages of project initiation, we design and implement the formal risk-management methodology. This defines roles and responsibilities, databases, and control reporting.

It is hoped that, as with decision policy, the procedures and systems are not reinvented with a new project. Rather, the process is a proven, consistent, and well-understood part of the way the organization operates. Special circumstances may require some modification, and the purpose of Risk Management Planning is to fix the process for this project. Appendix 8B, Risk Management Plan, discusses plan elements in more detail.

11.2—Risk Identification

In detailed project planning, the project team creates, as applicable, the bill of materials, WBS, and an activity network diagram. The project model details elements in schedule and cost estimation.

Risk Identification is about reviewing every input variable, activity, key material, and resource. What are the threats and opportunities? Checklists built-up from others' experiences are valuable in getting started and in ensuring completeness. Influence diagrams are able to represent relationships not evident in the activity network diagram. Classifying risks helps identify common and redundant entries. Also, consider potential changes in the environment as risks—i.e., the assumptions may change.

❖ As you might have guessed from the book's subject and this chapter's title, the emphasis in PRM will be on **quantifying** judgments about risks and uncertainties. *Qualitative Risk Analysis* (*PMBOK® Guide* Section 11.3) has its place, if desired, to preliminarily classify risks into three categories: "Important," "Not Important," and "Possibly Important." Beyond this, I strongly urge quantification.

11.3—Risk Assessment

In my scheme, this replaces PMBOK® Guide Section 11.3, Qualitative Risk Analysis.

The project *base plan* is a single scenario where the inputs are *EVs* for continuous chance variables. For a discrete variable, I use the outcome nearest the *EV*. Stochastic calculations at an appropriate level, perhaps the asset model, are the means to evaluate schedule, cost, and performance.

We need judgments for the values of every input variable in the model. The list includes, especially, risks from Risk Identification. Typically, the most capable available persons judge these values. Their assessments include:

- Single values for variables that are well known or can be calculated with precision; single values also suffice for less-important variables (prioritized subjectively at this stage)
- Probability distributions for important uncertain values in the project model
- Probabilities for discrete risk events
- Probability distributions for impact variables that become relevant when the associated risk events occur (e.g., remedial action cost incurred because of a delayed shipment)
- Single-value or probability distributions for contingency plan implementation costs.

❖ These are the "known unknowns" explicitly appearing in the model. I also suggest assessing risk for "unknown unknowns" (things we haven't yet thought about) and an aggregation of risks individually too small to warrant specific inclusion.

In PRM, the most common risk representation is in two parts:

(a) A discrete *risk event* for which someone judges a probability of occurring. I often use the word *contingency* for such events. These risk events can be either desirable (*opportunities*) or not (*threats*).

(b) The cost or time *impact* on the project as a continuous distribution given that risk event (a) happens. In probability language, the impact is *conditioned* on the occurrence of the risk even happening.

As we've discussed, a probability distribution completely describes a judgment about uncertainty for a single chance event. However, there may be interactions between variables (see Chapter 12). We further need the experts to describe how judgments, described earlier, are associated (correlated) with one another. Influence diagrams are useful in mapping interrelationship and designing detailed submodels.

11.4—Risk Analysis

In my scheme, this replaces PMBOK® Guide Section 11.4, Quantitative Risk Analysis.

Risk Analysis is about understanding overall project risk. The stochastic asset model is the basis for credible forecasts. Some practitioners carry stochastic calculations through the detailed project model as well, though this may be overkill.

A common display of project risk is a cumulative distribution diagram, such as the solid curve in Figure 8.2. The Base Case is only one scenario, used here as the zero reference. Cumulative distributions show the possibilities. Here we view project cost distributions (which may incorporate cost-equivalent considerations for schedule and performance) both before and after implementing risk-mitigation actions. An asset's value distribution would be similar (assuming the model includes all life-cycle effects), though the x-axis would instead be the asset value outcome (usually *PV*).

Sensitivity analysis (described in Chapter 9) quantifies how uncertainty and changes to input values affect the outcome. Usually, the target outcome is either asset value or project cost, depending upon the model. The purpose of sensitivity analysis is to help prioritize input variables and model construction details.

Prioritizing risk events is important in PRM and done here in Risk Analysis. The popular graph type of Figure 8.3 (either side) shows discrete risks versus their conditional EV impacts. (Many practitioners use a *quali-*

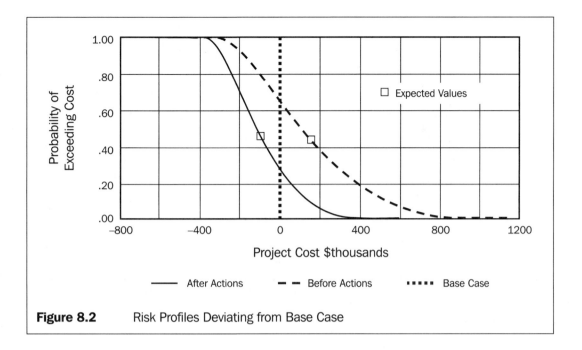

Figure 8.2   Risk Profiles Deviating from Base Case

tative matrix instead.) Project cost and asset value uncertainty are among the outputs of a feasibility study. Figure 8.3 characterizes the importance of identified (discrete) risks [1]. Risk mitigation actions affect the probability of the risk event or its impact, or sometimes both. For clarity, the illustration omits "opportunities" (favorable effects). Importance of a risk depends upon both its probability and impact. Risk management attempts to move threats "southwest" and opportunities, "northeast." Iso-EV cost contours are one way to segregate risks into importance categories. Appendix 8B, Risk Management Plan, describes more about evaluating candidate actions.

We should maintain and embellish, as appropriate, the project model part of the asset model.

11.5—Risk Response Planning

What we do about the risks? This is the topic of Risk Response Planning. Figure 8.4 shows the hierarchy of this process.

Use brainstorming and checklists again to identify candidate actions for mitigating each risk (or enhancing opportunities). Appendix 8C, Mitigating and Avoiding Risks, may provide you with some ideas. For this discussion, we will assume risks are only of the "threat" variety. Actions typically reduce or eliminate risk or affect the impact, should the risk event occur. From among the potential actions, which are cost effective to implement? The optimal project plan incorporates the combination of actions that adds most value to the organization.

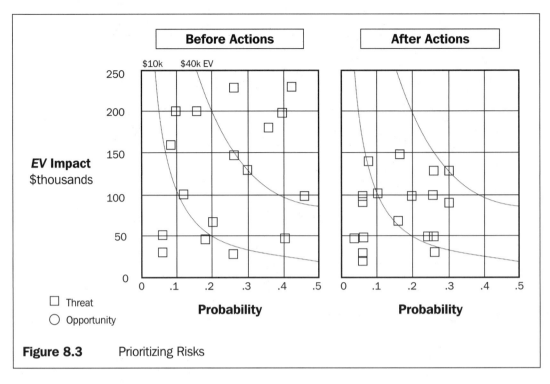

Figure 8.3   Prioritizing Risks

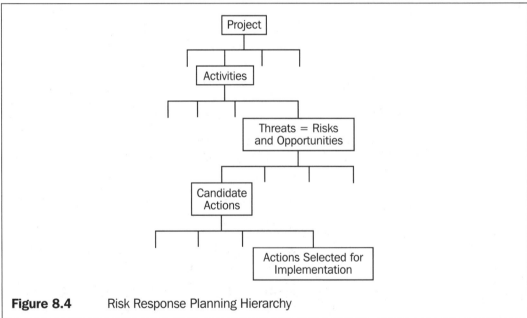

Figure 8.4   Risk Response Planning Hierarchy

Before-and-after graphs, as shown in Figure 8.2 and Figure 8.3, are good formats for illustrating the benefits of Risk Response Planning. We can calculate before and after distributions differing by a single action. It is the difference between curves *EV*s, such as those in Figure 8.2, that is the basis for evaluating the candidate action.

In a simple world, we could do a risk/cost/benefit analysis on every candidate action. The decisions would be simple: Implement those actions that add more EV benefit than their EV cost. However, correlations cloud the picture:

- A risk mitigation action may affect more than one risk. Synergies: "Killing two birds with one stone."
- Several actions may be candidates for mitigating one risk. Either action may appear feasible, but together they are not. "Diminishing returns."
- Implementing actions may affect the feasibility of mitigating other risks and the effects of other actions (both in probability and impact).

These are common problems in portfolio analysis. Here, instead of a portfolio of investments, we have a suite of actions and are selecting portfolio of response actions. There is much subjectivity in analysis work, and part of the analysis discipline is focusing on elements that matter most.

What if there isn't enough money (or other constraining resource) to perform all worthwhile risk-abatement actions? Like elsewhere in life, we prioritize. Instead of implementing everything with a positive *EMV*—notwithstanding the portfolio issues just mentioned—we would prioritize to do the best with what we have. Most practitioners use a return on investment-like criterion. I mention the most popular ranking criterion, discounted return on investment (*DROI*), in Chapter 3:

$$DROI = \frac{EMV}{E(\text{PV Investment})}$$

Choose to implement those actions with the highest *DROI* first.

11.6—Risk Monitoring and Control

An inventory of risks and actions is core to risk management. A database repository is the foundation. Data fields include various classifications, responsibilities, watch points, and time windows. Recording original estimates and actual outcomes is key to judgment performance feedback. Appendix 8B, Risk Management Plan, provides more details about this database.

At major milestones or other suitable points, post-implementation reviews are essential for participants' learning and for capturing knowledge. This is perhaps the single most important way in which to improve an organization's planning and evaluation processes and skills.

Keep Your Perspective

While the earlier outline appears linear, the process is iterative and features rework cycles. The asset and project models should be coordinated, and we alternate between looking at the forest versus looking at the trees.

Building asset and project models is the most fun in analysis work. Conditional branching is key to making the model realistically dynamic. It is always interesting to experiment—learning about what is important and how the project behaves under different circumstances.

There are four appendices to this chapter:
8A—Quick-and-Dirty Decisions
8B—Risk Management Plan
8C—Mitigating and Avoiding Risks
8D—Comparison with the *PMBOK® Guide* - 2000 Edition.

APPENDIX 8A

QUICK-AND-DIRTY DECISIONS

There is a common misconception that decision analysis is time consuming. Many evaluations require only a few minutes with pencil, paper, and a hand calculator. Once you are clear about the best course of action—stop the analysis! No further value will be added.

Decisions that warrant more extensive analyses have one or more of these characteristics:

- Outcomes are difficult to value (requiring detailed cashflow modeling).
- Outcome values are significant for the entity, and warrant serious attention to the decision.
- The best alternatives appear to have similar values or cost.
- There are too many variables, compounded by correlations, to process in one's head.

Common Simple Situation

Decision tree analysis is your solution method of choice if you are ever marooned on a desert island. A solar calculator will help! Regardless, you can sketch a decision model on the back of an envelope or in the sand, and do some quick calculations.

Suppose you have created a base project plan. Upon further reflection, you now recognize a contingency that could affect project cost (and/or schedule). Figure 8A.1 shows a simple tree-like model of this contingency.

Brainstorming about the possibilities is an important project management function. Corporate planners call it SWOT analysis: identifying **S**trengths, **W**eaknesses, **O**pportunities, and **T**hreats. Note that contingencies can be either *unfavorable* (threats or risks) or *favorable* (*opportunities*). A large project may have hundreds of identified risks and opportunities.

Once we identify a contingency, the manager should seek actions to exploit or mitigate the situation. This is when project management can be **proactive**, rather than waiting and possibly having to *react*. The actions we implement may change the probability that the contingency event will occur, affect the project cost distribution (i.e., impact) should the contingency event occur, or possibly *both*.

We can often meet a contingency with several candidate abatement (or exploitive) actions. An action can preempt the contingency event. More often, actions result in only partial control. Flexibility and contingency plans are among the ways to reduce the impact of negative contingencies that do occur.

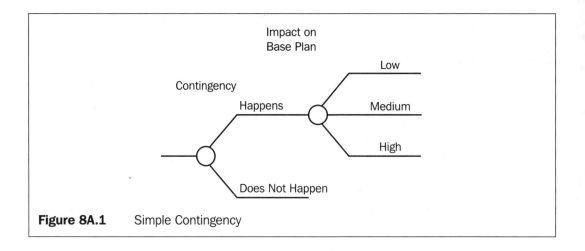

Figure 8A.1   Simple Contingency

Upgrade to	Probability[1] of Being Adequate	Cost[2] to Rebuild
Thicker Stock	.40	$5,000
Premium Grade Stock (but more difficult to machine)	.90	$10,000
Machined Casting	1.00	$30,000

[1] Conditional, given that the original stock and fabrication prove inadequate.
[2] Includes monetary-equivalent penalties for project delay.

Table 8A.1   Improved Base Plate Material

Here is a typical situation where a quick-and-dirty decision model is adequate. Suppose your project involves building several electromechanical instruments. Alignment is critical for certain components mounted on a base plate. The intended aluminum stock for fabricating the base plate is easy to work, but may prove too flexible and nondurable in the application.

Your team assesses a .12 chance that the aluminum-based plate chosen for fabrication will be inadequate. There are three upgrade alternatives, shown in Table 8A.1.

You could upgrade to one of these other choices now, or see how the originally planned aluminum stock works out. Assume that if an initial base plate is not satisfactory, you will have sufficient information then to know what solution is required.

We can use the Figure 8A.1 template to express judgments about the risk and impact of the contingency. Figure 8A.2 shows how we can appraise the contingency. The EV cost of the contingency is $1,200. Whatever alternatives we consider must reduce the EV cost by more than the cost of implementing action. We decision analysts call this a *value of imperfect control problem*.

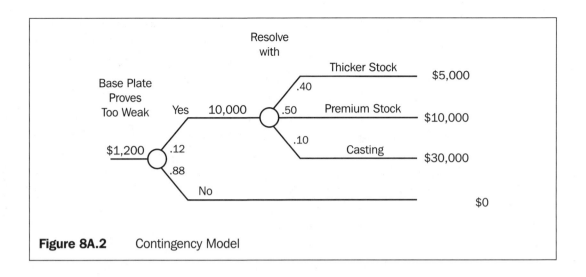

Figure 8A.2   Contingency Model

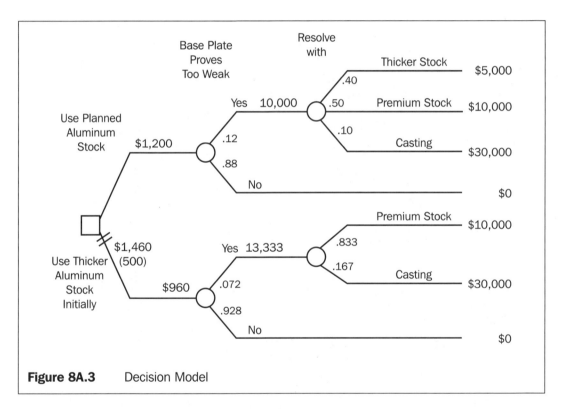

Figure 8A.3   Decision Model

An alternative. Your company can decide *now* to use thicker aluminum stock in the initial fabrication. This initially will cost $500 more. Is this prudent? Since the $500 is less than the $1,200 EV cost of plate inadequacy, the action alternative passes the first feasibility test.

Figure 8A.3 shows the decision model. You want to evaluate whether this conservative approach is a justifiable precaution.

The thicker base plate reduces the contingency probability from .12 to .072. If it is inadequate, then the probability that we need the Premium Stock increases from .50 to .833. Similarly, the probability of Need Casting increases from .10 to .167. In this case, the candidate action (Thicker Stock Initially) affects *both* the probability and the impact of the contingency.

The EV cost of refabrication drops from $1,200 to $960 if initially we use the thicker plate. However, the case with the thicker plate costs $500. Thus, the initial comparable EV cost with the thicker plate is $1,460. Therefore, *choosing Planned Aluminum Stock is most appropriate* (for a risk-neutral decision maker or an organization that has an EMV decision policy). The Thicker Stock Initially is a worse option, having a $260 higher EV cost.

Thus we obtain a logical, defensible basis for the decision. This type of quick-and-dirty decision analysis fits many situations. A basic understanding of decision analysis should be in every project manager and professional's toolkit.

APPENDIX 8B

RISK MANAGEMENT PLAN

I resist suggesting outlines and formats for economic evaluations and project plans. The formalism you need depends upon the situation. However, three topics in this appendix may serve well as the elements of a PRM plan:

- Sensitivity analysis
- Evaluating alternatives
- Inventorying risks and actions.

Sensitivity Analysis

Modeling is the heart of evaluating a system and the alternatives that we have to affect the behavior of that system. *Sensitivity analysis* is the *quantitative* process of determining which variables are most important in the analysis, through determining their influence on the outcome value. Sensitivity analysis is a full section in Chapter 9, Modeling Techniques.

Judgment plays an important role. Some risks are clearly not important. We should merely document those risks identified and considered "insignificant." Briefly describing our rationale is good practice (in case something proved significant after all).

Evaluating Alternatives

We only need to model in sufficient detail to make an informed decision. For most decision situations, we do not need to model the enterprise or even the entire project. Typical decisions are sufficiently localized so that great simplifying assumptions are reasonably valid.

Adding value is the goal in decision making. Quantitative methods are much more likely to produce consistent, meaningful results. Lots of books and articles describe matrices of risk versus impact. Figure 8.3 shows an improved, quantified version.

For choosing risk abatement actions, many practitioners advocate a *return-on-investment* decision criterion:

$$ROI = \frac{\text{Profit Improvement}}{\text{Cost of Action}}$$

Most people deduct the Cost of Action in the numerator. If not, this is usually and more properly called a *benefit/cost ratio* (*BCR*). Either way produces the same decisions. The decision rule is to implement the action if the $ROI > 0$ or if $BCR > 1$.

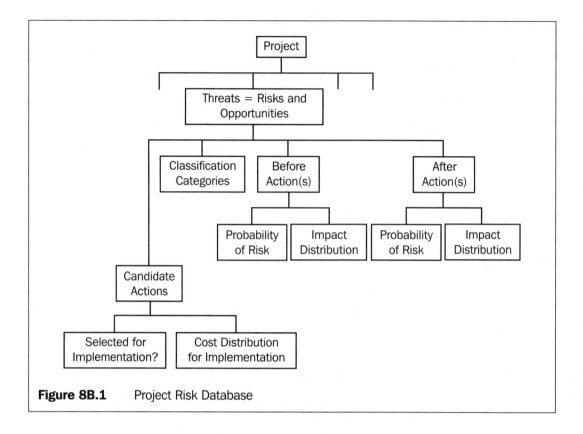

Figure 8B.1   Project Risk Database

We usually measure costs and benefit values as PV cash flow. Then this improved criterion is the *DROI*. Of course, since we're talking about risk, then the numerator and denominator should also be *EVs*.

It is simpler and less confusing just to talk about *EMVs*, though I point out these alternatives because they appear so often.

Inventorying Risks and Actions

As mentioned earlier in the 11.6—Risk Monitoring and Control subsection, the heart of PRM is the database of risks and actions. Figure 8B.1 illustrates the structure of this database.

An inventory of risks and actions is core to risk management. A database repository is the foundation. Here are some example data fields in addition to the elements in Figure 8B.1:

- Area or department owning the risk
- Person responsible for the risk
- Relevant time horizon (a Gantt chart would be a useful display of risks and actions)
- Activities affected
- Response resources needed if risk event occurs
- Watch points and early indicators.

I am unaware, at present, of any computer solution that ties everything together. These elements are usually managed separately: the stochastic asset model, the (usually deterministic) detailed project model, and the risks and actions inventory. Putting all this together is a complex application-design problem. Perhaps we await an intelligent assistant, such as an expert system described in Chapter 17, to seamlessly integrate these project management elements.

APPENDIX 8C

MITIGATING AND AVOIDING RISKS

It is an unhappy fact of life that there are usually many more things that can go wrong with a project than can unexpectedly go right. Although this section focuses on the downside, the project manager should be constantly vigilant for potential opportunities.

PMBOK® Guide Section 11.5.2, Tools and Techniques for Risk Response Planning, classifies actions into four areas.

.1 **Avoidance**. Changing the project plan to eliminate the risk.

.2 **Transference**. Move the risk to a third party, usually by contract. Insurance, options, guarantees, and fixed prices are examples.

.3 **Mitigation**. If we are unable to avoid or transfer the risk, we might find a way to reduce the probability of a threat and/or impact, should the risk event occur.

.4 **Acceptance**. This is the default, "do nothing," when we are unable to find a cost/effective action to deal with the risk.

The following outline describes some ways that you might find useful when avoiding, transferring, and mitigating risks.

Portfolio Risks

- Share risks by having partners (dilution or diffusion).
- Spread risks over time.
- Participate in many ventures (diversify).
- Group complementary risks into portfolios.
- Seek lower-risk ventures.
- Specialize and concentrate in a single, well-known area, where the company enjoys advantages.
- Increase the company's capitalization.

Commodity Prices

- Hedge or fix prices in the futures markets.
- Use long- or short-term sales (price and volume) contracts.
- Tailor contracts for appropriate risk sharing.

Interest Rate and Exchange Rate

- Use swaps, floors, ceilings, collars, and other hedging instruments.
- Restructure the balance sheet.
- Denominate or index certain transactions in a foreign currency.

Environmental Hazards

- Buy insurance.
- Increase safety margins.
- Develop and test an incident-response program.

Operational Risks

- Hire contractors under turnkey contracts.
- Tailor risk-sharing contract clauses.
- Increase safety margins; overbuild and overspecify designs.
- Have backup and redundant equipment.
- Acquire additional inventory and spares.
- Increase training.
- Operate with redirect and bail-out options at project milestones.
- Conduct tests, pilot programs, and trials.

Analysis Risks (Reducing Evaluation Error)

- Use better techniques (i.e., decision analysis).
- Seek additional information.
- Monitor key and indicator variables.
- Validate models.
- Include evaluation practices with project post-reviews.
- Perform parallel analyses with alternative approaches, models, and people.
- Involve multiple disciplines, and communicate cross-discipline.
- Provide better training and tools.

APPENDIX 8D

Comparison with the *PMBOK® Guide* - 2000 Edition

I support professional standards efforts, and I wish that I could have invested more time in the *PMBOK® Guide* revision. Despite important improvements, there are several areas in the PMI standard that are not quite right, in my humble opinion. These standards are mostly a volunteer effort, and I appreciate that many people devoted what time they could spare to the 2000 Edition.

In mid-2000, I submitted twenty-four comment forms to the *PMBOK® Guide Exposure Draft*. The project committee chose to reject or only partially implement some suggestions. Key points I offered include: (a) requirement of a clear decision policy; (b) risk management can apply to continuous events; and (c) emphasis on risk quantification. Below, I'll expand on these topics.

Asset Value Perspective

My background is corporate planning and economic evaluation, and I encourage project managers to begin risk management during the feasibility study. The feasibility study needs an asset life-cycle model so as to value different alternatives for the organization. We will assume your organization is a for-profit corporation for this discussion.

The corporate-asset perspective is especially important in decision policy: How do we measure value? In order to make decisions *during* the project, we need to know how project delivery affects the asset value after handoff. In Chapter 4, we discuss how schedule and performance outcomes affect net cash flow, and, hence, asset *PV*.

So, I would like to see the next *PMBOK® Guide* edition be more emphatic about encoding decision policy: objectives, time value, and risk attitude. Corporate decision policy should apply to all projects. That's why I omitted an "identify decision criteria" step in Chapter 2's ten-step decision process.

Continuous Risk Events

I *am* pleased that the *Guide* defines *risk* in a way so that the effects on the project can be either *favorable* or *unfavorable*. **Uncertainty** didn't make the *Guide*'s Glossary, and I'm happy to suggest a definition in this book.

The *Guide*'s Section 11.4.3.1 contains the only mention of classifying risks into *threats* and *opportunities*. The taxonomy is useful, and I would like to see this in the next edition. I suspect these terms would be easier to incorporate into the *Guide* if people could (would) agree on terminology usage.

Project *risks* are not always discrete events, despite my *uncertainty* definition in this book suggesting that this is the customary case. During a long project, for example, inflation might be important. I would normally call a continuous distribution an *uncertainty*, but this is splitting hairs. We don't want to get hung up on arguable definitions.

My point, however, is this. In the context of PRM, there may be actions we can take to mitigate or exploit an uncertainty (risk) that is other than a binary event. It might be a continuous-chance event, such as inflation (further complicated by the time dimension), or a discrete chance event with more than just true/false outcomes. A continuous distribution, in some circumstances, represents both the risk and the impact.

Another point is that most people oversimplify the risk and actions. The traditional risk model has us experience the impact only if the risk event occurs. Let's talk threat, the potential for undesirable effect. We implement a risk abatement to reduce the probability and/or impact of the risk. However, the world is not always so simple.

For example: A risk management plan might implement a contingency action (e.g., increase the flexibility of a crew availability) if an early-warning condition occurs (e.g., several predecessor activities are forecasting to finish late). If the risk event occurs (e.g., the activity cannot start when planned), the impact might be higher costs with overtime. So in this example, we have multiple discrete risk events, contingent decision points, and at least two occurrences that may affect project costs and schedule.

Risk Prioritization Needs Quantification

My biggest outstanding issue is about qualitatively characterizing and prioritizing risks. Assigning grades such as high/medium/low to a risk is asking for confusion. Using numbers—probabilities and distributions—provides unambiguous communication and a legitimate ranking and decision-criterion calculation (risked *DROI* or EV, respectively).

Modeling is key to planning and decision making, from conception to abandonment. I offered suggestions throughout the *PMBOK® Guide* about recognizing the importance of an asset model that parallels, though in less detail, the project model.

I'm hoping that the next *Guide* revision will mostly eliminate Qualitative Risk Analysis, and that its functions will be attributed to a quantitative Risk Analysis process. Maybe these together should be called Risk Analysis.

In this chapter, I described what I believe is best practice in applying decision analysis to PRM. That is largely the reason for this book!

Endnotes

1. Figure 8.3 is adapted from a chart produced by PROAct™ project risk management software, by Engineering Management Services, used with permission (see Appendix B, Decision Analysis Software).

2. In this situation, the revised probabilities are easy to calculate. More often, we would use Bayes' theorem.

PART II

MODELING AND INPUTS

The model is the heart of most analyses. The project model captures and expresses our understanding of the project as a system. Chapters in this part further describe evaluation methods, especially for dealing with uncertainty.

CHAPTER 9

MODELING TECHNIQUES

For most systems, such as projects, developing a model is the key to understanding the possibilities. The model represents the dynamics of the project and its behavior under different decisions and circumstances.

Decision analysis and the associated techniques help decision makers choose wisely under conditions of uncertainty. A decision analysis approach is applicable when:

- The situation has two or more alternatives.
- At least one alternative has multiple possible outcomes.
- The range of possible outcomes is significant enough to warrant attention to the decision.

This chapter focuses upon quantifying outcome values. Most often, a model is constructed and used to project different possible futures. Each projection, or scenario, is summarized into an outcome value. This single value measures goodness or progress toward the organization's objective.

Forecasts from Models

Forecasting is the most important analytic problem in business. Nearly every decision presupposes a forecast: What might happen with each alternative?

A *projection* is a scenario that reflects a particular set of assumptions. A model predicts what will happen if the assumption values are realized. Most often, a projection is a solution of a *deterministic* model—that is, a model without probabilities. The assumptions may be single-point forecasts of the input variables or merely what-if values. A base project plan, for example, is one projection of what might happen.

A *forecast* is a projection based upon forecasts of the individual input assumptions. These inputs should be probability distributions when the values are unknown. Here we are talking about a **stochastic**, or *probabilistic*, model. The term *forecast* implies an analytic process of estimation and calculation. In the context of this discussion of decision analysis, the best *forecast* is the expected value (EV) outcome.

In addition to input values, the forecast model includes assumptions about the *structure* of the system. This structure is the fabric of the project model, the work breakdown structure (WBS), or activity nodes network, for example.

Forecasting Approaches

There are three general approaches to forecasting:

- Using intuition or guessing
- Extrapolating the past, such as by linear regression
- Modeling the system, and then using the model to generate a forecast.

Intuition provides forecasts of questionable value. The prediction is believable only if the source person possesses recognized superior experience and a record of reasonably accurate judgments. Seldom are the assumptions or reasoning adequately stated. Because intuition is hard to define, it is difficult to achieve consensus and train successors.

Extrapolation requires suitable historical data and assumes that circumstances and behavior in the future will be similar to what was experienced in the past. This implies that conditions tomorrow will be like conditions yesterday.

Modeling involves designing and building a representation of the system. The model is an abstraction of the real world, based upon one's best understanding. Modeling is particularly valuable in situations that are new, unique, or complex.

Traditional forecasts use single-value forecasts of the model inputs. Example inputs include activity costs and completion times. Single-value input assumptions calculate through the model to result in a single-value outcome. Recall that such models are termed **deterministic** because every value is *singly determined*.

Deterministic Project Models

You may skip this section if you are already familiar with CPM, PERT, and PDM.

Among the quantitative techniques that I learned in business school, project scheduling models were perhaps the most interesting. These models are in-

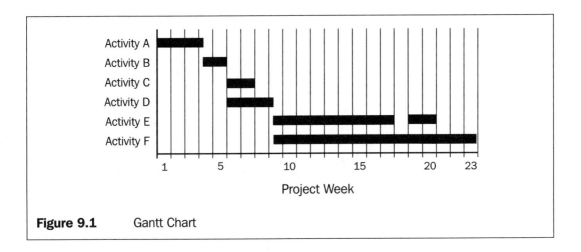

Figure 9.1   Gantt Chart

tuitive and an elegant way to think about projects. This section is an intro-duction to the methods, for those who may have missed this.

Gantt Charts

American industrial engineer **Henry Gantt** (1861–1919) originated a form of bar chart that bears his name. He developed this in the context of World War I military projects. A *Gantt chart*, illustrated in Figure 9.1, displays the activities in a project, and when they occur.

This charting tool, still popular, helps break down the project into a rea-sonable number of activities. It shows time to complete and sequence for every activity. It might also help determine schedule dependencies and re-source balancing, though it is just a graph and has no calculation method-ology.

Critical Path Method

Perhaps the most popular project planning tool came from the chemical and construction industries. The critical path method (CPM) grew out of a joint effort between DuPont Company and Remington Rand Univac during 1956–59.

A CPM diagram is a directed network representing the sequence of project activities. Originally the representation was:

> Activities as arcs

and these connect

> Nodes (also called "connection points" or "events").

The "activity–on–arc" method clearly shows each activity and its se-quence in the project, as illustrated in Figure 9.2.

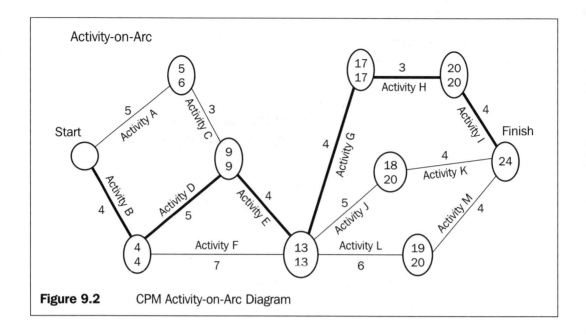

Figure 9.2 CPM Activity-on-Arc Diagram

The assessed completion time for each activity is the number on its arc. The connection points contain two numbers: The upper number is the earliest time that this point can be reached, and the lower number shows the latest time to reach this point. Solving the CPM model involves these steps:

1. Calculate the earliest times by working left to right, chronologically, through the network. The earliest completion at a node is the *latest* time from all of its activity connections coming from the left.

2. Calculate the latest times by working right to left. The latest completion time at a node is the *earliest* time, back-calculating times from the activities at the right.

3. The difference between numbers inside the nodes represent *slack*, indicating that connecting activities can be somewhat late and not delay the project.

4. Find the activities connecting nodes with zero slack. This sequence is the *critical path* (CP). Any delay in these activities correspondingly lengthens the time to complete the project.

In recent years, it has become standard to represent activities on nodes. Nonetheless, the CPM label persists, and the critical path is a key determination in project planning.

If there is value in shortening the overall completion time, we can examine time-versus-cost tradeoff alternatives for each activity along the critical path. The value of accelerating, or "crashing," an activity is approximately:

Value added by a crash program =
Days shorted by the crash program × Value/Day shortened
– Cost of the crash program.

This calculation is an approximation because the critical path is seldom certain, and other activities may become (more) critical as we accelerate one activity.

Program Evaluation and Review Technique

The United States Navy and Booz, Allen and Hamilton developed the Program Evaluation and Review Technique (PERT) during the 1950s for the Polaris submarine project. It is similar to CPM, but with the addition of probability distributions.

The foundation of a PERT analysis is an activity network diagram, with activities on the nodes. Most practitioners call these either CPM or PERT diagrams.

In PERT, we obtain estimates of completion time for each activity. Traditionally, these are in the form of three points:

- Optimistic completion time (L)
- Pessimistic completion time (H)
- Most likely (mode) completion time (M).

Here are the traditional formulas for the statistics (using "moment methods" of Chapter 1). The mean time to complete a task is:

$$\mu = \frac{L + 4M + H}{6}$$

The standard deviation of the completion time is approximately:

$$\sigma = \frac{H - L}{6}$$

These formulas approximate the statistics for a beta distribution. Then, the project has a mean completion time for activities along the CP:

$$\mu_{CP} = \sum_{\substack{\text{Activities } i \\ \text{along the CP}}} \mu_i$$

The standard deviation is:

$$\sigma_{CP} = \sqrt{\sum_{\substack{\text{Activities } i \\ \text{along the CP}}} \sigma_i^2}$$

These calculations have two serious problems:

- In PERT, we choose the CP deterministically. In a stochastic model, we would find that other paths might become critical.
- The standard deviation formula assumes activity independence.

Despite these issues, PERT is a tremendous invention and is the underlying concept in some commercial project-planning programs. These deficiencies are sometimes serious and warrant more-rigorous calculation methods—notably, **Monte Carlo simulation** (simulation).

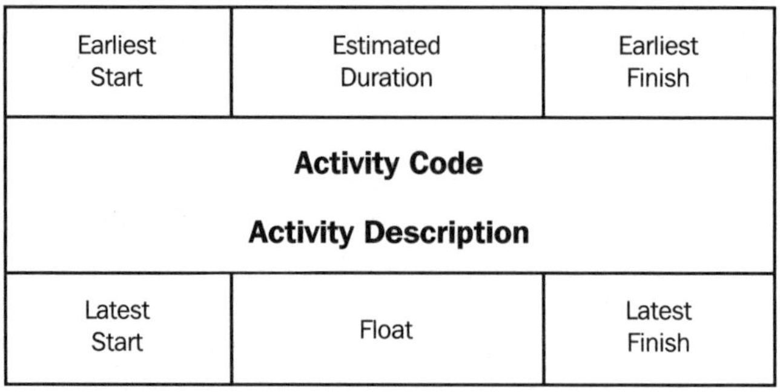

Earliest Start	Estimated Duration	Earliest Finish
Activity Code **Activity Description**		
Latest Start	Float	Latest Finish

Figure 9.3   Typical Activity Node Representation

Precedence Diagramming Method

"Industrial-strength" project-planning software has evolved to use a more flexible activity-on-node notation. Figure 9.3 shows a typical node representation. The project team supplies the Activity Code, Activity Description, and Estimated Duration. The other boxes will contain values calculated by the program. Estimated Duration would be a single value for a deterministic model. It could be a probability distribution in a stochastic model.

Critical path analysis has evolved to a more general form, called *precedence diagramming method* (PDM). The chief advantage is more flexibility to represent activity starting and finishing conditions.

The four relationships possible between predecessor and successor activities include:

- Finish-to-Start (the only relationship recognized in traditional CPM and PERT methods)
- Finish-to-Finish
- Start-to-Start
- Start-to-Finish.

Although cumbersome, we can represent the last three relationships, using dummy nodes in PERT or CPM. PDM eliminates the need for dummy nodes for overlapping activities. The arrows in Figure 9.4 show the four relationship types.

A further PDM embellishment is the ability to include a time delay on a link. This allows a simple way to show delays, such as for paint-drying time.

Deterministic Cashflow Models

This discussion describes decision making from the perspective of a business enterprise, although the techniques apply to all entity types.

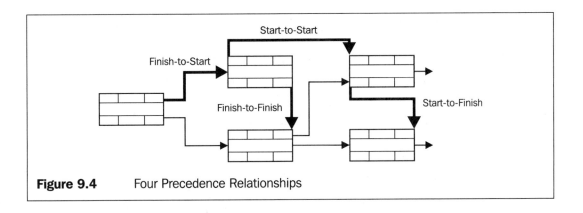

Figure 9.4   Four Precedence Relationships

Chapter 3 and Chapter 4 describe valuing outcomes through decision policy. Project managers are traditionally concerned with performance, schedule, and cost. One needs a logical way to trade off one dimension in terms of another. While these dimensions are important, it is impossible to make consistent decisions without a way to determine a composite value.

Cash Counts

In business, **value derives from net cash flow** (*NCF*). The present value (PV) calculation transforms an incremental *NCF* forecast into incremental corporate value. Presumably, this cash flow is available to distribute to investors or to reinvest in the business. Discounted cashflow (DCF) analysis is the basis for most modern financial analysis. There are many arguable details, such as inflation rate, tax rates, and cost of capital assumptions. The general process, however, is straightforward and reasonably consistent.

Decision making is easiest if a single value measure expresses the quality of the outcome. For most purposes, I recommend converting nonmonetary dimensions into money equivalents. This is the simplest way to deal with multiple objectives or multiple decision criteria. Thus, project performance and schedule translate into cashflow impact. Everything important to the decision is reflected in either revenues or cash expenditures. PV of the net cash flow is the single-value measure. Alternatively, this is often called *net present value* (*NPV*).

Figure 9.5 illustrates this evaluation approach. Shaded blocks in the figure indicate common project outcome criteria that inherently lead to multi-criteria decision making (MCDM, in Chapter 4). Information generated in the development model and feasibility model can be used to generate *NCF*, and then the *PV* or *EMV*.

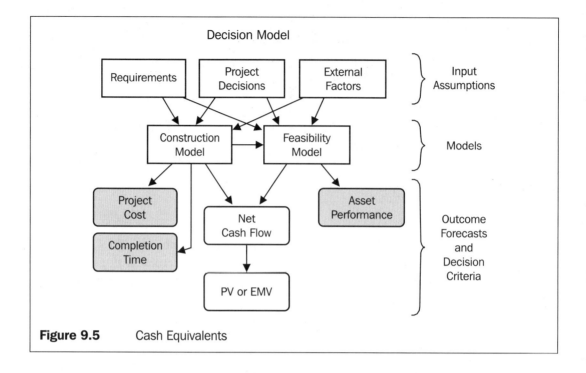

Figure 9.5   Cash Equivalents

Problem and Model Scope

A good project model contains sufficient operating and financial detail to reasonably represent the impacts of the relevant decision alternatives. The **appropriate level of detail** depends upon the decision at hand. Sometimes a quick inspection of the model outputs will indicate an obvious decision. In other situations, the relative differences in outcome values may be small. When this is the case, further analysis effort is warranted, perhaps incorporating further detail in the model.

The model's *scope* is one of the most important analysis-design decisions. The subject system of the analysis may be all or part of an industry, a business, a project, or a transaction. The scope usually needs to consider the remaining life cycle of the project and sometimes the life cycle of the product of the project (asset), as illustrated in Figure 9.6. Decision analysis techniques are fully general, and apply to construction or nonconstruction projects equally. Sometimes managers concern themselves only with a development or construction phase; this is usually inadequate. Completion time and asset performance also impact value by affecting cash flows. All important details and aspects of the problem should be incorporated into the model, at least to the point when the best alternative is clear.

Projects often influence other areas of corporate operations, and even other projects. Simplifying assumptions are usually necessary. We want to avoid modeling the entire corporation for every decision. However, we need sufficient detail to adequately forecast the impact on corporate *NCF*. The incremental effect on corporate *NCF* and its *PV* are generally the most useful model outcomes. Accuracy is usually better—and more significant for our

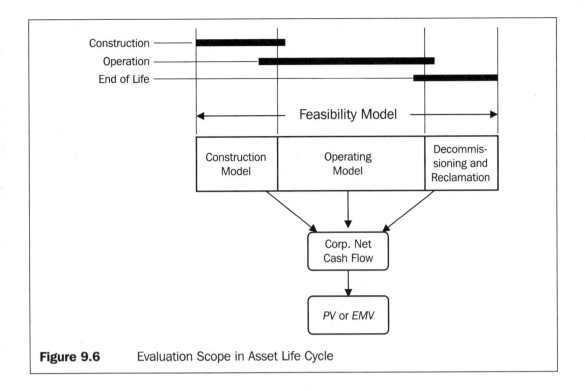

Figure 9.6   Evaluation Scope in Asset Life Cycle

purpose—regarding the *difference* between alternatives than for the actual alternative values.

The scope of the problem-solving process is important. The need to estimate *incremental* corporate value drives the scope of the decision model.

Modeling Process

Typically, an evaluation process is initiated when a problem surfaces. Something happens, or a new idea or information surfaces. It usually involves a choice about allocating resources such as time, money, or materials. The situation may be where a modest effort or investment potentially frees or safeguards much greater resources.

❖ Recall that Proactively Identify Decision Opportunities is the first step of the decision analysis process, described in Chapter 2. It is unfortunate that most people are so busy and reactive that they do not have time to create decision-making opportunities.

Increasingly, businesses *are* recognizing the value of *proactively creating new alternatives*. We professionals should continually ask, "What can we do to improve the value of this project?" And, "What might happen, different from plan, and what can we do to protect from or exploit the contingency?"

Often, a cross-disciplined project team is involved or assigned to the problem. The team should first define the problem (Step 2 in the ten-step process) and include a situation description.

Modeling Flows

Understanding the project and its elements is essential to developing a valid model. The model represents our understanding of how the project (or asset) behaves under different conditions.

We must choose a logical framework for developing the model. Factors in the model may have inherent flow relationships. It usually works well to adopt one or more of the following as a theme for the modeling process:

- Sequence of activities
- Flow of information
- Flow of physical units
- Flow of labor hours and material quantities
- Flow of cash
- Flows of income and expenses (accounting book basis).

The idea of conservation of mass, money, etc., is widely applicable. It is wise to build-in checks to ensure that all resources units are accounted for.

We build these models with mathematical formulas and variables. Here are two example statements:

Net_Cash_Flow = Cash_Margin – Income_Tax – Capital_Expenditures

Date Prototype Testing Begins = Maximum (Prototype_Construction_Finish, Testing_Facility_Construction_Finish).

System Diagrams

The first step in any modeling effort is to identify the objective of the analysis. If one is selecting the melt process for a casting plant, three alternatives are available: cupola, induction furnace, and arc furnace. It is not the accuracy of the estimates that is important in decision making. Rather, it is *the relative values* between alternatives. If the best two alternatives have similar values, further analysis is usually appropriate to refine these choices and discriminate the better value. This may include optimizing operating design and parameters for each major strategy choice.

Determining the appropriate model detail is a balancing act. The model should encompass all important features of the system. The project team and decision makers should be confident that the model behaves in a way that is consistent with their understanding of the situation.

Before beginning to actually construct a model, it is helpful to conceptualize the model's organization or structure. The general planning rule applies: "An investment in planning has a ten-fold savings in execution." A modeling conceptual error, found at an early stage, is much easier and less risky to correct.

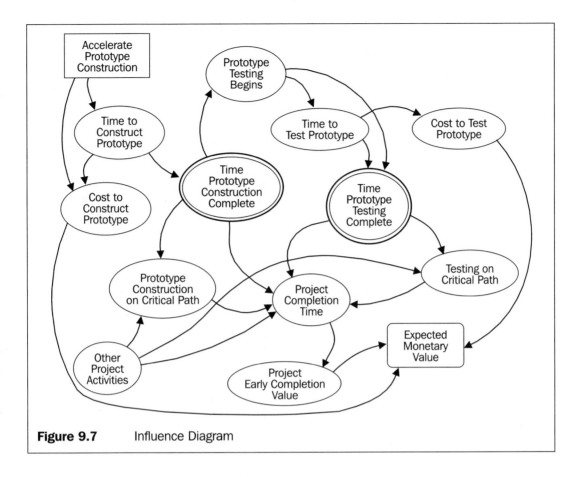

Figure 9.7   Influence Diagram

A diagram of the problem is a good early investment. We can do this with little time and effort, before laboring with the details of formulas and values. A system-flow diagram is useful in depicting essential features.

In project management, the starting point may be the project plan as a WBS. This provides a list of the project's activities and the precedence relationships. The graphical equivalent is the CPM, PERT, or PDM diagram. Costs and, possibly, performance details can be built upon the base project-schedule model.

A similar diagramming approach, focusing more on the variables, is an *influence diagram*. Figure 9.7 shows an example.

The arrows on the arcs in Figure 9.7 show the direction of influences or causality. Common symbol shapes in influence diagramming include:

■ Rectangles or squares for decisions
■ Ovals or circles for risk or uncertainty variables
■ Double-ovals for deterministic calculation variables (i.e., formula calculations)
■ Rounded-corner rectangle for payoff variable(s), the basis for decisions (such as *EMV*).

In Figure 9.7, the subject decision is whether to accelerate an activity, Construct Prototype. This activity is part of a much larger program or project. Prototype Testing follows, although there may be a delay. The Prototype Testing Start Date affects the activity costs and the project's overall time to complete. Whether an activity is on the CP determines whether delaying the activity directly delays the project's overall completion time.

Influence diagrams are a great way for a project team to begin working on a new, unfamiliar problem. Members can discuss the variables and their relationships while drawing the diagram on a whiteboard. Sometimes teams resolve problems through the insights gained just by developing the graphic model, without resorting to quantitative modeling.

Such diagram drawing is the central practice in *system dynamics*, the discipline of modeling dynamic systems with rate-of-change (differential) equations. "Loops and links" are often positive or negative *feedback* connections, illustrating (qualitatively) how the system behaves.

Detailed modeling should not proceed until everyone is satisfied that the diagram adequately and faithfully expresses the team's understanding of the system and decision alternatives.

Other Modeling Concepts

Modeling proficiency comes with practice. Simplicity is a hallmark of a good model; there is elegance in a minimal representation that adequately matches the project manager's view of reality.

Following are several useful concepts in modeling.

Decomposition is the process of breaking down something complex into understandable and workable components. This technique pervades most analyses. Decomposition enables better intuition and allows dealing with more detail than would otherwise be possible. We can break out submodels for organization convenience, and link them into a main model.

Synthesis is the process of combining components into a larger whole. In modeling, synthesis would naturally follow decomposition. Having decomposed the problem into smaller parts, we can combine the components into the overall model. Often, we can develop a submodel to better understand a portion of a system. Typically, we are interested in a probability distribution that is difficult to judge directly. We can then copy the submodel's distribution into the higher-level model.

Sensitivity analysis is very important in deciding which elements significantly impact the outcome. It permits the modeler to examine the degree to which an outcome variable is affected by changes in input variables. If a relationship is found to be important, additional analysis may be warranted to further define the probability distribution of the input variable, or to more precisely define the formula relationships in the model.

Unfortunately, new situations most often require partially or wholly custom models. Typically, 60 percent of the effort of a decision analysis is in constructing the deterministic cashflow model. Research has shown how to construct model logic modules for phenomena in typical projects. Reusing standard modules will lead to more efficient model development in the future.

The deterministic project model is the core of a planning or an evaluation analysis. The model aids in making forecasts, regardless of the probabilistic technique involved. Its main function is to generate projections and, hence, values for each possible outcome scenario. We then use probabilities to weigh the outcome values into the EV forecast of a decision variable such as *EMV*. Usually, we evaluate every path through a decision tree, and every trial scenario in a simulation with a deterministic model.

Modeling Tools

Computer assistance is preferred for all but the simplest decision problems. Computers allow us to include a much greater scope of considerations in the models.

There is a well-established industry in project-scheduling software. Much of the commercial software is limited to certain aspects of project management, including controlling cost, resources, or completion time. Models to calculate construction costs are often the most detailed. However, project cost is but one component of corporate NCF. Other tools are being developed (or are available, but not used extensively) that permit more sophisticated modeling of project network diagrams (PNDs). These rely on PNDs that permit other logical relationships between activities that are not typically available in commercial programs for project planning, scheduling, and control.

Often we need a custom model, tailored to the situation at hand. Available tools include:

- Computer spreadsheets
- Formula-based modeling tools, such as Javelin® or Lotus® Improv™
- Procedural, high-level programming languages, such as Microsoft® Visual Basic™
- Graphical modeling tools, such as High Performance Systems' ithink®
- Modeling languages, some that now permit visual display of the results of dynamic interactions, e.g., CACI'S SIMSCRIPT II®
- Task-specific modeling programs, such as Microsoft Project
- A variety of other tools to aid in defining and refining logical relationships between variables, such as flow charting and diagramming programs.

Spreadsheet programs are the most popular business-modeling tool. For larger problems, formula-based tools provide a more manageable and productive environment. For the largest models, or for those with complex formulas or conditional branching, procedural programming languages have an advantage: detailed modularity. Microsoft Visual Basic™ is powerful, and well-done models are mostly readable by nonprogrammers. The graphical modeling tools will become increasingly functional and popular.

There are many tools available for project planning. An increasing number of these solve the project activities network with simulation. These tools generate forecasts of cost and completion time as distributions. At this writing, there are at least three add-in simulation programs for Microsoft Project. Other vendors of project management software have added simulation capabilities.

Beyond the current tools, we can potentially reduce much of the modeling effort through rule-based expert systems (a subset of artificial intelligence, discussed in Chapter 17). Actually, the amount of work is unchanged; we delegate more of it to the computer.

Sensitivity Analysis

Project models are comprised of variables and formula relationships. We combine input variables in formulas to determine how the project system behaves and the corresponding outcome value. Obviously, some variables are more important than others. Sensitivity analysis is the process of analyzing the relative importance of elements in the model. Usually we focus attention on the input variable assumptions and not on the model structure.

A nonprobabilistic, or deterministic, cashflow model provides the basis for valuing each possible outcome. Monte Carlo simulation and decision tree analysis are ways to recognize uncertainty in input variables. These represent judgments about risks and uncertainties. Applying decision tree analysis, Monte Carlo simulation, or other probabilistic techniques turns the deterministic model into a stochastic model.

The real purposes of sensitivity analysis are to:
- Identify key variables warranting special attention
- Provide information to back up a presentation and recommendation.

The analyst may want to allocate time for obtaining expert judgments in rough proportion to the importance of the variables. Typically, two to five input variables cause over 90 percent of the uncertainty in the outcome value.

Sensitivity to Individual Inputs

In the simplest application, we perform sensitivity analysis by making alternative "what-if" trials of a deterministic model with step changes in one or more of the variables. These can be either chance or decision variables.

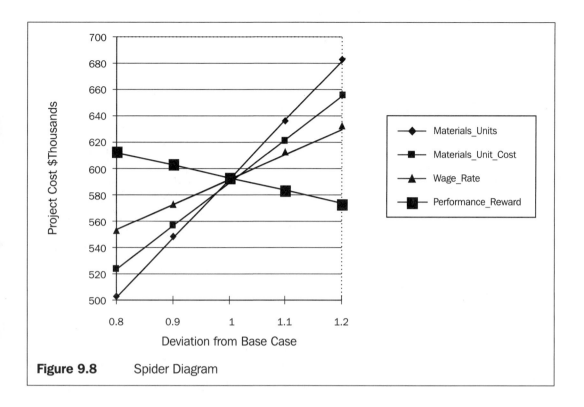

Figure 9.8   Spider Diagram

Usually, only one variable is changed at a time, holding the other variables at their *base case* value. This form of sensitivity analysis is easy to perform, and does not involve probabilities.

A **spider diagram**, such as in Figure 9.8, is a popular way to present simple sensitivity analysis. The x-axis is a factor deviation from the base case. Although the y-axis can be any dependent parameter (*PV*, *internal rate of return* [*IRR*], and so on), the outcome value measure is most meaningful.

❖ *IRR* is the discount rate that makes *PV* = 0. This popular decision criterion represents the yield of the unamortized investment, and is often used for ranking investments under a capital constraint.

Figure 9.8 shows the model's outcome sensitivity to changes in individual input variables; the more sensitive the model to a variable, the steeper the slope.

A drawback to the spider diagram is that percent deviations do not indicate the *range* of uncertainty for each variable. A variant of this diagram adjusts the lengths of the "legs" to confidence bounds (for example, 80 percent confidence limits) for the respective variables. Some practitioners further embellish the graph with "webs" connecting the confidence points.

Figure 9.9 shows a popular *sensitivity chart* in project evaluations, where the project can either succeed or fail. This is a single-variable spider diagram, with chance of success as the input variable and *EMV* as the outcome value.

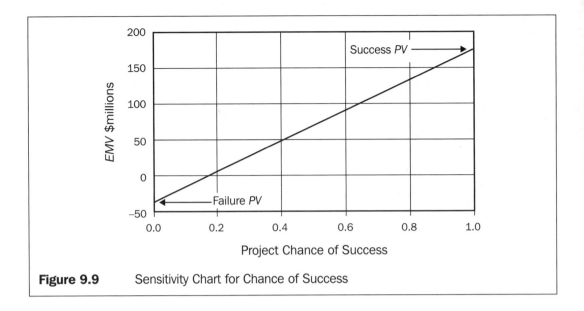

Figure 9.9   Sensitivity Chart for Chance of Success

A recently more-popular sensitivity graph is the ***tornado diagram***, shown in Figure 9.10. This has the benefit of expressing the combined effect of the variable range and model sensitivity to that variable. We run alternative what-if cases, changing one variable at a time to a low confidence bound (e.g., 10 percent), then to a high confidence bound (e.g., 90 percent). The graph in the figure prioritizes variables in sequence of importance, according to the range of the resulting outcome values. When the graph is oriented in the manner shown, the outline of the bars resembles a tornado. Note that the top four or five variables account for most of the outcome uncertainty.

Leverage Model

Both deterministic and stochastic models are suited to sensitivity analysis. Stochastic models show the additional effect of uncertainty in the input variables. Variables having a high degree of uncertainty have a correspondingly greater influence upon project outcome uncertainty.

In the tornado diagram featured in Figure 9.10, two effects determine the importance of a variable to the analysis outcome value:

■ The sensitivity of the model to changes in the variable's value (i.e., the slope of the line in a spider diagram)

■ The uncertainty, or range, of the variable.

These two aspects combine in a "leverage" effect, as illustrated in Figure 9.11. Symbolically, we have this formula relationship:

(variable's importance) ≅ (uncertainty in the variable) ×
(sensitivity of the model to this variable).

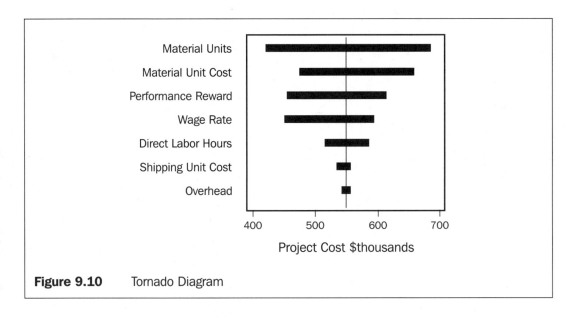

Figure 9.10   Tornado Diagram

Variable Interactions

Sometimes in performing sensitivity analysis, we simultaneously change two or more variables to determine the joint, or combined, effect. The joint variance (change) is usually different than the sum of the component variances. Analysis of joint effects is cumbersome with conventional sensitivity analysis utilizing the deterministic model.

There is a relatively new way to do sensitivity analysis that recognizes the possible interactions of variables in the calculations. Run a Monte Carlo simulation, saving the trial values of the input variable values in addition to outcome values. For each input variable, calculate a **correlation coefficient** between the input and outcome variables. The correlation coefficient formula is in Appendix 1A, Moment Methods.

This statistic represents the degree of association (correlation) between the variable's random sample values and the project's trial outcome values. The magnitude of the correlation coefficient is a measure of sensitivity to that variable.

The correlation coefficient (ρ) ranges from +1 if the variables have a perfectly positive correlation to –1 when they have a perfectly negative correlation (both rare). A +1 would mean that the sequenced (ranked) input variable values and outcome values are perfectly paired. If the correlation coefficient is close to +1 or –1, then we should simply use a formula to express the dependent variable as a function of the independent variable. A zero correlation means that there is no apparent pattern (correlation) between an input and the outcome variable.

Figure 9.12 is a **sensitivity chart** illustrating the relative importance of each input variable, according to variable rank correlation. (This graph was generated with Crystal Ball. @RISK produces a similar chart. See Appendix B.)

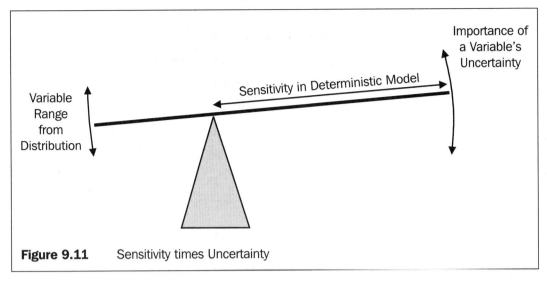

Figure 9.11   Sensitivity times Uncertainty

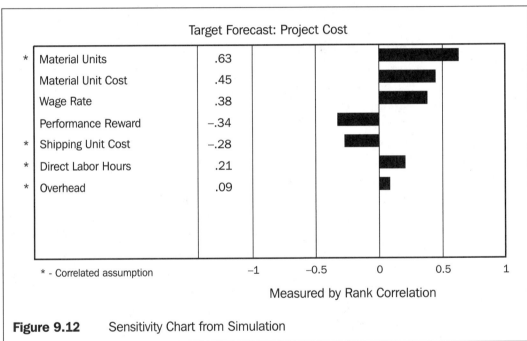

Figure 9.12   Sensitivity Chart from Simulation

❖ **Rank correlation** uses the rank sequence of data values (ordinal scale data) rather than the values themselves (ratio scale data) in computing the correlation coefficient.

As with a tornado chart, we prioritize input variables by the width of the bar. We can obtain a similar sensitivity chart, with the same ranking of variables, by approximating each input variable's contribution to the variance (σ^2) of the outcome variable.

If I could use only one form of sensitivity graph, this would be it. There is one little problem, however. Sometimes we have a strong correlation between a minor variable and an important variable. In the model in Figure 9.12, Shipping Unit Cost is of minor importance, but is highly correlated to Material Units ($\rho = -.5$ in the model). Disabling correlation allows such minor variables to drop out. Thus, sometimes we want to temporarily disable correlation in doing sensitivity analysis to get a better prioritization of input variables.

Dynamic Simulation Models

In most Monte Carlo project simulations, uncertainties are resolved at the start of a simulation trial. Random samples of input probability distributions (trial values) are substituted in the deterministic model. The system then solves the model to determine the forecast outcome and its value for that trial.

The typical analysis has many assumptions. Decision points during a project can greatly complicate the model.

A **dynamic model** makes adjustments as the project simulation progresses. Decisions are based upon the then-current forecasts, policies, and rules of thumb. At subsequent decision points, for example, forecasts will use then-current conditions and apparent trends. Example intermediate decision points include:

- Evaluating whether to continue a project after test results
- Changing specifications to adapt to a changed outlook for market demand
- Expediting activities to make up for project delays.

A decision tree analysis can explicitly represent only a few subsequent decision points. Solving such a decision tree defines choices that will be based upon event outcomes realized up to that point. *A decision tree is perhaps the simplest form of a dynamic project model.* Several decisions and chance events, however, can overwhelm a decision tree approach.

We can accommodate more detail and flexibility in a simulation model. These dynamic simulation models are some of the most interesting to develop. Key decision points are placed where management interventions can occur. Such models reflect the adaptive nature of real-world project management. We can make projects *self-healing*, in effect, much as the real system where a manager can intervene. Situations where dynamic simulation is applicable include:

- Shared resource loading
- Activity duration and cost dependent upon actual start time versus original plan
- Effects of contingencies, which often ripple through the system (when things start to go wrong, often a chain of unpleasant surprises is set into motion).

Simulation is the only technique that can represent such diverse and important details in a decision model.

The key to dynamic modeling is representing conditional branching. Decision rules in the project model, representing the company's decision policy, can drive the model's behavior. IF statements accomplish this in spreadsheets. Modeling in this detail enables more realistic project planning and evaluation.

Summary—Toward Credible Evaluations

The aim of decision analysis is **faster, more confident decisions**. Model building looks time-consuming, and it can be. The extent of the analysis, however, should always be appropriate to the decision being made. *Analysis only adds value when the analysis outcome may affect the decision*. The alternative to decision analysis is intuition. While the intuition of the experienced manager can add significantly to the decision-making process, the wise decision maker supplements intuition with logical and rational decision methods. Of course, the extent of an analysis is often subject to time and resource constraints, and should consider the value of further analysis.

Modeling is a key method of gaining insights into the behavior of a complex system or any reasonably sized project. It is difficult to overstate the importance of a good model.

CHAPTER 10

PROBABILITY DISTRIBUTION TYPES

Probability is the language of uncertainty. A common anxiety among people learning decision analysis is choosing the type of probability distribution to represent an uncertainty. Here we examine the most popular distributions and situations where and why they apply.

Representing judgments about uncertainty is key to using stochastic (probabilistic) project models. Usually, the most qualified people available are asked to provide their opinions about values that go into the model. When the expert does not know a significant parameter with confidence, a probability distribution can completely express his judgment about uncertainty. Here we examine the most popular distributions and situations where and why they apply.

In the example figures, the numbers in parentheses are the "arguments" of the distribution function. These are typically the way we specify the respective distributions to a **Monte Carlo simulation** (simulation) computer tool. In this chapter, I'll use *mean* (μ) instead of expected value (*EV*), though they are synonymous. Some distributions also use the *standard deviation* (σ) statistic as an argument. We will use p to represent probability of success.

Probability Distributions

Probability refers to a number, 0–1, representing chance of occurrence. Most people are comfortable with this everyday idea. A phrase such as "a 40 percent (.4) chance of delivery delay" seldom presents confusion, so long as we are clear about what "delivery delay" means.

Often a risk is a *binary event*. It will be either true or false. A contingency event either happens or not. Often we assign values of 0 (false) and 1 (true) as outcome values of a binary distribution. Spreadsheet IF statements are a prime example of using binary chance events.

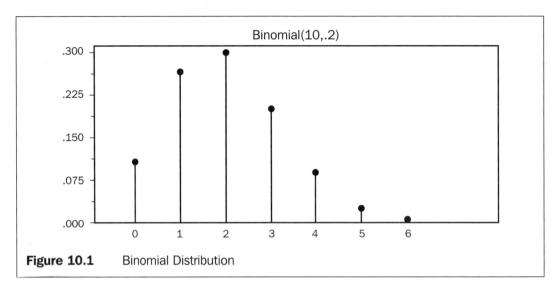

Figure 10.1   Binomial Distribution

For more-complex situations, we have other types of discrete probability distributions. If the outcome value is along a continuum, we have instead a *continuous distribution*. Probability distributions represent the range of possible values and the probabilities of values within the range. We will look at the distribution shapes that are most useful in project evaluation and in project management.

Discrete Distributions

Does the chance event have two, or perhaps several, distinct possible outcomes? If so, we are talking about a discrete probability distribution. Frequently, the potential outcomes are integers, such as "number of work interruptions." The parameter name often begins with "number of." Examples include number of equipment breakdowns, number of people available, number of units needed, and so forth. Each possible outcome is assigned a probability, and these probabilities must sum to 1.

Simple systems often produce discrete distributions. Figure 10.1 and Figure 10.2 show the most popular discrete distributions, after the binary risk event. Though we don't have the distribution formulas printed here, because of space, most are simple enough. Software tools, even some hand calculators, are widely available with functions for the distributions described in this chapter.

Binomial Distribution

A collection of independent events, each with the same probability of success, would exhibit a *binomial* distribution. For example, suppose that we have ten independent research projects, and we judge each as having a p =

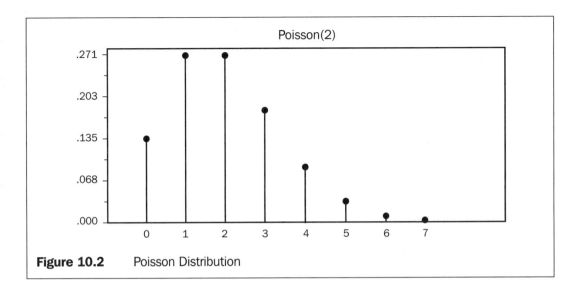

Figure 10.2   Poisson Distribution

0.2 chance of success. The binomial distribution characterizes this situation. Though elements in actual systems may not be fully independent or have the same probability of success, the binomial distribution is often a reasonable approximation for a simple portfolio model. Figure 10.1 shows a binomial distribution with n = 10 trials with p = .2 probability of success on any trial. This distribution is often a starting point for representing simple portfolios, such as research projects.

Poisson Distribution

Sometimes events happen randomly, such as defects and work interruptions. The number of such events in a time or other interval is described by a *Poisson* distribution. The only parameter needed to specify this distribution is the average (μ) number of events occurring during an interval. Figure 10.2 shows a Poisson distribution with μ = 2 occurrences. This distribution is widely used in simulating queuing (waiting-line) systems, such as representing the number of work requests during a time period.

Three-Level Estimates

In decision tree analysis, we can use only discrete distributions. Thus, we must convert continuous chance events into discrete approximations.

Typically, three branches are adequate: high, medium, and low case. These are called "three-level estimates." We should choose these three values and their probability weights, so that the original continuous distribution's statistics are preserved. More than three outcomes can be used, if you want more resolution.

Suppose that your expert judges the uncertainty in volume of a natural gas reservoir as a lognormal distribution with μ = 120 and σ = 50 billion

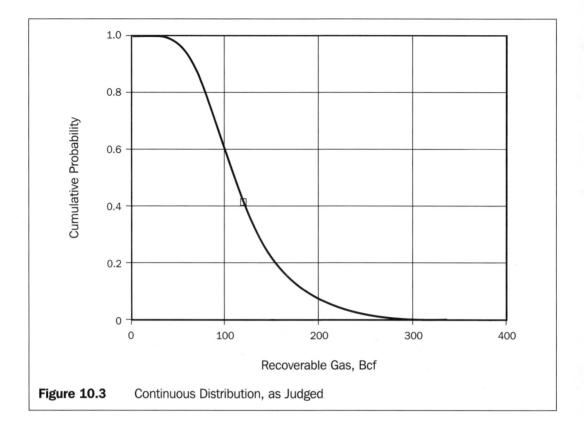

Figure 10.3   Continuous Distribution, as Judged

cubic feet (Bcf). Figure 10.3 illustrates this judgment. With simulation, we would use the continuous distribution directly, as is. For a decision tree analysis, I *discretized* the distribution into the form in Figure 10.4.

Continuous Distributions

In project management and other types of planning and analysis, most uncertainties will be continuous. Cost, time, and quality metrics are prime examples. Figures 10.5 through 10.10 show the most popular continuous distribution types.

Normally a scale is omitted from the y-axis. It is possible to show a scale, though the units are unnecessary. You should remember that the y-axis is scaled such that the total area under the curve—representing probability—equals 1. The probability of an x-axis value is proportional to the height of the curve above that point.

Uniform Distribution

The simplest continuous distribution is the *uniform*. This is often called a rectangle or boxcar distribution, because of its shape. If (a) one knows the

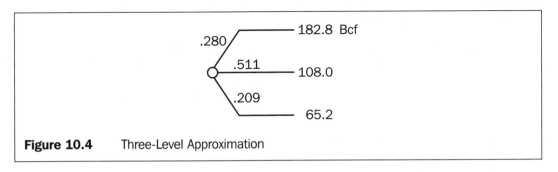

Figure 10.4   Three-Level Approximation

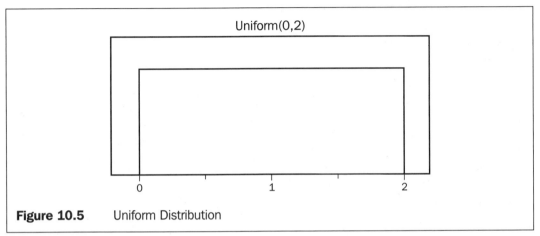

Figure 10.5   Uniform Distribution

upper and lower bounds of the range of possible values, and (b) if every value within that range is equally probable, we are describing a uniform distribution. Figure 10.5 illustrates a uniform distribution bounded at 0 and 2 units.

Many people incorrectly assign this distribution shape to uncertainties. However, it is a rare system that generates values that are uniformly distributed. More often, values in a central part of the range are more probable. Examples of uniform distributions include: position of a rotating shaft that stops randomly, position at which a cable breaks, and a small section of a broad distribution.

Triangle Distribution

The triangle distribution is very popular, though I've never seen a system in business or in nature generate values with a triangular shape. Simplicity is the appeal. Just three values fully describe the triangle distribution: minimum (*L*), most likely (*M*, mode), and maximum (*H*). Figure 10.6 shows an example. Even people without training in probability can relate to these points.

The shape of a particular distribution is usually less important than its position (μ) and width (which we might characterize with σ). Let me offer two cautions when using the triangle distribution:

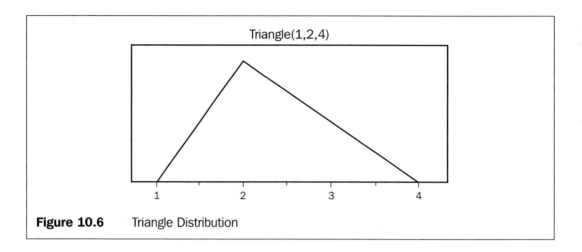

Figure 10.6   Triangle Distribution

- People tend to judge distributions too narrowly. The low and high parameters are the actual extremes, and not just pessimistic and optimistic cases.
- Many people will confuse "most likely" (the *mode*) with the best single-point estimate. It is not, unless the triangle happens to be symmetric. Drawing the distribution will help eliminate the confusion. The best single-point estimate is the mean (μ, *EV*), and this happens to have a simple formula: $\mu = (L + M + H)/3$.

Normal Distribution

The most commonly observed distribution is the *normal*. Galileo observed the familiar bell-shaped distribution when measuring the positions of stars and planets. Figure 10.7 shows a normal distribution with a $\mu = 2$ and a $\sigma = 1$ unit.

The normal distribution occurs often in nature and in business. When we sum many independent, continuous chance events together, the total tends to be normally distributed.

Simple project models often assume that activities are independent. Then if the activities have similar duration, the distribution for time to complete a chain of activities is approximately normal. Amazingly, this is true regardless of the shape of the component distributions. In statistics, the *central limit theorem*—one of the fundamental principles in statistics—describes this key behavior.

Most every statistics book includes a table of the standard normal distribution ($\mu = 0$, $\sigma = 1$). You can obtain the same values from the NORMDIST function in Excel. From a table or the function, one can determine confidence intervals. For example, an interval $\mu \pm \sigma$ represents a 68 percent confidence interval for a normal distribution. The vertical dashed lines in Figure 10.7 show σ intervals. In theory (and equation), the normal distribution is boundless. As a practical matter, for planning and evaluation work, there is virtually no chance (0.3 percent) of being outside the range of $\mu \pm 3\sigma$.

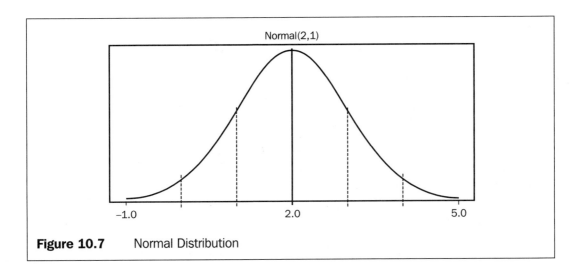

Figure 10.7   Normal Distribution

Lognormal Distribution

We often observe data where the frequency distribution is positively skewed—that is, having a longer tail to the right. When two or more distributions are multiplied, such as time × hourly cost, the product is typically positively skewed. As we multiply more independent components together, the product becomes more lognormal in shape. (This, too, is a result of the *central limit theorem.* Some older readers may remember adding logarithms on slide rules to multiply.)

Figure 10.8 shows an example lognormal distribution, with μ = 2 and σ = 1. This is a common distribution shape for uncertainties that are positively skewed.

❖ The log of values obtained from a lognormal population plot as a normal distribution. Special "probability graph paper" is available for plotting the cumulative frequency distribution. This has one axis linear in standard deviations of a normal distribution. If the cumulative frequency of the data plots as a line on a linear value scale, then the data are normally distributed. If the data plot as a line on log value scale, then the data are lognormally distributed.

Both the normal and lognormal distributions are completely described by μ and σ. Some computer tools accept alternate statistics to specify the distribution, such as the 10 percent and 90 percent confidence points.

Exponential Distribution

The *exponential* distribution is a counterpart to the discrete Poisson distribution. The exponential distribution is most commonly used to represent time between arrivals of random events. Figure 10.9 shows an exponential distribution with μ = 2 units.

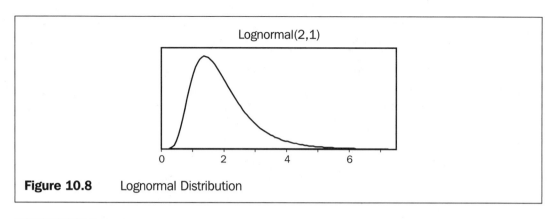

Figure 10.8   Lognormal Distribution

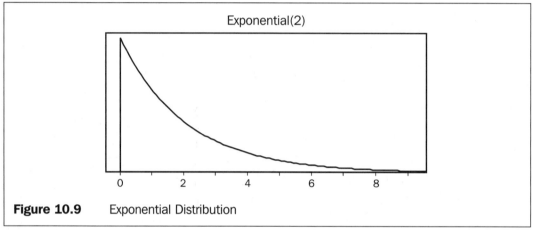

Figure 10.9   Exponential Distribution

Like the Poisson, we use the exponential distribution in discrete-event simulations, such as of queuing systems. Common uses include representing the time until the next arrival of a service request or unscheduled work interruption.

Beta Distribution

The *beta* distribution is a mathematical function that assumes a variety of profiles, depending upon two shape parameters. The basic distribution is bounded by 0 and 1. In the distribution illustrated in Figure 10.10, the shape parameters are 2 and 5, and 3 is a scaling factor. With the shape factors, we can make many different symmetric and asymmetric shapes.

We can reposition and rescale the distribution as needed. Project management professionals have used beta distributions since the 1950s to represent activity times-to-complete in PERT project models.

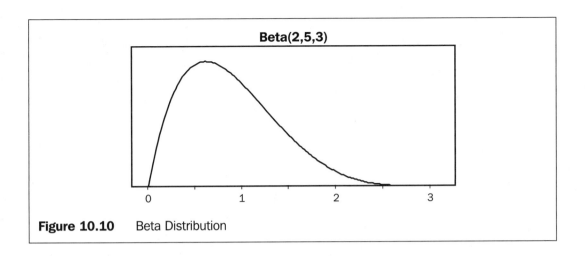

Figure 10.10   Beta Distribution

Which Distribution Is Best?

If you are the expert, the best distribution is the one that completely expresses your belief about the uncertainty. Often we have data that suggest that a system is producing a common distribution shape. Be aware that mathematicians have described hundreds of distributions, and your system need not produce a distribution with a recognizable mathematical function. Fortunately, the distributions listed earlier usually suffice. Importantly, the popular software tools allow users to specify custom distribution shapes.

Without data, perhaps the best way to obtain a distribution is to model the subsystem that causes the uncertainty. If the expert can explain how the process works, we can model it and use the model to generate a distribution shape. The amount of effort in detailed modeling should be consistent with the importance of the variable to the decision at hand.

Usually our best available experts provide judgments that go into the project models. Delegating responsibility for these inputs is a responsibility of the decision maker.

A probability distribution completely describes a judgment about a single variable. There is an additional dimension of expert opinion: Are there influencing relationships among the variables? That is the topic of Chapter 12. First, we will discuss the source of these probability distributions in Chapter 11, Judgments and Biases.

CHAPTER 11

JUDGMENTS AND BIASES

*Psychology is often a part of decision science: many investigators are interested in better understanding how people **do** make decisions. We would like to avoid biases and cognitive illusions. Our discussion here is about how people **should** make decisions.*

Decision analysis is a mostly quantitative discipline. Previous chapters describe forecast and evaluation models. This chapter focuses on the expert judgments that are inputs to these models.

Three Roles

There are three roles in the decision process, as shown in Figure 11.1:

- **Experts** or **assessors** provide the judgments that go into an evaluation. Usually, the most knowledgeable people available provide these inputs.
- **Evaluation analysts** are primarily responsible for developing the quantitative project models, models that generate scenario outcomes and forecasts for each alternative.
- **Decision makers** review the forecasts and judge whether the analysis is credible. They make the selection (usually accepting the team's recommendation) and initiate implementation.

Overlapping duties are common, as people "wear different hats."

Judgments

A *judgment* is a value assessment performed by a person. There are two basic approaches to judgments, or assessments, as inputs to an evaluation:

- **Deterministic Assessments** (non-probabilistic)
  - ◆ Single-point values (e.g., a particular cost)
  - ◆ Single-line forecasts (e.g., inflation rate over time).

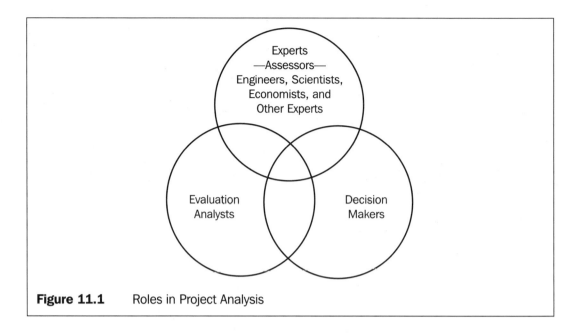

Figure 11.1   Roles in Project Analysis

A conventional deterministic analysis uses only input variable forecasts. Even in decision analysis, this is adequate to represent minor variables or those known with high confidence.

■ **Probabilistic Assessments** (stochastic)

◆ Continuous probability distributions (e.g., hours to complete an activity)

◆ Discrete probability distributions (e.g., number of subcontractors bidding)

◆ Event probabilities—that is, whether or not an event happens (e.g., whether a task will require rework). This binary event type is the simplest of discrete distributions.

When a value is uncertain, the representation takes the form of a probability distribution. Considering a single variable alone, a probability distribution can completely represent an expert's judgment about the possible outcomes of a chance event.

Risk analysis is the process of assessing the probability distribution for one or perhaps several variables. *Decision analysis* is more encompassing, and is about evaluating alternatives in the context of decision policy. There may be several risk analyses as part of a decision analysis.

Objective and Subjective Probability

Because a human performs a judgment, the resulting probability distribution is called a *subjective probability*.

The extreme opposite is *objective probability*. This is supported by a comprehensive understanding of the system or by conclusive evidence: either knowing the value and likelihood of every possible element in the pop-

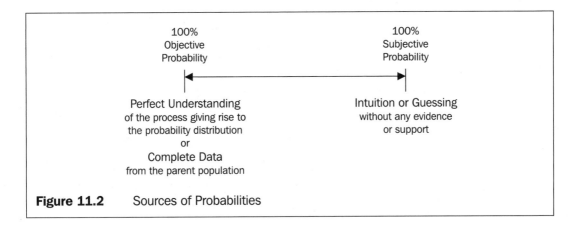

Figure 11.2   Sources of Probabilities

ulation, or completely understanding the stochastic process providing variable outcome values.

Figure 11.2 shows the continuum between the two extremes. Most judgments lie somewhere in the middle, far from either end. Even with considerable data from similar situations, the expert must assess to what degree the data still apply.

With sufficiently complete data or system knowledge, which is rare, we could approach a 100 percent objective probability assessment. Fully objective assessments are rare. Examples would be probabilities associated with cards, dice, and other elements of chance, where we have essentially complete knowledge of the system.

Judgments, as inferred by their name, always involve a degree of subjectivity on the part of the expert. Subjective probability assessments reflect someone's belief. Here are two common and illogical statements:

■ "I judge that the probability is 30 percent, but I may be wrong."

> ❖ There is no such thing as an *incorrect* probability, so long as it faithfully captures the expert's understanding. The opinion is personal. Two people, given the same information, will often arrive at somewhat different assessments. For a binary risk event, nature or whatever is being judged, the outcome will be 0 or 1 (false or true). The probability is not an outcome prediction, or it would *always* be wrong. Rather, the probability reflects the expert's degree of belief that the event will occur.

■ "The probability is 30 to 40 percent."

> ❖ When someone judges the likelihood of an event, the assessment should be a single number. A range is nonsense (unless predicting where the final judgment will lie). The expert should settle on a single fraction, despite often incomplete information.

It is important that judgments be as objective as possible. Being "objective" as to *source* (see Figure 11.2) reduces the effect of emotion. Possibly confusing is also using "objective" when referring to judgment *quality* as meaning free from bias. Biases (i.e., not objective to quality) are more likely when the source of the judgment is subjective. For this reason, we often hear a question like, "How *objective* is that assessment?"

In decision analysis, subjective probabilities are often all that are available. In most evaluations, you will find several key variable assessments that are highly subjective. Nevertheless, appropriate use of even soft judgments about important variables leads to improved decisions. The decision model provides a logical way to use everything important that we know about the problem.

A *good decision* is consistent with the data and with the organization's decision policy, but does not guarantee a *good outcome* in a particular case. We use decision analysis in believing that there is a correlation between good decisions and good outcomes. Consistently making good decisions increases the likelihood of favorable results over time.

Eliciting Judgments

Eliciting means to bring out or draw out the judgment of an expert. Unless the expert has been well trained in probability concepts, eliciting a judgment is usually best accomplished through an interview process. The interviewer, often a decision analyst, acts as an interested but objective party. Different perspectives of the variable are discussed and quantified until the expert is confident that the resulting probability distribution accurately reflects her best judgment.

In formulating an opinion, we ask the expert to consider the possibilities. Is this the right variable? Have we clearly defined what it means? Is this the right level of detail? What is assumed in this assessment? What is the worst (or best) possible outcome? What has to go right for this to occur? What might go wrong?

In the interview, it is important to first determine range of the distribution. Then work inward. Do not fall into the trap of starting with the best value and attempting to build a distribution around it. If you do, you will likely fall into the trap of the *anchoring bias* (discussed later in this chapter). Bracketing the possibilities and working inward avoids anchoring on an initial central value.

Some experts are uncomfortable with quantifying their judgments directly as probability distributions. In such cases, analogs may help diffuse the probability anxiety. One means is to use a *probability wheel*, such as that illustrated in Figure 11.3, which uses pie-shaped sections to represent the possible outcomes. The expert adjusts the size of the pie sections until she feels that the areas are proportional to the likelihood of the respective outcomes. A scale visible only to the interviewer shows the corresponding probabilities. A similar approach would be to use a device where linear distances represent probability weights.

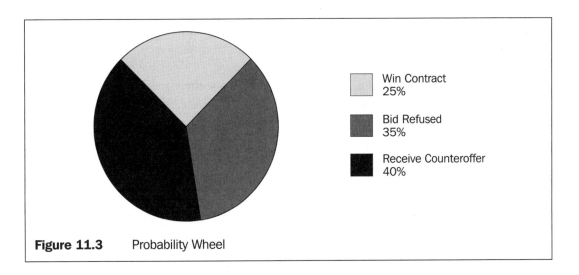

Figure 11.3 Probability Wheel

A classic analogy to uncertainty is an urn or other container of colored balls or marbles. An interviewer chooses colors and number of balls to represent different possible outcomes of a chance event. For example, a project manager might be considering which component to use in a critical application. Component X is reliable but expensive. Component Y has a "high" probability of working in the product application and costs one-third as much. If the company implements Component Y and it fails, then the losses will bankrupt the company. Assume white marbles represent Component Y's "success," and black marbles represent "failure." The interviewer adjusts the mixture until the manager is indifferent between:

- Choosing the safe but expensive Component X
- Randomly drawing a marble from the urn, and realizing the project outcome corresponding to the marble color.

If the fraction of black marbles is less than the actual risk of Component Y failure in the application, then choose Component Y.

Overconfidence about Our Knowledge

Actual forecasting behavior and clinical experiments repeatedly show that people are overconfident about their knowledge. Consider persons asked to provide, say, an 80 percent confidence interval for a parameter.

❖ An 80 percent confidence interval is defined by two bounds, such that there is only a 10 percent chance of the outcome being lower than the lower bound, and a 10 percent chance of being higher than the upper bound.

It makes sense that the *less* someone knows about a variable, the *wider* her confidence interval should be. Typically, only about half of survey participants have the true outcomes contained in their judged 80 percent confidence intervals. That means the typical person is responding with a 50 percent confidence interval, when the request was for an 80 percent confidence interval. Other interesting results from such surveys (see Capen 1976) include:

- People without knowledge of a topic are often unable to differentiate between 30 percent and 98 percent confidence intervals.
- Asking for a 95 percent interval typically gets about a 65 percent confidence range.
- The more people know about the general subject (not the specific question), the larger the confidence interval that they assign (they more fully appreciate the possibilities). The more a typical person knows about the topic, the less chance that their interval includes the true value.
- Even when told beforehand that "most persons are overconfident about their knowledge," survey participants continue to make their confidence intervals too small.

Asking the person to judge two confidence intervals will help. For example, first ask for a 90 percent, then a 50 percent, confidence interval.

The solution to this overconfidence bias is *practice* and *feedback*. Expert assessors should practice and be given feedback on the quality (outcomes) of their assessments. If artificial situations are necessary for practice, it helps to make the exercise as meaningful as possible, such as by putting some real money at stake.

If we elicit the judgment by using an interviewer, he will often first ask the expert for a *plausible* range. This represents a confidence interval, but not the whole range. Then, they can discuss reasons why more extreme values might occur.

Biases

One hallmark of a credible evaluation is *objectivity* (discussed in Chapter 1). This is not *objectivity* used in the sense of what was the *source* of the probability assessment (data or intuition). In the discussion that follows, *objectivity* is synonymous with *lack of bias*.

A **bias** is a repeated or systematic distortion of a statistic, being too high or too low on average. The statistic of most interest is the *EV*. The average error (actual minus estimate) should tend toward zero over many forecasts.

Achieving objectivity, or low bias, requires attention in three areas of the evaluation:

- Bias-free assessments of input variables
- A value function, embodying the decision policy, which faithfully measures progress or goodness toward the organization's objective
- Integrity in the decision model structure, so that calculations themselves do not introduce any biases or other errors.

Common Biases in Evaluation or Decision Policy

Decision policy has three elements, any of which can introduce bias:

- **Objective**. If the value or quality measure does not directly correspond to the organization's purpose, there will be a bias. Different stakeholders have different objectives, therefore biases. Most businesses profess to maximize shareholder value, and should be measuring monetary value.
- **Time value**. Present value discounting adjusts cash flows to reflect time value of money. Most companies use a discount rate that is too high for probability-adjusted forecasts, creating a bias against long-term projects.
- **Risk policy**. Many managers believe that they have a responsibility to act conservatively. They will willingly sacrifice a *risk premium* (see Chapter 4) in terms of reduced *expected monetary value,* to lower risk. This practice may be intentional and appropriate. An organization's management should look carefully at what objective is to be maximized in decision policy. An *objective value measure* will be a statistic that corresponds directly and logically to the objective of the organization.

Belief and Perception Errors

Several obvious biases arise from emotions and motivational effects; others are from relying on ill-founded heuristics or rules of thumb. Additional biases arise because of poor understanding of statistics or probability theory. There are also perception biases, similar to optical illusions, because our mental model may not be consistent with reality.

Listed below are the more common biases that might be inadvertently introduced into an analysis.

Personal feelings. The natural tendency is to shade judgments to reinforce what we want to do. If members of a project evaluation team will be able to work on an enjoyable project, they may inadvertently deliver optimistic assessments.

Feelings about the effects of certain outcomes. A contractor may have an excessive desire to win a bid in order to appear busy and successful.

Biases toward new information. People often seek new information only when a "favorable" report is expected. A study is more likely to be commissioned if the decision maker expects it to support her present opinion. "Bad news doesn't sell." Even when delivered, bad news is often discounted, faulted, or ignored.

Believing what one wants to believe. Projects (or bids) with unreasonably optimistic projections are often selected over projects (or bids) submitted with more reasonable projections.

Insensitivity to sample size. Often there is insufficient data to draw a conclusion. People are prone to make hasty generalizations.

Availability. We remember cases that are more famous or where we were more closely involved. Some scenarios are easier to imagine than others, such as those in our industry or area of expertise. The most recent data or experience is weighted most heavily. The easier it is to imagine or remember, the higher the believed likelihood of occurrence.

Insensitivity to prior probabilities. Discrepant and unusual events, even though rare, are given undue weight. Exceptions are remembered and weighted as if commonplace. Judgment bias occurs when the current situation is rare, neither common nor unique.

Sensitivity to the cause of the problem. People are willing to do more to save a species endangered by hunting than endangered by natural change. Life-threatening risks are more acceptable if the person has a choice about being exposed to the risk (e.g., drives a motorcycle without a helmet).

Anchoring. People do not like to change their minds, especially if the earlier position was publicly stated. They "anchor" to the previous position. Later, they are more likely to recognize information that reinforces the original judgment or decision.

We also mentioned anchoring when judging an uncertainty. If one has an initial impression of the best forecast, then he often keeps this constantly in mind when building-out the distribution. It is therefore difficult to objectively consider the possibilities. Psychologists have demonstrated that people assessing a probability distribution shape should not try to build around an initial "best guess." The expert inadvertently anchors to the original number. This effect is minimized if the assessment starts at the extremes of the distribution and works inward.

Framing. We are sensitive to the wording and context of outcomes. This is called the *framing* of an event description. Very different judgments can result from the way we ask (frame) questions.

Consider a major project that will earn a $20 million profit for the company if it succeeds, but will lose $2 million dollars if it fails, asking:

- "What minimum *probability of success* would you require to be willing to approve this project?"
- "What maximum *probability of failure* would you accept and still be willing to approve this project?"

Such questions often evoke a response different from the complement question. If any person were to answer both questions, the responses should add to 1. Often they do not. Surveys about *losing* (saving) jobs or lives often show that the answers depend upon the form of the questions.

Improving Evaluations

Consistent, objective evaluations require good analysis practice. Here are some recommendations:

- Make a conscientious effort to **best capture the experts' judgments** in assessing input variables. Some of these assessments may be highly subjective. Whether additional investigation is warranted can be evaluated as a *value of information* problem (see Chapter 6).

- Strive to avoid judgment biases in assessing input variables. **Everyone upstream from the decision maker should be as objective as possible**. Otherwise, the analysis is questionable and of little value. Note that if everyone is slightly conservative, the resulting analysis can be overwhelmingly conservative.

- Some situations demand conservative decision making. A conservative attitude is a bias—but is often appropriate. **Apply a consistent risk policy**. This is done, in effect, in the final stage of analysis. Most often, the decision maker simply compares risk-versus-value (or cost) profiles of the different alternatives and chooses the best one (see Chapter 3 and Chapter 4 for a more consistent, quantitative approach).

- We can detect some errors by **validation**. Sometimes we can develop models to validate outcome data. Conversely, data can be used to validate models.

- In developing a valid model, it helps to **decompose** the project system into submodels. Quantify subjective assessments, and model interrelationships between variables. A **suitable stochastic method** (e.g., Monte Carlo simulation) correctly propagates the probability distributions throughout the calculations.

- Recognize that biases do exist. We can avoid or minimize some of these by **carefully structuring the problem**. Use an appropriate value measure, and separate judgments from preferences. A common error, for example, is to increase the present value discount rate to compensate for risk. It is far better to use probabilities to deal with uncertainty, and use the discount rate only to represent preference for time value of money.

- Perhaps the most powerful way to improve decisions is *post-implementation reviews*, also called *post-evaluations* or *post-audits*. These are follow-up analyses of decisions after the general results become known. There is a psychological bias toward rationalization, and many people have difficulty reconstructing their thought processes after learning the outcome. It is important to preserve the original reasoning by documenting the analysis. Provide **performance feedback** to the individual assessors, and use lessons learned to improve the evaluation process.

Summary

As professionals, most of us spend a great portion of our workdays processing or preparing information for others to act upon. This work is either evaluation itself or preparation for evaluation. Employers and clients are better served by ensuring that evaluations are objective—a hallmark of professionalism.

A colleague approached me once, saying, "I could use the decision analysis methods *if only I had good data*." When do we ever have "good" inputs to planning evaluation models? Rarely!

My response is always to point out that we are going to make the decision regardless of whether we have good data. A decision analysis approach lets us do the best we can, given what we know, even when some of those inputs are very subjective. Chapter 12 continues our discussion about judgments, next focusing on relationships among variables.

CHAPTER 12

RELATING RISKS

In modeling projects, a common beginner's mistake is assuming that chance events are independent. Often, a chance event (risk or uncertainty) is related to one or more other chance events. Decision variables can influence chance events also. Characterizing the association between events is a second dimension of assessing uncertainty.

When something starts to go wrong in a project, often many things begin to go wrong together. Positive feedback can quickly drive a system to spiral out of control. A delay in one activity delays a chain of subsequent activities. Encountering unexpected complexity or bad weather increases activity completion times. These are examples where we have *correlations*, or *associations*, between variables in the project model.

In stochastic modeling, if any two variables are related, we should express that relationship in the model; otherwise, the analysis results will be wrong. In this chapter, we will discuss some of the causes of correlation and ways to represent this in project models.

Correlation

Association and **correlation** are synonyms. Either term refers to a causal relationship between two or more variables. At least one of the variables is a chance variable—that is, a risk or an uncertainty. For example, Activity Cost is typically associated with Activity Time to Complete.

If data are available, the easiest way to determine whether two paired data variables are related is to plot and inspect a **scatter diagram** (also called an x-y plot or cross-plot). If we see a pattern in the points, then there is correlation between the x and y variables. Alternatively, we can use a statistic, called the **correlation coefficient**, to measure the degree of linear association (correlation). Usually, understanding the system is sufficient to identify whether one variable is dependent upon another. Figure 12.1 demonstrates a relationship between Person-Hours to Complete Project and

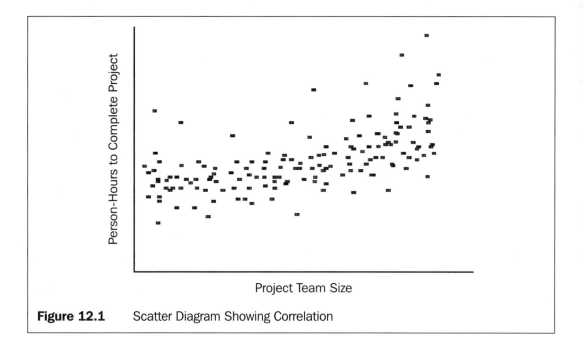

Figure 12.1   Scatter Diagram Showing Correlation

Project Team Size. We see that an increase in Project Team Size is generally associated with an increase in Person-Hours to Complete Project. This is *positive correlation*, and the *correlation coefficient* is about +0.7 in this case.

Most analyses involve at least some conditional (i.e., non-independent) probabilities. Typically, one or more chance variables are partially dependent on another event outcome.

Decision trees are especially well suited for representing conditional probabilities. For example, in value of information problems (Chapter 6), the information-event outcomes (symptoms) are correlated with an event of interest (affecting value). A convenient way to represent the relationship between the chance events is by using a *joint probability table*.

A well-known deficiency in deterministic project models is *optimistic completion times*. This is not necessarily due to optimism by the project professionals, whom we asked to judge activity completion times. Standard PERT analysis (in Chapter 9), for example, considers only activities on the deterministic critical path. Such simple models do not consider near-critical paths that have a probabilistic influence on project completion time. Further, simple approaches usually assume independence between activity duration times.

Most often, *correlation adds to uncertainty* in a project. If variations in time and materials increase together, for example, the effect on the project is greater than the sum of the variances in time and materials alone. That is, total project uncertainty is worse than if time and materials were independent. (A negative correlation would be welcome, in this case, because it would decrease overall uncertainty.)

Sources of Correlation

The following paragraphs describe situations where correlation arises.

Direct cause-and-effect relationship. Often one variable is partially dependent upon one or more other variables. For example, Vehicle Cost is determined, in part, by Distance Driven, weight of the vehicle, and average load.

Common drivers. Two variables may share a common influence. The number of people on a project team obviously affects salary expenses. Having more people also means more communication channels, which leads to higher costs in coordination efforts. Thus, salary and coordination costs are correlated. Other correlation examples include:

- Low unemployment level—the driver—affecting recruiting lead-times and salary levels
- Inflation, materials, and wage rates—affecting many activities across the board
- System or problem complexity, which may be unknown at the project start
- Estimation biases
- Changes in project scope.

System constraints. Bottlenecks, exclusive use, and other resource constraints can cause correlations. For example, higher demand for shared resources and common materials usually results in longer lead-times. Similarly, competition for a resource results in the customary inverse relationship between price and demand.

Ways to Represent Correlation

We should balance the effort in representing correlation with its importance in the model and decision situation. In the subsections that follow, I will describe several correlation modeling methods.

An influence diagram (discussed in Chapter 9) is an excellent way to map relationships between elements in a system. In this method, we connect decision, chance, calculation, and payoff variables with "influence" arcs showing the direction of cause-and-effect relationships and calculation-precedence relationships.

Probability Tables

In Chapter 6, we use joint probability tables to represent probability relationships between two events. In *value of information* problems (options), we have one or more information chance event(s) (symptoms). One or more chance events of interest affects the symptoms we observe.

For example, the underlying demand for our product (perhaps we want to forecast *next* year) affects the results we obtain with a market survey this

Market Study Result	Market Demand			
	High	Medium	Low	
"Favorable"	.12	.15	.06	.33
"Inconclusive"	.06	.20	.12	.38
"Unfavorable"	.02	.15	.12	.29
	.20	.50	.30	

Table 12.1   Joint Probability Table

year. Product demand, in turn, drives our project's profits, which we learn about later. Fortunately for our calculations, most often we need deal with only one pair of chance events at a time, such as is shown in Table 12.1.

There is correlation between the Market Study Result and Market Demand. Otherwise, the survey information would be worthless.

Asset and project models are more likely to use Monte Carlo simulation, instead, as the stochastic calculation process. With simulation, we have additional techniques for representing correlation.

Sampling Actual Data

A data set consists of values sampled together. For example, for different drugs introduced to the marketplace, we might have data of unit volumes at monthly intervals after introduction. If we have a collection of representative data sets, we can use it for sampling by either:

- Randomly selecting a data set, with or without replacement, and using the data-set values as trial values in the simulation. This has an advantage of not needing analysis in order to understand the relationships. Of course, we might miss an opportunity to gain important insights.
- Analyzing the data, and finding a way to represent the relationships mathematically. This is the approach for the remaining three subsections.

Fitting to Data

As seen in Figure 12.1, a scatter diagram shows a pattern when there is correlation. Figure 12.2 shows another data collection where a clear pattern exists. Direct Labor Hours explains most of the Total Task Cost, and the relationship appears approximately linear. Workforce composition, materials, and other variables also affect total cost.

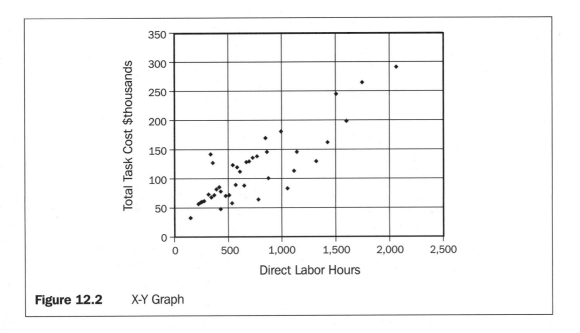

Figure 12.2   X-Y Graph

We could "fit" a dependent variable to one or more "driver" variables using regression. *Regression* is a statistical technique that finds the best fit of equation coefficients to one or more independent data variables. Most popular is the "least squares" method, where the best set of equation parameters provides the lowest sum of the errors squared. The simplest method—and probably well suited to the data included in Figure 12.2—is a "linear regression" to the formula:

Total Task Cost = $a + b \times$ Direct Labor Hours

where a computer routine chooses coefficients a and b to best match a line through the data. Many hand-held calculators now provide linear regression functions. To make the synthetic data more realistic, we might add a noise function (such as a normal distribution about the best-fit line). Noise in real and synthetic data represents other variables and effects not recognized in the model.

Fitting a function to multiple variables and curve-fitting to a more complex equation (e.g., a polynomial equation) are extensions of the same idea. For truly difficult problems, *neural networks* (discussed in Chapter 17) may be a suitable "massive regression" approach.

Correlation Coefficient

If an increase in one variable is generally—though not always—associated with an increase in another, they are said to have a *positive correlation*. The opposite effect is negative correlation.

A statistic, called a *correlation coefficient*, measures the degree of linear association between paired data values. The formula for the (Pearson moment-product) correlation coefficient is in Appendix 1A. Microsoft Excel's CORREL function is a convenient way to obtain the correlation coefficient statistic, ρ. Perfect positive correlation has $\rho = +1$, and perfect anti- or negative-correlation has $\rho = -1$. In these extreme cases, one variable is simply a deterministic function of the other variable. Unrelated variables have $\rho \cong 0$. The two strongly related variables shown in Figure 12.2 have $\rho = 0.85$.

The popular @RISK and Crystal Ball tools for Monte Carlo simulation with Excel spreadsheets both provide convenient ways to relate chance events with correlation coefficients. A correlation coefficient for any pair of variables is perhaps the simplest way of expressing correlation.

If there are many relationship pairs, then a *correlation matrix* is used. This is a matrix of correlation coefficients of all variables involved.

There is a trick to the way popular simulation programs use correlation coefficients. Instead of using correlation calculated with actual data values, @RISK and Crystal Ball use **rank correlation**. That is, the correlation coefficient refers to the rank order of the variables, rather than to the actual values. If you want to calculate the rank correlation coefficient, you will first need to convert the values to their ranks. For example, if you have 100 data values for a variable, sort the data and then replace the values with the rank numbers 1 to 100. Do this for the other variable as well. Then calculate the correlation coefficient using the ranks of the variables. I understand that the rank correlation mathematics works better than value correlation when the distributions have different shapes.

Correlation coefficients are a quick and easy way to represent correlation in a model. This way presumes that there is a *linear* relationship between the variables, which is another deficiency of the method. The next technique is the best if circumstances warrant the extra modeling effort.

Detailed Modeling

The superior modeling approach, if doing the work is justified, is to model the system in detail. We represent the functioning of the system, such as a project, as best understood. Correlation is a characteristic of many systems when there are cause-and-effect relationships and when there are common "driver" variables. My motto is, "If you can describe it, we can model it." How are these variables related? What is the calculation hierarchy? Can we further decompose these elements? If you can explain why or describe how the project and its environment work or behave, then we can express that knowledge in a model. Again, an *influence diagram* is a good way to map the relationships.

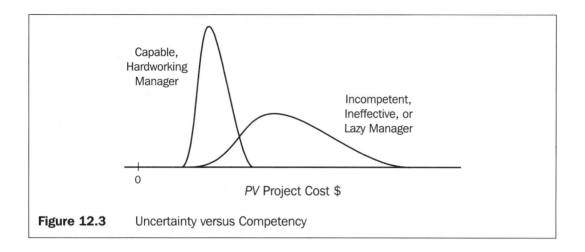

Figure 12.3   Uncertainty versus Competency

Human Factors

Analysis is always easier with good data. Fully objective probabilities are possible when we completely understand the system, such as with most games of chance. Unfortunately, biases creep into our judgments about uncertainty. Further, human behavior affects the outcome of a process in progress. The following two subsections describe examples where human behavior affects chance events.

Competence

Often, we estimate cost or time to complete without sufficient consideration as to who will be doing the work. Who does the work often is as important as how the work gets done. Factor the people into the project plan and forecasts. With programmers, for example, individual productivities can range by a factor of ten or more. Similarly, a project manager can have a dramatic influence on the project team's productivity, as illustrated in Figure 12.3.

Response to Progress

As I read Eliyahu Goldratt's book, *Critical Chain* (1997), I was struck by his clear explanation of human behaviors in project performance. Despite being a novel, the book, in my opinion, vividly explains why judgments about uncertainty so often are biased.

In project planning, we may detail the work to be done and then apply metrics and various methods in estimating time and cost. This is straightforward planning and cost estimation.

People often spoil the plan. You will probably recognize the following behaviors.

Multi-tasking. Our original intent may be to work systematically on tasks in a logical sequence, one at a time. Urgencies and waiting delays often necessitate overlapping different tasks and different projects. The resulting inefficiency worsens matters, creating need for further multi-tasking. (This is *positive feedback* in the system, working to our detriment.)

Wasting slack times. This is largely procrastination, what Goldratt calls the "student syndrome" in *Critical Chain*. Early finishes are not reported, while late finishes push back successor activities.

Embellishment. If you are ahead of schedule and cost budget, why not add more features or make it a better work product? This is especially true in software development. Gold-plating. Less-driven workers may be inclined to coast a bit.

Catch-up. If behind schedule and budget, most conscientious people are inclined to work harder. Beyond a point, however, some people will give up.

Project progress reporting bolsters a feeling of control. Some companies have found that this is an illusion, and that reporting provides little impact on project success (perhaps because some organizations do not share the progress reports with the people actually doing the work). The procrastination and embellishment behaviors, mentioned earlier, suggest why.

People like to work toward objectives. Just knowing a time to complete target provides an achievement incentive. This is why "stretch" budgets are so popular.

Garbage in produces garbage out. Decomposition is a key method that project planners use for making better forecasts. Breaking down tasks into details reduces biases in estimation and the undesired behavior effects. Plus, planning the details leads to a more realistic work assessment. For example, we can segregate contingencies from the normal portion of an activity's work (and address them with project risk management, Chapter 8).

Correlation affects the forecast quality in a stochastic model. The next chapter describes what I think is the most important reason for people to use decision analysis—you get a better number!

CHAPTER 13

STOCHASTIC VARIANCE

One of the benefits of decision analysis is improved accuracy. Using expected value (EV) inputs in a project model does not always provide the EV result (however measured). Sometimes the difference, stochastic variance, is dramatic. This chapter discusses the causes of stochastic variance and how to reconcile a decision analysis to a conventional, deterministic analysis.

When planning your project, suppose you had used a stochastic (probabilistic) model to forecast expected value (EV) Completion Time. What if, through extraordinary coincidence, your team completes each activity in the same time as the EV estimate for each activity? That is, suppose you realized your base-case project model? Would this ensure that the project is completed in exactly the forecast time? Generally, *no*. This chapter explains **stochastic variance**, that portion of the deviation, actual minus estimate, attributable to the stochastic calculations.

Base Case versus Stochastic Model

Deterministic refers to traditional project models with single-point inputs. *Stochastic*, or probabilistic, refers to project models where we represent uncertain inputs as probability distributions.

Base Case

Usually, a *base case* projection (the base project plan) is a projection made with a deterministic model. For example, this might be a ***base plan*** for a project—what happens if everything goes according to the input parameters, and the project executes exactly as modeled. Customarily, the best single-value assessments are the inputs to the base-case model, and those values are *EVs* if the experts assess distributions for the input variables. This base case is but one scenario, one that is especially useful as a reference for discussion. Although of interest, you should not use the base-case scenario for making decisions. The reason is that the base case is often an *incorrect forecast*.

Stochastic Forecast

Of course, a project team should incorporate its best information in forecasting. Probability distributions (and correlation details) express complete judgments about uncertainty. We would like the effects of probability distribution inputs to propagate through the model calculations. Thus, the outcome variables will be distributions. Two key points:

- The best single-point input values are their *EV*s. For discrete variables, normally we use the outcome nearest the *EV*. The deterministic project (or asset) model solution is the base case.

- The EV of the completion time distribution is often *different* than the base case, and that difference is the *stochastic variance*. The stochastic variance phenomenon arises with other variables as well.

(Stochastic Variance) = (Base Case Outcome) − (EV of Outcome Distribution)

I chose this name in reference to *variance analysis*, the process of reconciling a forecast with actual.

❖ The stochastic variance effect is certainly not new, but I have seldom seen any reference to this calculation phenomenon in the literature. Cost accountants do *variance analysis*; so I thought *stochastic variance* would be a good name.

Deterministic and stochastic calculations provide different best estimates. This surprises many people who think that decision analysis is an embellishment mainly to characterize risk. This calculation difference can sometimes be dramatic.

In one analysis (see Appendix 13A), the venture required a $2.8 million investment. The base case *present value* (*PV*) was $1.2 million; however, the stochastic model's *expected monetary value* (*EMV*) was $4.6 million! Thus, the real value of the project was almost four times the value of the conventional analysis!

In summary, in order to get an EV projection of a time-spread variable, such as costs across time, we need to calculate with probabilities. Anything less rigorous may introduce a bias or calculation error into the forecast.

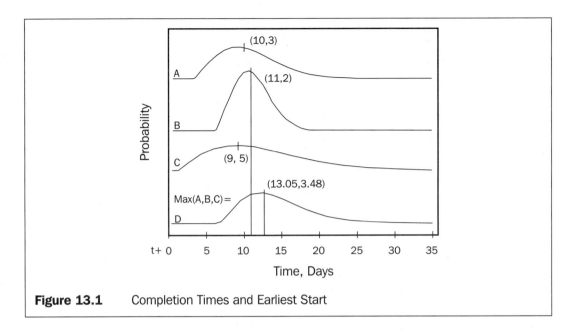

Figure 13.1   Completion Times and Earliest Start

Merge Bias

In project management, one source of stochastic variance is *merge bias*. In Chapter 9, we see activity networks where often two or more *predecessor activities* must finish before a *successor activity* can begin. Regarding stochastic behavior, I once heard a project modeler say, "Nothing good every happens at a merge point."

Consider the following, illustrated in Figure 13.1: Activities A, B, and C must be completed before a successor activity, D, can start. In a conventional, deterministic project analysis, the latest completion time, Max(A,B,C), determines when D can begin. The notation Max(A,B,C) is read "maximum of A, B, or C" (completion dates). This corresponds to the MAX function in Excel.

Assume that A, B, and C all begin together. Each has a probability distribution representing judgment for its activity duration. The EV start date for D is often *later* than the latest EV completion date for *A*, *B*, and *C*. Thus, projects with uncertainty in activity completion times usually take longer than the base case schedule than if there were no uncertainties. This **merge bias goes unnoticed without using a stochastic project model**. Neglecting this "joining" or "merging" effect is one reason why many projects complete later than forecast.

Here are the calculation details for the example, with distributions, as shown in Figure 13.1. Activities A, B, and C start together at time 0, and have EV (same as mean, μ) completion times of 10, 11, and 9 days, respectively. There are uncertainties in these estimates, as shown in the figure. The judged activity-completion times are skewed, lognormal probability distributions. The μ, or *EV*, is the first value in parentheses. The width or uncertainty of each distribution is characterized by its *standard deviation*, σ, the second value in the parentheses.

With a conventional activity network model (CPM or PDM), Task D can start in 11 days (see Figure 13.1). This is the EV completion time for B, the latest of the best single-value estimates for A, B, and C. However, using 11 days to schedule the D start is unwise. Task D's EV start date would be 11 days only if the completion times of A, B, and C were known precisely, or at least within narrow ranges. This would also be true if the distributions for A and C had no chance of exceeding 11 days. This is not the case shown in Figure 13.1. Any of the preceding activities could delay D's start beyond 11 days.

A simple Monte Carlo simulation demonstrates the effect. With the assumed lognormal distributions, as shown in Figure 13.1, the EV start date for Task D turns out to be 13.05 days (excess calculation precision is retained to illustrate the concepts). This 2.05-day increase beyond the largest EV completion date for any prior activity is the merge bias.

If a project's schedule lengthens 2.05/11 = 19%, what is the effect on costs? A stochastic model of the project system helps with the answer. Whenever the forecast or estimation is important, we should explicitly incorporate distributions in representing risks and uncertainties.

The deterministic solution had the successor activity starting in 11.0 days, while the EV start under uncertainty was 13.1 days. The 2.1 days difference, *merge bias* or *stochastic variance*, is the effect of uncertainty in the network project model. This is one way that stochastic variance can arise from the model structure.

❖ The project manager probably should not use 13.05 (or rounded) days for planning Activity D's start. The optimal project value will likely be a different planned start for D, and this optimization process is the subject model in Chapter 15.

Many people first become interested in risk and decision analysis as a way to *characterize* the uncertainty in estimates. An even greater benefit is **more accurate** estimates for decision making. Sometimes, the difference between forecast and actual can be substantial through no fault in project execution. When reconciling a forecast with the project's actual outcome, the variance analysis should separately recognize the component attributable to stochastic variance.

Variance Analysis

Variance analysis (not to be confused with the *variance* statistic) identifies the component causes for an actual outcome deviating from its forecast or budget. Cost accountants are often the ones who prepare variance analyses.

When we use decision analysis techniques to make forecasts, the difference between forecast and actual:

Total Variance = Actual Outcome – Forecast Outcome.

We can split this into two components:

Total Variance = Deterministic Variance + Stochastic Variance.

Decision analysis provides a more accurate forecast for many problems. It also helps the decision maker better understand the business or proposed transaction. The example *variance analysis*, discussed later in this chapter, shows one format for explaining what happened in reference to the calculated forecast.

Forecasts Are Usually Wrong

A stochastic model produces a more accurate forecast because it correctly recognizes uncertain variables and how they interact through the calculations. The stochastic variance can arise from common situations:

- Asymmetry and non-linearity (perhaps the most common cause), e.g., a bonus when the team meets a performance target
- The merge bias, caused by constraints on activity starts and finishes in the activity network structure
- Contingency plans and other subsequent decision points represented in the project model
- Correlation, or association, between variables.

Stochastic modeling better represents reality. When done properly, the EV projection is an objective forecast. This means that it is unbiased. The forecast is unbiased if the input values and model calculations are unbiased. Bias can arise from an improper model structure: its formula relationships and constraints.

We started this chapter with the question: What if for every input variable:

Actual outcome value = EV of the assessed probability distribution?

Using these EV input values provides the **base case** deterministic analysis. The problem is that the base case answer is often different from the EV of the outcome variable's distribution. The difference is the **stochastic variance**. Because this situation arises, it is important that a post-analysis recognize that portion of the total variance attributed to the stochastic calculations.

Example Simulation Analysis and Variance Report

Let's examine a simple model calculated with Monte Carlo simulation to show the projection and a variance analysis:

Net Cash Flow = NCF = Volume × Price – Cost.

Variable	Statistics			Distribution Type	Correlation Coefficients	Assumptions
Volume	$\mu = 10$	$\sigma = 2$		Lognormal	Independent	10.000 k units/mo.
Price	$\mu = 30$	$\sigma = 5$		Normal	−0.5	30.000 $/unit
Cost	l = 140	m = 180	h = 280	Triangle	−0.5	200.000 $k
						NCF 100.0 $k

Table 13.1   Spreadsheet Model

Trials	10,000
Mean, $\bar{x}$	$95.09k
Standard Deviation, s	$69.79k
Mean Std. Error, $\sigma_{\bar{x}}$	$0.70k

Table 13.2   NCF Distribution Statistics

Assume that a company's experts provided the following assessments for the three random variables:

- *Volume*: Lognormal distribution, with μ = 10,000 units and σ = 2,000 units. Independent variable.
- *Price*: Normal distribution, with μ = $30/unit and σ = $5/unit. Correlated with Volume with a correlation coefficient ρ = −.5.
- *Cost*: Triangle distribution, with low = $140,000, most likely = $180,000, and high = $280,000. This has μ = $200,000 and σ = $29,400. Correlated with Volume with ρ = −.5.

The deterministic solution is simple. Using the *EV*s for each parameter, Table 13.1 shows that the base case forecast is:

$NCF_{\text{deterministic}}$ = 10,000 units x $30/unit − $200,000 = $100,000.

This would be the forecast with the conventional, single-point calculation approach.

In a decision analysis, we capture experts' complete judgments about uncertainties in the form of probability distributions. The result of a Monte Carlo simulation model forecasts (EV) *net cash flow* (*NCF*) at $95,090, as shown in Table 13.2. I developed this example with one of the popular spreadsheet add-in products (see Decision Analysis Software, Appendix B).

Figure 13.2 displays the simulation *NCF* distribution. The EV *NCF* is $95,090. Although the distribution in the figure appears approximately centered at about $100,000, the bias is significant. The stochastic variance is $100,000 − 95,090 = $4,910, or about a 5 percent difference. Often the stochastic variance is substantially greater in proportion to the mean forecast (as with the example in Appendix 13A).

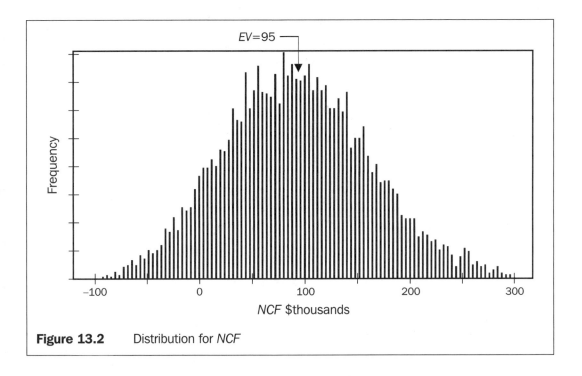

Figure 13.2   Distribution for *NCF*

Table 13.3 is an example variance report for the NCF projection. We should separately recognize the stochastic and deterministic variances in a post-analysis. This table illustrates one possible format.

The *joint variance* in Table 13.3 results from simultaneous changes across multiple variables in the calculation. Cost accountants sometimes define certain item variances to include joint components; that is, they define component variances to include all parts of the joint variance(s). I recommend separating the individual and joint contributions.

Figure 13.3 shows the cumulative distribution for the NCF projection. An example interpretation: There is about a 57 percent chance that *NCF* will be less than $100,000.

Notice that the graph in Figure 13.3 conveys much more information to the decision maker than a single-value estimate would provide. As a decision maker, wouldn't you prefer the graph, with *EV* annotated?

Summary

*EV*s provide the best single-point assessments for each continuous parameter in an analysis. Also, EV of the outcome distribution provides the best, single-point project forecast.

What if, through extraordinary coincidence, the project realizes the *EV* of each input parameter? This is the base case, and the outcome would be the actual result. However, the outcome value is often different from the *EV*

Project/Budget Variance Report
for December 2000

	μ		σ	
	Mean		Std. Deviation	
Original Projection:				
Volume	10.0k		2.0k units	
Price	$30.0		$5.0/unit	
Cost	$200.0k		$29.4k	
NCF from EV Parameters				$100.0k
Less Stochastic Variance				4.9
				———
NCF Forecast (from simulation)			$s = \$61.4$	$\overline{x} = \$95.1k$

Post-Analysis:			Contribution to	
	Actual	Variance	$ Variance	
Volume	8.244k	(1.756)k	(52.7)k	
Price	$31.08	$1.08	10.8	
Cost	$144.835k	$55.165k	55.2	
Joint Variance			(1.9)	
Deterministic Variance			11.4k	+11.4

Check:	NCF (actual parameter outcomes)	$111.4k
	NCF (EV parameters)	100.0
	Deterministic Variance	$11.4k

Stochastic Variance	+4.9
	———
Total Variance	+16.3
	———
Actual NCF Realized	$111.4k

Notes: NCF = Volume × Price − Cost

Variance amounts in parentheses are *unfavorable*.

Symbols E(x), *EV*, and mean (μ) are synonymous.

μ and σ are symbols for the mean and standard deviation, respectively, for distributions representing judgments about input variables.

$\overline{x}$ and s are the sample mean and standard deviation of the simulation results; these are *approximations* for the true solution μ and σ.

For illustration here and elsewhere, more digits are being shown than are significant. Here, the standard deviation, σ, is huge compared to the mean. The resulting standard error of the mean for 10,000 trials is only $700.

Table 13.3   Example Variance Analysis

forecast. This difference is the stochastic variance. The post-analysis sepa-rately recognizes this correction effect that arises with the more accurate stochastic calculations.

A more precise and unbiased EV forecast is perhaps the most important benefit of a decision analysis approach. Post-analyses are perhaps the single

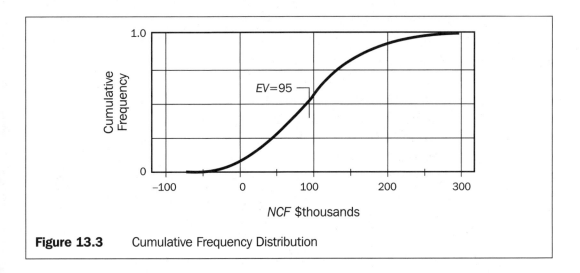

Figure 13.3   Cumulative Frequency Distribution

best way to improve our decisions; it is important to recognize the individual sources of deviation from forecast.

The variance analysis format described in this chapter supports a *distinction between **good decisions** and **good outcomes***. With a solid decision analysis process, we should reward people for good decisions, not for being lucky with chance outcomes. We should judge the evaluation team members based on their creativity in generating ideas, and on the completeness and integrity of their analyses.

APPENDIX 13A

NEW VENTURE ANALYSIS

Several years ago, Mr. Devereux Josephs, a fellow certified management consultant, and I were analyzing a new venture. This was a real-to-life example as part of a joint presentation to the Institute of Management Consultants. Dev was showing traditional DCF analysis. He developed a Lotus 1-2-3 spreadsheet model for a typical new product venture. His model showed:

Base Case

Deterministic Model

$2.8 million investment in plant and working capital

Yielding

$1.20 million net *PV* discounting at 10 percent/year
14.7 percent internal rate of return (IRR)
9.5 years to payout (time to make cumulative *NCF* positive)
$8.8 million total *NCF* = net profit

While not a thrilling value, $1.2 million *PV*, the new venture appears economic. This was the ***base case*** analysis. This traditional analysis shows that the project has a *PV* of $1.20 million, net of capital recovery, operating expenses, income taxes, and cost of capital.

I modified Dev's deterministic model to make it a stochastic model, as would be used in a decision analysis. *PV* as a value measure is appropriate and widely accepted. Many of the model assumptions are uncertain, such as rate of unit sales growth. I replaced the ten most important input variables in the model with probability distributions—making these parameters "fuzzy." I built the distributions around the original, single-point values so that these original values were the distribution *EVs*. I also put in some correlation between key variables.

I solved the model using Monte Carlo simulation. In effect, the calculation propagates the probability distributions through the model. Now, instead of a single *PV*, we obtain a *PV* distribution. Figure 13A.1 and Figure 13A.2 show two forms of the resulting *PV* distribution.

The simulation outcomes ranged from –$2.5 million to over +$42 million. This range is useful information in characterizing the venture's uncertainty. I suggest focusing on perhaps an 80 percent confidence interval (about –$2 to +$19 million) and not get too excited about the distribution tails. From the cumulative distribution, we see that there is almost a 50 percent chance that the project will have a positive value.

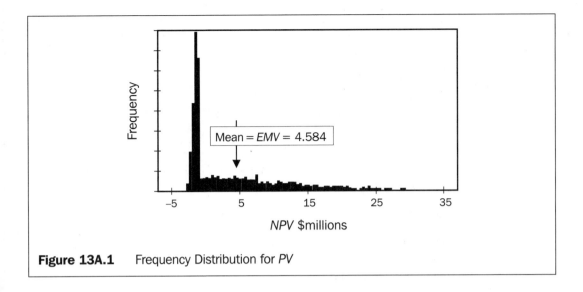

Figure 13A.1   Frequency Distribution for *PV*

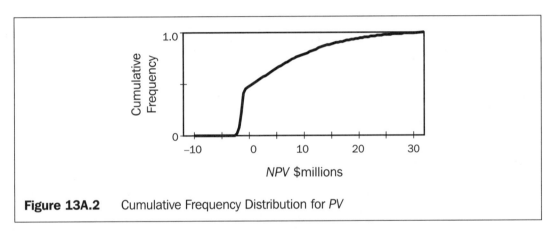

Figure 13A.2   Cumulative Frequency Distribution for *PV*

The *EMV* is what counts most. For the $2.8 million investment, our *EMV* is $4.6 million. This is the value added to the corporation beyond recovering the investment and interest.

- To small, risk-adverse companies, this risk profile would also warrant a value adjustment to reflect their attitudes about risk. Note that a portfolio of projects quickly dilutes the effect of individual projects having high risk.
- To a large, adequately funded, and (essentially) risk-neutral company, the *EMV* may be all that is necessary for decision making.

The best assessment of value, or forecast, is the *mean* or *EV*. In recommending this new venture, the project team might say, "The venture is estimated to add $4.6 million to the company's net worth." This is quite a difference from the base case, isn't it?

The stochastic results reflect a $3.4 million *correction* to the base case value. This adjustment is the *stochastic variance*. If, through extraordinary coincidence, the EVs of the input variables were realized (their best individual forecasts), then the actual outcome in the look-back analysis would be PV = $1.20 million.

The unit manager might reasonably ask:

> You forecast this venture to have an *EMV* of $4.6 million. Coincidentally, internal and external circumstances were such that we realized the values of the individual input forecasts. That's good, isn't it? Yet, you are saying our value added is only $1.2 million. **What happened to the missing $3.4 million?**

In this example, the principal cause of the discrepancy is something not seen in the deterministic model. If we launch the new venture and, after a while, it fails to cover its cash operating costs, management will terminate the venture and sell the assets. This is an *option* to truncate losses, yet keep all of the upside potential. The stochastic model incorporates these possibilities to which the deterministic model is blind.

Dealmakers should be alert to hidden value. If one party can better assess value and risks, it possesses much better information for negotiating.

PART III

SPECIAL TOPICS

This part discusses topics of interest at the fringe of mainstream project management. Additionally, a chapter on probability concepts provides the fundamentals for working with probabilities, the language of uncertainty.

CHAPTER 14

EXPLOITING THE BEST OF CRITICAL CHAIN AND MONTE CARLO SIMULATION

Critical chain project management is a hot new method that can improve a traditional decision analysis approach to project planning and risk management. This chapter describes an even better approach by adding-in techniques of decision analysis.

Critical Chain

Many people regard Eliahu Goldratt's book, *Critical Chain* (1997), as the most significant project management publication in recent years. In this book, written as a novel, he applies *theory of constraints* (TOC) to project management. The obvious constraint in projects, of course, is the critical path. **Critical chain project management** (**CCPM**) extends critical path analysis to the constraining resource. Many managers have seized upon the radically different critical chain approach as an improved way of planning and managing projects.

CCPM addresses several key problems in project scheduling. However, in my opinion, the method ignores much of what we have learned in decision analysis about understanding and modeling risk. CCPM uses, primarily, deterministic calculations. In this chapter, I will compare and contrast my understanding of CCPM with a traditional decision analysis approach. Then, we will discuss ways to blend the best features of the two styles.

Theory of Constraints

Many consider Goldratt to be the father of *theory of constraints*, which is widely heralded in manufacturing. His first best-selling book, a novel called *The Goal: A Process for Ongoing Improvement* (1984), is about de-bottlenecking manufacturing operations. Simply put, greater throughput can be achieved by attacking the bottleneck constraint. His process, whether talking about manufacturing inventory or project time, is essentially the same:

- **Identify** the constraint.
- **Exploit** the constraint, making sure that the constraining resource is fully used.
- **Subordinate** other activities to the constraint. Don't start work prematurely, yet ensure that the constraint resource is never waiting for work.
- **Elevate** the constraint: Seek ways to raise the productivity or availability of the constraining resource.

Managers want to ensure that the constraining resource is fully used. They avoid starting work prematurely as this builds excess work-in-process inventory.

Critical Chain Project Management

In the *Critical Chain* story, Goldratt applies his philosophy to project management. The analogy between production management and project management is effective. The obvious project "bottleneck" is the sequence of activities along the critical path. The analog of excess work-in-progress inventory is prematurely starting activities off the critical path. Manufacturing's throughput is much like project completion time. Focusing on project critical path activities is the manufacturing equivalent of concentrating on bottleneck production processes.

Critical Chain, both the book and approach, has been widely reviewed and discussed. Reading this book is an enjoyable way to challenge one's beliefs about project management and to gain new insights. Other references that I've found most helpful include articles by Leach (1999) and by Elton and Roe (1998), and a book by Newbold (1998).

Critical Chain defines CCPM, a powerful new approach to project management. The key features of the CCPM approach include:

- The schedule model is deterministic, with buffers to deal with uncertainty. *Deterministic* means that the inputs to the model are all singly determined values.
- Remove padding from activity estimates. Otherwise, people will usually waste the slack. Goldratt suggests estimating activity-completion times at 50 percent confidence points (medians). Eliminate buffers along the critical chain. Put a main buffer at the end of the project to protect the customer's completion schedule. Also place buffers at the end of "feeding" activity chains that merge into the critical path. Schedule high-risk activities early so that problems can be detected and addressed early.

- Determine the critical path and resource constraints. Adjust the project plan(s) as necessary to exploit the constraining resource(s). The driving objective is minimizing project completion time.
- Avoid wasting slack times. Part of this is accomplished by using median rather than conservative time estimates. Encourage early activity completions. Instill a culture where an activity team is ready to begin working on its critical activity, and will devote 100 percent of its effort to this activity for the duration.

❖ Contracting people and other resources to be 100 percent applied to an activity would be difficult in many situations. There are other projects competing for the resource that would similarly like 100 percent dedication upon demand.

- Work to plan, and avoid tampering. Monitoring and communicating buffer statuses are key to managing the ongoing project.

"It's *always* a people problem" is an old saying in management consulting. CCPM addresses project management's challenge to effectively deal with uncertainty. CCPM reduces the effects of two behavioral problems: biasing estimations and wasting slack times. However, there is much more that we can do to manage uncertainty.

Decision Analysis with Monte Carlo Simulation

Decision analysis is the discipline for making decisions and evaluations under uncertainty. It is characterized by analyses having three key features:

- *Judgments* about uncertainty, and often analysis results, are expressed as probability distributions.
- We determine the quality of an outcome by a numeric *value function* that measures goodness or progress toward the organization's objective.
- The *expected value* (*EV*) calculation compresses the distribution of possible outcome values into a single number.

The optimal decision policy is to choose the alternative having the best *EV*. Usually this means maximizing EV present value (*PV*) net cash flow or minimizing PV cost. (These decision rules are the same except for a sign change.)

We use a project model to forecast the behavior of the project as a system. *Monte Carlo simulation* (simulation) is perhaps the easiest and most useful way to add-in details about uncertainties. It is a straightforward process that allows distributions to represent activity time estimates and other uncertain inputs. Simulation solves the project schedule, providing distributions and *EV*s for outputs, such as time to complete and cost. There are several commercially available programs that provide simulation capabilities for models in Microsoft Excel, Microsoft Project, and various other project planning tools.

The key analytic benefit of simulation is that the result is a more accurate estimate. Project managers have recognized that uncertainty in merging activity paths produces a longer schedule. This is because it is the *latest* of predecessor completion times that drives the start of the next activity. With stochastic (probabilistic) project models, this is often called *merge bias*. In Chapter 13, I use a more general term, *stochastic variance*, for this effect.

Contrary to popular belief, summing activity completion times does not produce a normal distribution. Unfortunately, for people doing the calculations, most real projects contain many correlations. For example, often, when things start to go wrong, problems affect many activities and thus compound the effects. (This is *positive correlation*, even though the effects are quite *negative!*)

With the simulation model, the project manager can forecast such elements as:

- The probability that an activity lies on the critical path (looking back from project completion). This is called the **criticality index**.
- The distribution for time to complete the project or any sequence of activities.
- The distribution of project cost or, better, project value to the customer. We can perform cost/benefit analyses for candidate risk-mitigation actions and for evaluating possible activity-accelerating (crashing) efforts.

Traditionally, project scheduling starts activities as soon as possible. The intent is to minimize possible delays from time overruns for most noncritical activities. *Critical Chain* explains why we should avoid earliest possible starts by default.

Comparing Approaches

Table 14.1 highlights and contrasts features of the CCPM and decision analysis. Deterministic calculations are a deficiency in CCPM, in my opinion, from all implementations of which I've read. On the other hand, the critical chain approach remedies some problems with a traditional stochastic planning model.

Combining Methods

There are complementary strengths in both CCPM and decision analysis. Combining the methods—taking some of the best features of each—ought to be an improvement. Here is a strategy to realize benefits from blending critical chain and decision analysis approaches for project management:

- Develop the work breakdown structure and activity network diagram in the usual way.

	Critical Chain	Monte Carlo Simulation	Features of Both
Theme	Focus on the deterministic critical path or critical chain.	Manage priorities and risks using *criticality indexes* and calculated distributions.	Reduce or eliminate multi-tasking and wasting slack.
Plan Changes	Strive to keep fairly static, except for adjusting buffers.	Dynamically update the active project plan.	Recognize resource constraints.
Scheduling Starts	Pull (start tasks only as needed by finish date, with buffers).	Traditionally push (start tasks as early as possible).	Can be pull (start tasks only as needed by finish date, with buffers).
Calculations	Deterministic (single-values).	Stochastic (probability distributions).	
Execution	Work to plan—make it happen.	Work with the possibilities.	

Table 14.1   Comparing the Two Approaches

■ Obtain quality judgments about activity completion times and resource requirements, usually by interviewing the best available experts. These judgments should be expressed as probability distributions. Breaking apart important contingencies (probability, and impact distribution if the contingency occurs) is a good way to obtain a better representation and a more realistic estimate.

Figure 14.1 illustrates this *decomposition*. A baseline completion time (or cost) for managing an activity would be the EV time to complete, assuming no major contingencies occur. Task leaders provide the forecasts for activity time and materials, and so on. In the example activity, either or both of two significant contingencies could occur, lengthening time to complete Activity AE. The base case projection assumes that neither of the two significant risk events occurs, and we use the narrow distribution mean for the deterministic model input.

■ Learning is essential to improving future judgments. A graph of actual outcomes versus estimates is an excellent feedback tool (as we discussed in Chapter 1). Post-evaluations should be nonpunitive. A culture of trust and objectivity is essential for obtaining quality estimates and for other human facets of effective project management. The activity manager maintains the model inputs (more about this later) for time to complete the activity. This function, and the cost of the activity, can incorporate dependencies for delayed start and other dynamic conditions.

■ Develop a stochastic project model. We can maintain this perpetually throughout the project life cycle. As available resources permit, shorten the project plan to conduct more activities in parallel (being careful to recognize resource conflicts and multi-tasking inefficiencies). Schedule start times for low-criticality index activities to optimize project value. Simulation models confirm that delaying noncritical activity starts reduces multi-tasking, premature investment, and rework due to changes.

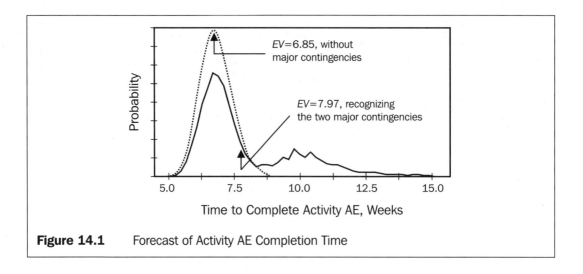

Figure 14.1   Forecast of Activity AE Completion Time

The stochastic project model is the core of effective project risk management. Cost/benefit/risk analyses for activity decisions can produce outputs such as Figures 14.1 through 14.3. (Figures in Chapter 15 illustrate additional types of graphic information available to Activity AE's manager.) Changes to the top-level project model may be necessary in extreme cases. Apply optimization techniques for planning starting times for each activity (the topic of Chapter 15). In complex situations of shared resources, we need to expand the scope of the stochastic model to incorporate multiple projects and their supporting resources.

- Provide activity leaders with convenient access to the project model. The project manager should be especially involved in monitoring ongoing activities (dedicated efforts to the extent possible; reporting early completion) and in alerting workgroups to be prepared as work on critical (or near-critical) activities approaches. Figure 14.3 shows a forecast of when predecessor activities will be finished, so that activity AE can begin.

Stochastic Model Benefits

Modeling major contingencies provides activity managers with information about such elements as:

- Probability an activity will be on the critical path, the *criticality index*, and affects the time to complete the project.
- The forecast, as a probability distribution, for when all predecessors to the activity will be complete (see Figure 14.2).

❖ In Figure 14.2, AE is the code for an activity, "Assemble Equipment." The distribution represents a forecast for when all of activity AE's predecessors will be complete. A subproject model is the source of the distribution. Here, the project model calculated a *criticality index* of 0.35 for this activity.

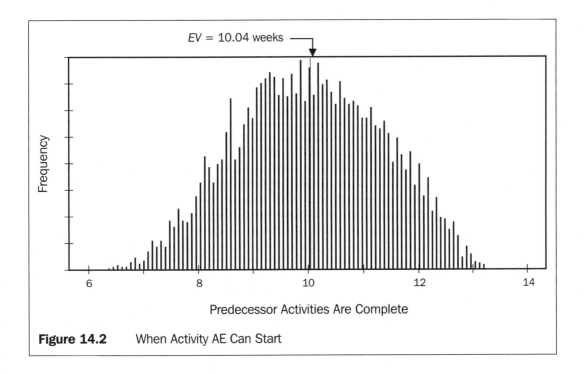

Figure 14.2   When Activity AE Can Start

- Time to complete the activity (such as in Figure 14.1), as either modeled or judged directly by the activity leader or best available expert. In some cases, it is useful to build a submodel of the activity that details the major contingencies.
- A graph of project EV cost versus the particular activity time to complete, such as is illustrated in Figure 14.3.

❖ Figure 14.3 shows total project cost as a function of time to complete Activity AE. This function and the criticality index, 0.35, are useful in evaluating alternatives to delaying, advancing, slowing, or accelerating work on this activity.

Chapter 15, about optimization, continues this example, and includes a distribution for Project Completion Cost and a sensitivity chart for EV cost versus an activity planned start date.

- A graph or other means comparing decision variables with project costs (the next chapter describes this optimization problem).

Summary

Project teams should stay flexible. A project is a dynamic system, and the best project and activity managers will be alert and responsive to changes as they occur. Regularly examine where resources might be better allocated.

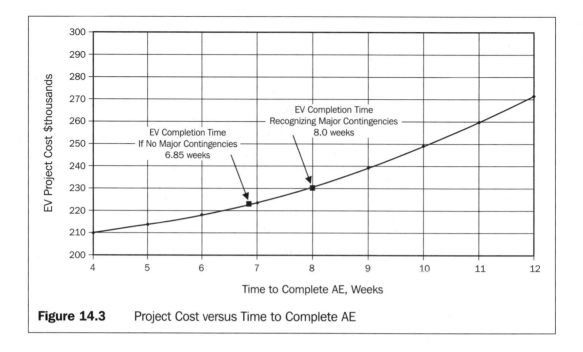

Figure 14.3   Project Cost versus Time to Complete AE

Capable leadership of a motivated, well-trained team is of paramount importance to project success. However, even skilled people perform complex planning processes poorly without the assistance of quantitative tools. The methodologies described here can be very helpful in bolstering human judgment.

This is an exciting time in project management. The project management body of knowledge has changed dramatically during the past twenty years. Low-cost software and computing power now enable modeling projects as never before. We have the means at hand to dramatically improve productivity in project execution.

The next chapter shows an example stochastic project model and the types of information this produces for decision making. This is built in Excel and incorporates probability distributions to represent chance variables.

CHAPTER 15

OPTIMIZING PROJECT PLAN DECISIONS

Here we look at project planning—especially project risk management—in a decision analysis context. A simple example project, optimized under uncertainty, shows the types of information available from a stochastic project model.

It's an Optimization Problem

Managers often face decision problems where the choices are more complex than simply yes or no. There are numerous decisions in project management. In project schedule planning, decisions fall into three primary decision categories:

- *Structure of the activity network.* Sequencing the activities, including which to execute in parallel. The decision about the network structure is discrete, choosing from among the available limited options, though the possibilities may be many.
- *Resources and resource levels.* Identifiable resources, with perhaps variable levels of commitment for each.
- *Planned start dates for each activity.* Date assignments, too, are usually variable, and these sometimes need to be planned around resources' commitments elsewhere. Even within the same project, a resource critical path (i.e., critical chain) controls.

The example in this chapter focuses on activity planned start-date decisions. The stochastic project model provides the means to optimize decision variables. Figure 15.1 shows one example. This chart shows project cost sensitivity to one decision variable, planned start date for activity AE. All other activity planned starts are at their optimal values.

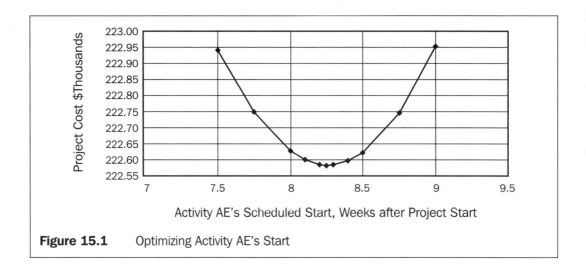

Figure 15.1   Optimizing Activity AE's Start

Chapters 10 through 12 discuss ways to express judgments about resource availability, productivity, and other uncertainties. In this chapter, we will focus on optimizing the schedule model already structured: choosing best planned activity-start times so as to minimize overall project cost (thus maximizing project value).

One of the tenets of *critical chain project management* (CCPM) is: Avoid having the same people work on parallel activities (multi-tasking) to the extent possible. This usually means restraint in starting activities. Small buffers at the end of "feeding chains" merging with the deterministic critical path minimize risk of project delay. The main buffer—to protect the customer—is placed at the end of the project.

However, this view oversimplifies. A better approach is to explicitly represent project uncertainties in a stochastic evaluation model. This chapter builds upon the last in demonstrating decision analysis as an alternative and improvement over traditional and critical chain deterministic methods.

Example Project Model

Figure 15.2 shows a simple project model for delivering a custom technology system. The stochastic model embodies uncertainties in two forms: activity completion times and possible rework. Ideally, a rework activity would be modeled as a looping-back cycle until we get it right. However, representing this in the model is much simpler if we can reasonably assume that only one rework pass is required to remedy defects. The Assemble Equipment activity, "AE," is singled out in this and in the prior chapter to show example information available for this activity's manager.

Having two potential rework activities realistically complicates this straightforward project. The arrows in Figure 15.2 show the precedence relationships.

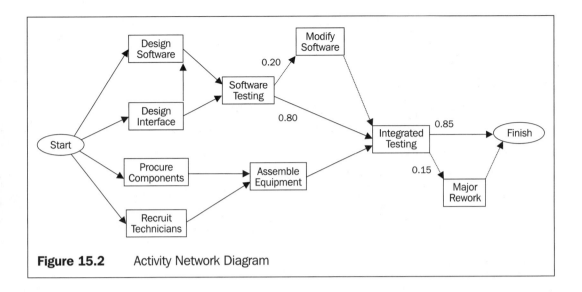

Figure 15.2   Activity Network Diagram

Branches with decimal fractions, representing probabilities, show two potential rework activities. All precedence relationships are Finish-to-Start, except the one Finish-to-Finish relationship: Design Interface (DI) must finish before Design Software (DS) finishes.

In addition to judgments about the need for the rework activities Modify Software (MS) and Major Rework (MR), project planning includes judging activity completion times, including contingencies. The planned activity start dates are the decision variables in this model.

What we really care about is *total project value*. Here, for simplicity, we are looking at project cost only, and we assume that minimizing the total project cost is the objective. Further, let's assume that the company is neutral about risk, and that expected value (EV or mean) cost is the appropriate project outcome measure. Figure 15.3 shows a distribution for project costs produced with the subject project model. The project outcome forecast is from Monte Carlo simulation. The best single-point forecast of total project cost is $223,000. The EV calculation simplifies decision making by reducing the distribution into an equivalent-value single number.

Optimizing Activity Starts

An *influence diagram* assists in modeling and understanding the elements of a decision. We discussed this method in Chapter 9. The influence diagram in Figure 15.4 shows an activity's start-date decision and elements in evaluating when to plan an activity start. Included in the analysis and the complete project model, though not shown here, is the effect of late or early finish on the overall project cost.

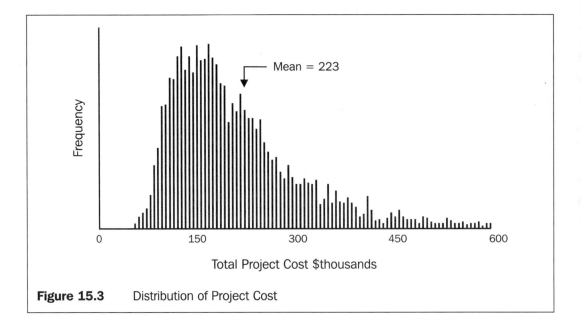

Figure 15.3   Distribution of Project Cost

This calculation model includes only cost penalties for idle crews. A more complete model might also include the effects of:

■ Changing requirements, with the amount of rework exacerbated by premature activity completions.

■ Multi-tasking inefficiencies, affecting time to complete and quality—premature activity starts worsen this also.

■ Correlations between times to complete various activities.

Everything important to the decision should be included in the model, despite that some of these details might involve highly subjective judgments.

❖ Note that there are no explicit buffer representations. Certainly there should be slack between completion of some activities and the start dates of their successor activities. Activity and resource buffers are intrinsic to the model, and not a focus item for the project manager. This reduces temptation to "waste the slack."

A project plan can be updated for progress and as other information becomes known. The project manager can optimize project start times and other planning decisions.

Activity managers focus on their respective pieces. One important perspective is *free float* (slack): How much can we delay this activity's start before affecting the early or planned start of its successor activities? Figure 15.5 shows the forecast of slack time after Activity AE and the beginning of its earliest successor. This is the distribution of the implicit buffer between AE and its successor. The mean slack time (free float) is 4.9 weeks.

Be careful how people use the information about slack time! You don't want the slack to be wasted, and knowing with high confidence that there is some slack might lead people to focus less on the task at hand. For me,

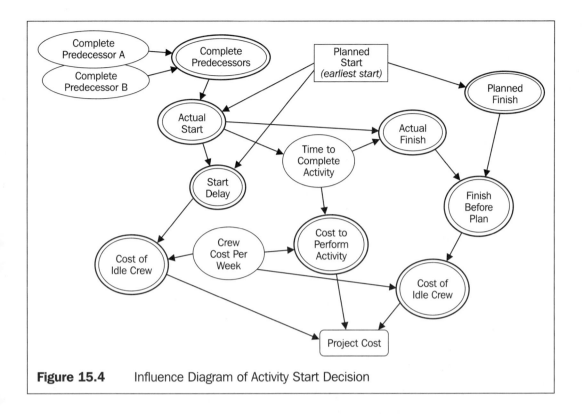

Figure 15.4   Influence Diagram of Activity Start Decision

this was a key message in Eliahu Goldratt's *Critical Chain* (1997). The stochastic model shows that there is about a .3 chance (see Figure 15.5) that Activity AE will be critical.

Incentives

This model recognizes all values as costs. Increased asset value, due to early completion, is incorporated as a negative cost.

Penalty functions represent the cost effects:

- A fraction, typically put at 30 percent, of crew time is wasted for the time after planned start before an activity can begin, due to precedence requirements.
- A finish before the forecast finish wastes, typically, 25 percent of idle crew time.
- Early project finish was valued at +$8,000 per week, and late finish was valued at −$10,000 cost per week.

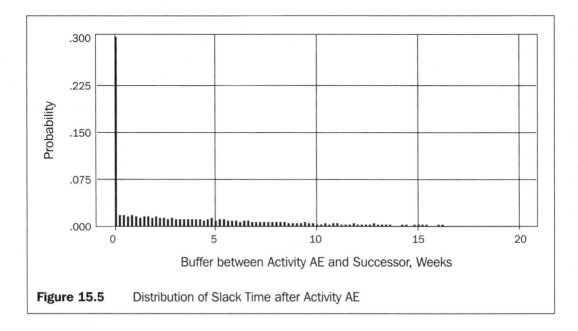

Figure 15.5 Distribution of Slack Time after Activity AE

Optimization Experience

Solving stochastic models is computationally more time-consuming than conventional analyses, because calculations with probability distributions are so difficult. Monte Carlo simulation solves a difficult calculus problem using a simple and elegant random sampling process. Because Monte Carlo is an approximation technique, we need 100 to 1,000 times more computer time to get reasonably precise results. Fortunately, computer power is continually becoming more accessible and inexpensive. Nonetheless, computation efficiency requires that project models be kept reasonably simple.

In the past two years, two stochastic optimization tools have become available for project models in Microsoft Excel spreadsheets. They use very different methods, though both have the same calculation goal:

- OptQuest® for Crystal Ball® by Decisioneering Corporation. This tool applies tabu search and neural network technologies for optimizing decision variables.
- RISKOptimizer™ by Palisade Corporation. This tool uses a genetic algorithm approach to optimizing @RISK® models.

See Appendix B, Decision Analysis Software, for more details.

Depending upon the problem, one tool may be better than the other. My limited tests thus far are inconclusive as to advantage; so I've disguised the exhibits as to the particular analysis tool used. Both RISKOptimizer and OptQuest optimization tools provide progress reports, similar to the one shown in Figure 15.6, for monitoring the program's progress.

An intelligent automated assistant could guide most or all of the optimization. Further, another automated assistant could guide the activity network

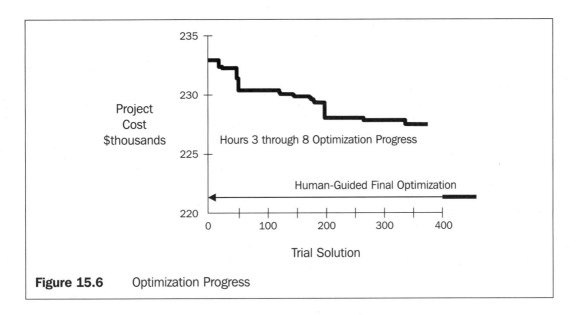

Figure 15.6   Optimization Progress

construction. These are among the topics of Chapter 17, Expert Systems in Project Management.

Table 15.1 summarizes selected deterministic and stochastic results. We see summary statistics for the distributions resulting from two traditional deterministic critical path method (CPM) solutions, using earliest starts and latest starts. Then, the table shows three progressive stages of optimizing (using a 300 MHz Pentium II) the stochastic model, starting from the latest-starts CPM solution. The decision variables are planned dates, in weeks, to start the respective activity. The base case in each column is the deterministic solution. The mean value—used for making decisions—represents the stochastic solution.

This project model behaves such that an early-starts solution is nearly optimal because the penalties for late finishes dominate. Comparing columns 2 and 3, notice that penalties for delay (in this model) are worse than costs of early starts.

Merge bias is the effect causing the difference between the *base case* and *EV* forecast. Most stochastic project models show that projects require more time than suggested by the base case. This is because the latest of predecessor activities typically determines when the next activity can start (the lines *merge* on an activity network diagram). Merge bias is an example of the *stochastic variance* topic of Chapter 13.

Use outcome *EV*s when making project decisions. The variance from the base case value results from carrying probability distributions through the calculations. Stochastic variance (Chapter 13) is useful as a component in explaining the difference between forecast and actual.

The automated optimization started with the "latest-starts" values for activity start dates. After three computer-hours, with one tool, the mean project

Activity Code	CPM Solution with Early Starts	CPM Solution with Late Starts	Best Solution after Three Hours	Best Solution after Eight Hours	Finished with User Guidance
Planned Dates to Start Activities, Days after Start					
DS	0.00	0.00	0	0.00	0.00
DI	0.00	2.00	1.98	1.00	0.00
PC	0.00	4.00	1.98	1.00	0.00
RT	0.00	3.00	1.30	0.00	0.00
ST	14.00	14.00	14.47	12.00	12.50
AE	7.00	9.00	9.32	8.51	8.25
IT	17.00	17.00	18.00	18.86	19.20
Analysis Results					
Base Case $k	170.36	184.69	171.59	171.03	170.86
Mean $k	225.29	242.14	232.89	226.48	222.58

Codes for Activities

DS	Design Software	PC	Procure Components	IT	Integrated Testing
DI	Design Interface	RT	Recruit Technicians	MS	Modify Software (if indicated in ST)
ST	Software Testing	AE	Assemble Equipment	MR	Major Rework (if indicated in IT)

Table 15.1   Project Cost for Five Cases

cost fell from $242k to $233k. Another five hours further reduced mean cost to $226k. Figure 15.6 illustrates the progress graph of this second period of automated optimization. Then I finished the job, manually adjusting decision variables in steps that brought EV cost down to $222.6k. With 5,000 trials, the standard error of the mean is approximately $0.6k [1].

Three figures in Chapter 14 show distributions useful for Activity AE's manager:

Figure 14.1 **Forecast of Activity AE Completion Time** (obtained in this case from a submodel for the activity).

Figure 14.2 **When Activity AE Can Start** (distribution of when all predecessor activities will be complete. However, this is insufficient to decide when to plan Activity AE's work start.).

Figure 14.3 **Project Cost versus Time to Complete AE** (useful for evaluating options to shorten or extend this activity).

Simplifying Project Decisions

The analysis in this chapter deals with decisions to plan activity starts. Most decisions are optimization problems where there is a *range* of choices for one or several decision variables. Figure 15.1, Optimizing Activity AE's Start, enables the activity manager to optimally plan her activity's start date.

The previous chapter shows a distribution for the time between Activity AE's completion and another distribution for the start of the earliest possible successor activity, Integrated Testing. These distributions are interesting, though perhaps unnecessary, for decision making. Further, people checking on the distribution of the implicit buffer might be tempted to waste slack.

The criticality index for AE is 0.35, meaning that AE has a 35 percent chance of being on the critical path and directly affecting time to complete the project. With a good system, Activity AE's manager should be receiving more definite information about whether AE will be critical. The criticality index will migrate toward zero or one as the project proceeds. Even when AE is under way, the activity team may be unsure whether its activity is going to be on the critical path.

Decision analysis provides a more realistic and more accurate representation of the project and alternative values. As such, the project manager has better information for making decisions under uncertainty.

The core theme in critical chain project management (CCPM) is to avoid wasting slack. Rather than planned intervals, the stochastic model reveals buffers as distributions. The reality is that there isn't a confident amount of slack available to waste. Focusing on optimizing project value provides a more rigorous way for project planning—and all other—decisions.

Endnotes

1. This is the ± uncertainty in the *EV* with 68 percent confidence. For conventional Monte Carlo sampling, the standard error of the mean is $\sigma_{\bar{x}} = s/\sqrt{n}$ where s is the sample standard deviation and n is the number of trials in the simulation. The *EV* error, σ, is typically one-third of this formula result when using Latin hypercube sampling (the standard technique), and we need other means to approximate this statistic.

CHAPTER 16

PROBABILITY RULES

Probability is the language of uncertainty. With just four algebraic rules, we can do a lot with probabilities.

It is a pity that our education was neglected. As soon as we learned fractions, we should have begun a lifetime of communicating and working with probabilities.

For most of us, at some point in our lives, our teachers presented the topics in this chapter. However, without frequent use, unfortunately, the skills are lost. Here is a short refresher if you need one.

Venn Diagrams and Boolean Algebra

A useful aid for visualizing events and probabilities is a *Venn diagram*, such as that shown in Figure 16.1. English statistician **J. Venn** (1834–88) invented the diagram that bears his name.

A Venn diagram represents "event space" and all of the possibilities that we relate together. The outer border is typically a rectangle, and we partition the area inside to represent the possibilities—*events*. The shapes are not important, although the graph is more meaningful if areas are drawn roughly proportional to the probability of the corresponding events. The areas, representing probabilities, are dimensionless, and the total area must equal one.

❖ In school, I sometimes worried, "What if we're on a line?" Or, worst of all, "What if we're on an intersection of lines?" One need not be concerned, I finally realized, because a line has no area and, thus, zero probability.

Each piece represents two or more events together happening or not happening, and we call these *joint events*. In Figure 16.1, we have five joint events.

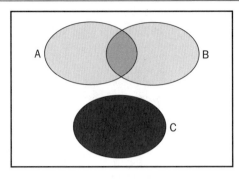

Figure 16.1   Venn Diagram

Here is some useful notation in what we call logic or **Boolean algebra**:

$\overline{A}$ means *not* A
P(A)   means the probability of A
AB or A · B   means A *and* B (the intersection)
P(A | B)   means the probability of A, given B
A + B   means A *or* B (the union).

In the scenario in the Venn diagram in Figure 16.1, there are five possible outcomes:

$A \cdot \overline{B} = A \cdot \overline{B} \cdot \overline{C}$ = A only
$B \cdot A = B \cdot \overline{A} \cdot \overline{C}$ = B only
$A \cdot B = A \cdot B \cdot \overline{C}$ = A and B = intersection of A and B
$C = C \cdot \overline{A} \cdot \overline{B}$ = C only
$\overline{A} \cdot \overline{B} \cdot \overline{C}$ = neither A nor B nor C.

Key Probability Theorems

There are three primary logic operations. And these take arguments, true or false. You may recognize these as Microsoft® Excel spreadsheet variables and functions:

TRUE or **TRUE()**
FALSE or **FALSE()**.

We can assign either value to a cell or the result of an equation. As examples:

= **TRUE()**
= **IF(AY_TimeToComplete <20.2,True,False).**

The parentheses behind **TRUE** and **FALSE**, if used, indicate that these are functions. You can omit the parentheses, since there are system variables, **TRUE** and **FALSE**, in Excel that work the same.

Complement Rule

Here is an obviously valid concept called the *complement rule*:

$$P(A) + P(\overline{A}) = 1.$$

For example, if we know that P(success) = .8, then we also know that P(not success) = .2 = P(failure).

Excel has a **NOT()** function. This returns the complement of the argument inside the parentheses. For example, if we have a cell named "Machine_Center_14_Available" that has a value of True, then:

= NOT(Machine_Center_14_Available)

evaluates to False.

The complement rule is closely aligned with the idea that the sum of the probabilities must always add to one. We call this the *normalization requirement*. If we have weights for several possible outcomes, then we can convert the weights into probabilities by *normalizing*. This is done by dividing each weight by the sum of the weights. The resulting numbers, now representing probabilities, will then always add to one.

Addition Rule

We represent the *union* of events with either a "+" or "∪" symbol. This means that either A or B is True, or both.

$$P(A+B) = P(A) + P(B) - P(A \cdot B).$$

This is called the *addition rule*.

The last term, P(A · B), surprises many people. Referring to Figure 16.1, we can see why it is necessary. If we add the areas for A and B together, we have twice counted the intersection area (overlapping portions of A and B). So, this last term in the addition rule is to correct for otherwise double-counting that intersection piece.

In Excel, suppose we have:

Cell B10: **Lathe1_Available**
containing a formula that evaluates to True,

Cell D10: **Lathe2_Available**
containing a formula that evaluates to False, and

Cell F10: **Lathe_Available**
contains formula: =   **OR(Lathe1_Available,**
                          Lathe2_Available)
that evaluates to True.

Modelers often use the addition rule when they want to calculate the probability of success when there are two or more teams working separately toward some goal. If either *or* both efforts succeed, then we have successfully achieved that goal.

In Figure 16.1, we see that there is no common area between A and C. These are said to be ***mutually exclusive***. In this special case, the addition rule simplifies:

$$P(A + C) = P(A) + P(C).$$

Multiplication Rule

This next rule calculates the probability of two events happening together. This is the logical "and" operation, and we symbolize this with the multiplication dot "·" or the "∩" symbol. Often people omit the dot, as with implicit multiplication between two symbols. Thus:

A and B = A · B = AB = A ∩ B.

The multiplication rule formula is:

$$P(AB) = P(A) P(B \mid A).$$

In Figure 16.1, this is the slightly darker area in common with both A and B. The probability of B *is conditioned by* (dependent on) the outcome of A, as shown in Figure 16.2. Every directed path through a tree, left to right, describes a *joint event*. The darkened topmost path is AB, and $P(AB) = P(A) P(B \mid A)$.

Independence

The three probability rules described in this chapter all work, whether or not the events are independent. In fact, we often use the multiplication rule as an expression and a test for independence:

A and B are independent if $P(A) = P(A \mid B)$.

This means, if true, then B tells us nothing about A. If independent, then the converse must also be true: $P(B) = P(B \mid A)$.

We usually know, from our understanding of the system (project), which elements are independent and which are influenced by others. We appreciate the cause-and-effect relationships. An interesting feature of probability is that if A depends upon B, then—at least numerically—B also depends upon A.

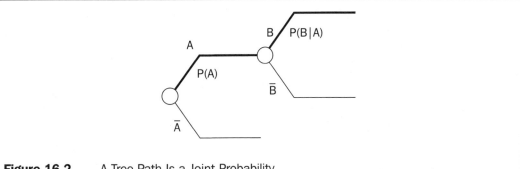

Figure 16.2   A Tree Path Is a Joint Probability

The multiplication rule has a simpler form for independent events:

$$P(A \cdot B \cdot C) = P(A) \times P(B) \times P(C).$$

We can string any number of events together in this fashion, so long as each element is independent. Thus, if everything has to work for the project to be a success, and each task is independent of the others, then the special case of the multiplication rule will calculate the probability of success.

❖ Warning: People often confuse *independence* with *mutually exclusive*. These are very different concepts. In fact, if two events are mutually exclusive (e.g., separate circles), then they are *not* independent, because if one is true, then the other cannot be.

Bayes' Rule

Appendix 6A presents Bayes' rule. I count this as the fourth probability rule, behind the three already discussed. Here is a somewhat different presentation of Bayes' rule:

$$P(e_i|A) = \frac{P(A \cdot e_i)}{P(A)} = \frac{P(A|e_i)P(e_i)}{\sum\limits_{j=1}^{N} P(A|e_j)P(e_j)}$$

where

e_i = outcome i of the chance event of interest
N = number of possible outcomes for e_i
A = attribute of new (imperfect) information, the outcome of an
     information event (symptom).

I added the center part to show that Bayes' rule is, in effect, just a rearrangement of the multiplication rule.

The *normalization requirement* explains both the multiplication rule and Bayes' rule. With new information, we cut away part of the Venn diagram and normalize probabilities for the pieces that are left.

Thinking Logically

The four probability rules are sufficient to do most operations with probabilities. As people become more numerically and logically literate, we can expect greater fluency with these probability concepts. I have observed that schoolchildren in Europe and Asia learn these concepts more thoroughly.

Some of the Internet search engines support Boolean searches using the same concepts. For example, you might search using:

"power plant" *and* nuclear *and not* "North America."

I once saw a search tool screen with a little Venn diagram indicating whether the *and* or *or* operation was in effect.

We will see more of this.

CHAPTER 17

EXPERT SYSTEMS IN PROJECT MANAGEMENT

Knowledge management is a hot topic in business today—and people are finding ways to capture knowledge and embed it in software. Artificial intelligence techniques, including rule-based expert systems, provide new ways to represent and share hard-won knowledge.

How does a project manager perform his job? How do you train a person to be a good project manager? The idea behind expert systems is that we can capture the knowledge needed to perform certain types of work in a knowledge base of rules. A computer program then applies these rules to guide a user in performing some task. The effective *expert system* (ES) can assist a non-expert in performing tasks, such as planning and analysis, at nearly expert-level performance. We will also discuss an allied technology, *neural networks*.

Smart Computers

Artificial intelligence (AI) is a broad area of computer science devoted to designing ways to make computers perform tasks previously thought to require human intelligence. The main applications of AI include:

- Natural language processing (computers that understand our speech and words)
- Vision systems (such as recognizing objects and patterns)
- Robotics and control systems
- ESs (rule- and frame-based, including "fuzzy logic")
- Neural networks.

Some people bristle at the name, "expert system," because such programs are vastly inferior to the overall capabilities of a human expert. Instead, ESs and neural networks are often called "knowledge systems."

Some of us think that we humans are inventing our successors (see Moravec 1999a and 1999b). Our tools may replace us. That possibility is at best (or worst) a few years away. Meanwhile, smart computer programs promise better tools in project management.

Expert Systems

An *ES* is a computer program that solves a procedural problem in much the same way that a human expert would. The ES is a computer program that contains expert knowledge about a narrow problem. The ES assists a less-experienced person in performing a particular task in a manner similar to and with nearly the performance of a human expert.

The most popular ES applications include:

- Diagnosis and prescription
- Classification
- Planning and configuring.

These are all functions that project managers perform. As such, ES technology offers software developers a way to build-in project management expertise. This technology is often operating behind the scenes in software systems. You have probably used ESs already, such as the "wizards" often found in some popular computer programs.

In project management, following are principal areas where knowledge systems have special potential.

Cost estimation. There are already fielded ESs and neural networks (described later) for this application, and we're sure to see more commercial offerings in this area.

Model building. Knowledge about generating projection models, forecasting formulas, and industry accounting practices are example knowledge areas that we can encode as rules.

Analysis. An ES is an appropriate approach to the manual tuning of the project optimization described in Chapter 15. Almost any analysis procedure that we can carefully describe is suited to automated analysis. An ES is much easier to configure than describing the logic by hard-coding with IF statements.

Exception reporting. An ES can continuously monitor project data and conditions. It is then able to provide prompt warnings of exceptions and trends, matters possibly requiring intervention. Automated systems can communicate "this needs attention" alerts by email, pager, voicemail, or conventional paper reports.

Truck Transport Billing System

Type Project: New Development
Platform: PCs running MS Windows
Language: C++
Interfaces: General Ledger
Accounts Receivable

Figure 17.1   Example Frame Structure

IF Weather Forecast = Rain *and* Outdoor Activity
    then Expect Weather Delay   CF = 0.7

IF Change Order *and* electrical
    then Need Architect Approval *and* Need Engineer Approval   CF = 1.0

Figure 17.2   Example Rules

Representing Knowledge

There are two common ways of representing knowledge in an ES.

Frames are a way to store information about "objects" (chunks of data). Each frame represents a hierarchical data structure relating objects to each other and containing attributes of each object. Modern databases and object-oriented programming languages have increasingly incorporated this approach in recent years. Figure 17.1 is a simple frame example for a software project.

There is often a hierarchy of object types, and some of the attributes can be "inherited." In a project model, for example, the activities are often detailed as tasks, which in turn are further detailed into actions or steps. Certain features of the "parent" object can be inherited by its "children."

Rules are the action part of the knowledge base. They encode the logic for solving the problem. Figure 17.2 shows two example rules. A typical ES contains 50–500 such rules. Common-sense reasoning is not a feature of the system. We must clearly define the task and make the rule base as complete as reasonably possible.

Most often, the ES functions only as an advisor, and a human decides whether or not to accept the program's advice. Well-designed systems usually feature an "explanation facility." This is a way of backtracking through the rules that were used ("fired") in arriving at the recommendation or conclusion. By examining the system's reasoning, the program user taps into the wisdom of the experts who contributed to building the knowledge base. It is a great learning tool. Users can make notes about exceptions (overrides), and these are a common source of new rules to be added.

❖ I once invested most of a year in developing a prototype ES for financial modeling. Using the automated assistant, I could build custom evaluations models, much as we now do with computer spreadsheets, in one-twentieth the time.

The world isn't black and white, and builders of these systems often want to recognize shades of gray. Sometimes data are incomplete and uncertain. Not all rules apply to every situation. The most popular way to represent confidence in knowledge is by "fuzzy logic," where we rate knowledge completeness as confidence factors (CFs, also called *certainty factors*, appended to the rules in Figure 17.2) on a 0-to-1 scale: Sometimes people confuse CFs with probabilities, though they are not. Zero means "no information or knowledge," and 1 means "absolutely true." See Appendix 17B for more about this.

We can attach confidence factors to: (a) assertions provided by the user or knowledge base, (b) rules in the knowledge base, and (c) conclusions "inferred" by the ES as it operates. If the problem has multiple solutions, then CFs provide a means to rank the proposed solutions.

With these knowledge representations, it is difficult to imagine a procedural problem that cannot be solved with ES technology. Some among us believe we humans are inventing our successors, and that our tools will replace us (see Appendix 17A, Neural Networks).

Operation

The "reasoning" part of an ES is its inference engine (IE). The IE is a procedure that works through the frames and rules in order to draw conclusions. This is what gives an ES its power. The IE borrows from rules of logic, analysis, and search techniques.

Typical analysis tasks where we might want assistance include:

- Helping design the project to meet a list of target specifications; developing the work breakdown structure, bill of materials, and cost estimates
- Helping develop the project plan, while watching for resource problems and looking for ways to level workgroup loading and shorten the schedule
- Analyzing the project situation, while reporting problem areas (elegant "exception reporting"), and suggesting remedies
- Monitoring for risk events and early warning signs, generating action lists.

Here's an example "utility" ES. Teknowledge Corp. developed the Wine Advisor several years ago to demonstrate its ES software. The company acquired permission to extract wine-selection rules from a respected wine authority's book. Knowledge engineers encoded the expert's wisdom into a knowledge base of about 200 rules. Suppose your project is to prepare an elegant meal for your family or friends. The Wine Advisor assists you in deciding what type of wine to buy. The ES asks questions about what food you are planning to serve: Will you have meat? If so, what type? Will there be a sauce? Tomato or cream? And so on. The program asks only pertinent questions based upon rules in the knowledge base and inferences drawn from answers that you provided earlier. The interactive process takes only a couple of minutes. The Wine Advisor then presents a list of recommend wines, prioritized according to the selection expertise of the expert.

In over two decades of popular use, ES technology has diffused into some of the project management applications. Following are several examples:

- Digital Equipment Corp. developed an early, large-scale ES to configure complex computer orders. Millions of combinations were possible from among thousands of components. Everything had to be shipped, fit together, and work.

- Engineering design and cost estimation are prime application areas for ES developers. Much of the work in design and estimation is procedural, and frame structures and rules work well for representing this knowledge.

- Part of my experience has been in developing an ES for project cashflow modeling. The knowledge base and inference engine represent the process of developing feasibility models (functionally equivalent to what an analyst would develop with a computer spreadsheet). The knowledge base can recognize different types of projects in different industries and in different countries.

- Even if we do a good initial project plan, maintaining the project database for all changes is often a major effort. Monitoring is especially time-consuming and tedious. An ES can manage many of the details.

Applying the Technology

What makes a good candidate for an ES? Here are guidelines for qualifying a problem for an ES solution:

- The problem is important.
- A body of knowledge related to the problem exists.
- There are recognized experts who are substantially better at solving the problem than non-experts.
- Experts are scarce and expensive.
- We can teach the skill, i.e., explain the process and reasoning of the experts.
- We can recognize a good solution.
- Solving the problem currently requires several hours to several days.

Software tool developers have long recognized the need for dynamic programs—those that change their function and presentation to suit the circumstances. The old, and still most common way, to provide flexibility is by embedding conditional branching logic using IF statements. When we hard-code the logic this way, the program is "brittle" (easily fails) and difficult to change and maintain. ESs take more computer time to operate, but generate fresh reasoning as needed. Expressing the logic as rules is much simpler for tasks suitable for an ES design approach.

The future of project management includes tools to help us work faster and improve our performance in an ever-accelerating world. We don't have time to learn everything, and we don't have time to do all that we're supposed to be doing. Intelligent assistants—utilities—will increasingly appear in the marketplace, ready to help us with selected tasks. With ESs, we don't have to be a specialist to perform some tasks at an expert level of proficiency. Further, we can accomplish work faster, more alertly, and more rigorously. Our "assistant in the box" never gets tired and never has a bad day.

Two technologies closely allied to ESs are *neural networks* and *fuzzy logic*. People are already using these methods in project management applications. The two following appendices describe these emerging technologies.

APPENDIX 17A

NEURAL NETWORKS

An artificial **neural network** (**NN**) is a simple arrangement of calculation nodes, called neurons, used for pattern recognition. We design NNs to operate in ways approximating, and perhaps improving upon, the operation of a living brain. Don't worry about becoming obsolete quite yet: the human brain has approximately 100 billion neurons, while a typical *artificial* NN has perhaps fifty neurons.

NNs mathematically process complex data. One can view this as sometimes massive, multi-variable, nonlinear regression.

❖ Recall from Chapter 12, Relating Risks, that regression determines equation coefficients in which a calculated variable is a function of one or more other variables. We are most familiar with linear regression, where we find the best line to represent a relationship between values plotted on an x-y graph. All but the simplest hand-held calculators will do linear regression, calculating a "least squares" fit through data points of y versus x.

An NN relates {several to many inputs} to {one to several outputs}. The reasoning is difficult for the user to decipher. However, we care mainly whether the "black box" generates good predictions. (Additional detail is in McKim 1993.)

In an NN structure, such as that displayed in Figure 17A.1, we relate various inputs to one or several outputs. Also, there may be one or more "hidden" layers of nodes to improve performance. Weighted values of the input nodes determine what happens at successor nodes. Knowledge is represented solely by the network configuration and the weights assigned to the branches.

The key is "training" the network—that is, cycling through data to establish the best configuration and best weights for each connection. Once trained, the network can examine new data and predict the outcomes, sometimes with astonishing accuracy. Estimation is an obvious application in project management. Given the parameters of the project or activity and historical data, an NN can predict time and cost to complete.

Low-cost PC software is available for building NNs. Some of the programs require little user knowledge, automatically training the network with the available data and testing the performance of different network structures.

Applications include forecasting project performance, estimating best competitive bid amount, estimating cost, filtering data, recognizing patterns, analyzing trends, controlling processes, and optimization. Both ESs and NNs capture knowledge and experience. An NN can process data, and an ES can process the information further. The two methods are very different and complementary.

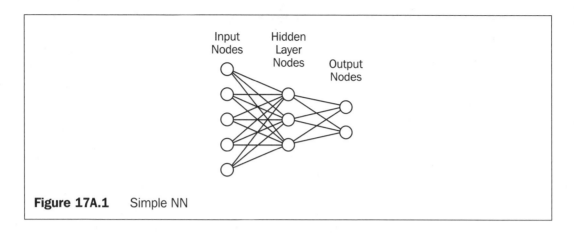

Figure 17A.1   Simple NN

Aspect	Neural Networks (NNs)	Expert Systems (ESs)
Knowledge	More fuzzy.	More concrete.
Knowledge Representation	Network pattern and connection weights; don't know the rules.	Rules and frames.
Capturing Knowledge	Data, though domain expertise helpful.	Domain expert plus knowledge engineer.
Databases Structure	Many suitable, including frames.	Frames (objects with inheritance).
Decision Making	Judgment and intuition.	Thinking in rules.
Changing Data	Progressive learning (plastic).	Need to revise the knowledge base (brittle).
Explanations	Elusive.	Common feature.

Table 17A.1   Comparing ESs and NNs

ESs are feasible only with procedural problems. We need to be able to describe the rules for solving the problem, not by "recognizing" the solution. Sometimes with an ES approach, it would be too expensive to build a knowledge base of rules. One graduate student trained an NN in an evening, and it performed sunspot forecasting comparable to an ES that took a sunspots expert months to build. Table 17A.1 compares and contrasts ES and NN technologies.

APPENDIX 17B

FUZZY LOGIC

Probability theory deals with propositions, or outcomes, that are either true or false. *Fuzzy set theory*, or *fuzzy logic*, deals with propositions that have vague meanings. If one is evaluating the chance that a project will exceed its scheduled completion time, we can express this judgment unambiguously as a probability. Alternatively, the assessment might be that a project will be "substantially delayed." The words "substantially delayed" are somewhat vague, but still describe the outcome. Fuzzy logic provides a quantitative approach to representing "soft" declarations. Some call this approach to uncertainty *approximate reasoning*.

Fuzzy set theory was invented by **Lotfi Zadeh**, professor at the University of California, Berkeley, in the 1960s to handle vague meanings in logical inference. The basis is the idea of membership. Suppose we polled many people regarding the height that divides classifications "Tall" and "Not Tall" for United States adult males. The responses might form a cumulative frequency distribution, such as that in Figure 17B.1.

The y-axis, Degree of Membership in Figure 17B.1, represents the fraction of people who classified the x-axis value as "Tall." This has the appearance and same dimension as a cumulative probability function; only here, we are representing the degree to which people would consider a height to be "Tall."

This function serves as a way to encode the quality or completeness of information. Degree of Membership measures the confidence that the proposition "Tall" is true. So, if we have an assertion that a person has the attribute, "Tall," that says something "fuzzy" about whether the person is a member of the class of people considered "Tall." While the membership function is not equivalent to a probability distribution, they appear similar in ways.

This degree of membership idea leads to its use as a *confidence factor* (CF). We can characterize the truthfulness quality of an assertion with a number, ranging from 0 to 1 (see Figure 17B.1), representing the degree of confidence in that piece of information. We can assign CFs to assertions and rules, and the program assigns CFs to resulting inferences.

The 0 to 1 CF range, which has the same bounds of a probability, does not have the same meaning as probability. CF = 1 means 100 percent probability. However, CF = 0 means only that the information has no value; it does not mean that the opposite assertion is assuredly false. Many ESs use CFs to represent the reliability of assertions, rules, and inferences.

❖ CFs may look and sometimes act similar to probabilities. However, they are not probabilities, and we should not use CFs for risking, in my opinion.

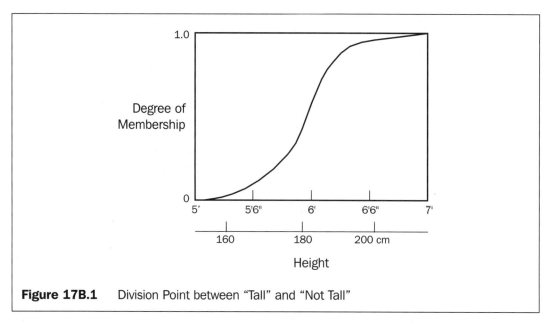

Figure 17B.1   Division Point between "Tall" and "Not Tall"

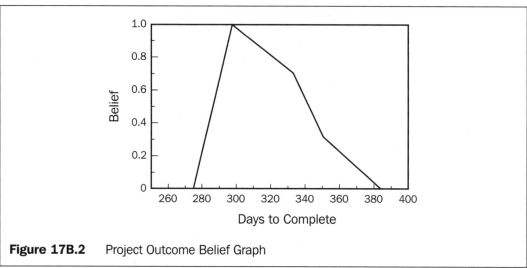

Figure 17B.2   Project Outcome Belief Graph

In project models, some people have used fuzzy logic assertions instead of crisp, single-value inputs. There is algebra, though somewhat arbitrary, for fuzzy calculations. Fuzzy set calculations are simple, and propagate quickly through a model. The result is membership functions for value, cost, schedule, and so on. Figure 17B.2 shows the outcome result of a simple project model. The fuzzy results propagate through the model in all calculations. The solution is fast and reproducible.

The main drawback to fuzzy logic is that the calculations do not have the logical rigor of probability theory. One can obtain strange "distribution" shapes from simple and seemingly innocent combinations of variables. Nearly unpredictable results occur with complex formulas and conditional branching (IF statements).

Fuzzy logic's mathematical operations are well suited to control systems and other situations where precision is less important. For some purposes, we can achieve adequate accuracy with perhaps 1 percent of the computational effort that probability calculations require. Control of air conditioners, elevators, and auto-focus cameras are common fuzzy logic applications.

APPENDIX A

SUMMARY OF METHODS

Decision tree analysis and Monte Carlo simulation are the most popular calculation techniques for evaluations under uncertainty. There are other quantitative techniques useful in dealing with uncertainty in specific situations.

Some Additional Methods

Table A.1 lists decision analysis and related techniques, along with their key strengths and weaknesses. Several appear only in this appendix:

■ Scenario analysis
■ Approximate integration
■ Design of experiments and Taguchi methods.

Scenario analysis is a planning technique focusing on plausible alternative futures and management responses. We consider possible events that would impact the organization or project. We next identify and evaluate actions to take advantage of opportunities and to protect against threats. The emphasis is not on a forecast, but on developing insights about what could affect the project. Few practitioners of scenario analysis apply probabilities to the individual scenarios, and that is the reason I omitted this topic from earlier discussion.

Design of experiments and Taguchi methods provide an efficient approach to sensitivity analysis for many-variable systems. This provides an effective way to prioritize alternatives for improving value or for reducing variance [1].

Approximate integration holds promise. The results are reproducible and fast. The method is known by several names: *convolution, quadrature,* or *cubic spline integration* (splines were flexible strips of wood used by draftsmen). Another term is *fast calculus integration.*

Method	Key Strengths	Key Weaknesses
Discussed in Chapters		
Decision Tree Analysis	Graphical layout of expected value calculation.	Must convert continuous into discrete distributions.
	Evaluating alternatives with sequential decisions (e.g., value of information).	Must limit number of decision alternatives and chance event outcomes.
		Requires decision policy value function.
Monte Carlo Simulation	Can accommodate complexity easily, such as dynamic behavior under contingencies.	Time versus accuracy tradeoff; solution can be computationally time-consuming.
	Very generally applicable.	Solution is approximate and changes with random number seed.
		Poor precision with low-probability events.
Influence Diagram	Similar to decision trees.	For EV calculations, the theory and calculations are more difficult.
	Better represents relationships between variables.	
Scenario Analysis	Simple.	Seldom quantifies risks and uncertainties.
Moment Methods (parameter method)	Medium complexity; fast; reproducible solutions.	Provide only statistics about the shape of the solution distribution.
		Calculations often ignore important details, such as correlation.
Fuzzy Logic	Low–medium complexity; fast.	Only approximates probabilistic reasoning.
	Reproducible solutions.	Potential developments needed to improve accuracy.
CPM, PERT, and PDM	Simple.	Simplistic project network model may be inadequate.
		Only one critical path is recognized and, with PERT, used in stochastic calculations.
Sensitivity Analysis	Simple.	Does not recognize risk versus value tradeoffs.
Multi-Criteria Approaches; Analytic Hierarchy Process	Simple if non-probabilistic.	Risk or uncertainty is merely one of several attributes; problems with consistency.
		Probabilities can be used if the criteria hierarchy represents the value function.
Other Methods		
Scenario Analysis	Simple.	Seldom quantifies risks and uncertainties.
Design of Experiments; Taguchi Methods	Value optimizing or variance reduction with efficient handling of many decision (controllable) variables.	Limited representation of uncertainty, noise, e.g., using Low and High for each chance event.
Approximate Integration	Fast, repeatable solution.	Little recognition in practice and literature; emerging technique.

Table A.1   Techniques of Uncertainty

Approximate integration provides suitably accurate results for simple probabilistic models involving addition and multiplication. One obtains the solution directly, in the form of an outcome probability distribution. The signal processing field has used these calculation techniques for perhaps three decades.

Deterministic or Stochastic?

Is stochastic analysis even needed? If so, what method types are appropriate?

Deterministic models. This book is about stochastic decision models. However, conventional deterministic models will suffice in some situations, such as when:

- Not very important
- Low risk: reasonably assured volumes, costs, and prices
- Preliminary evaluation
- Doing a base case projection or sensitivity (what-if) analysis
- Decision is made, already, and perhaps the projection is only for a budget plan.

Stochastic models. People often approach risk and decision analysis to determine the uncertainty in an estimate. This helps in contingency planning, for example. They are often surprised when the answer changes due to effects causing *stochastic variance* (Chapter 13).

People often ask: Which tool is better: decision trees or Monte Carlo simulation? The answer depends upon the problem. Neither technique is inherently superior. However, each technique is better at solving certain problems.

Table A.2 lists decision situation attributes versus tools. Check marks show, with all other things equal, whether decision tree analysis or Monte Carlo simulation would be preferred. There are a few other calculation methods, usually for special situations, but trees and simulation remain the workhorses of decision analysis.

Endnotes

1. See Santell, M. P., J. R. Jung Jr., and J. C. Warner. 1992. Warner wrote a contemporaneous three-part tutorial in *PM Network*: Part I, May 1992, pp. 36–40; Part II, July 1992, pp. 34–38; Part III, August 1992, pp. 69–74.

Selection Factor	Favoring Dec. Trees	Favoring Simulation
Decision criteria other than value or only *EMV*, *CE*, or *EU* decision criterion.	√	√
Sequential decisions in model.	√	
Optimizing a continuous decision variable.		√
Output distribution(s) desired.		√
Chance events much better represented by continuous outcomes (e.g., dynamic price model).		√
More than 5–8 chance events.		√
Correlations can be represented by joint probability tables or by correlation coefficients or modeled dependency relationship.	√	√
Outcome values easily obtained and few chance and decision nodes (hand solution feasible).	√	
Low probability events.	√	
Complex economic and competitive environments.		√
Analyzing portfolio strategy.		√
Complex, dynamic system.		√

Table A.2   Stochastic Method Selection Guide

APPENDIX B

DECISION ANALYSIS SOFTWARE

In recent years, many people who are not professional analysts have been developing sophisticated project models. Software is the great enabler.

Traditional analysis is deterministic—that is, without using probabilities. Most project software is deterministic, such as Microsoft Project. As project professionals become competent in spreadsheet or project modeling software, they might ask, "What's next? How can I improve the quality of these models?" Representing uncertainty is a logical and important step toward improvement.

Coupled with relentless competition and increasing computer power is an increasing awareness of decision analysis. Further, decision analysis' growing popularity is partly the result of low- to moderate-cost personal computer (PC) software.

This section provides brief descriptions and contact information for five programs. Two are for decision tree analysis, two are for Monte Carlo simulation, and another is for inventorying project risks and actions.

❖ **First a disclaimer**: I try to maintain objectivity about resources that I may be recommending to readers and clients. However, it is hard to be completely neutral. Though I am not on any company's payroll, I do have friends in these companies. I assist in marketing PROAct on my Web site, and I've delivered training and consulting in association with two of the other companies. A foremost duty as a consultant is to be independent, and I am trying to be as objective as possible in this section.

❖ **Trademarks**: 1-2-3®, @RISK®, Analytica®, Lotus®, Microsoft®, OptQuest®, RISKOptimizer®, and Palisade® are federally registered trademarks. DATA™, DecisionTools Suite™, DPL™, PrecisionTree™, PROAct™, RISK+™, TopRank™, and Visual Basic™ are also trademarks of the respective companies. The software screen shots are used with permission.

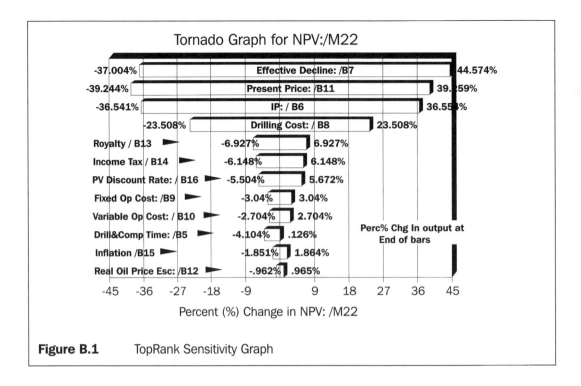

Figure B.1   TopRank Sensitivity Graph

Spreadsheets

The ubiquitous computer spreadsheet is powerful for many types of calculations, including *expected values*. The most straightforward are *payoff tables*, of course.

It is easy, also, to develop templates for small- to medium-sized decision trees. I recommend that you first sketch the decision model structure to be clear about the problem. Then lay out an organization of cells that will represent nodes in the tree model. Though unnecessary, it is helpful, visually, to draw the tree diagram on the worksheet. Use the Draw functions (in Excel) to superimpose a network of node symbols and connecting branches.

Developing a template provides documentation and ease of recalculation. However, if you are only going to solve the tree once, don't bother with the spreadsheet.

Microsoft Excel is the world's most popular modeling platform. Most people developing cashflow projection models are doing so in spreadsheets. Most of the popular decision analysis tools are able to link to models in or through Excel.

Palisade Corporation (vendor information listed later in this Appendix) has an interesting tool for sensitivity analysis for spreadsheet models. TopRank prioritizes input variables in terms of their importance in affecting a selected outcome variable. Figure B.1 shows an example tornado diagram from TopRank (graph modified slightly, for clarity, in this book). The what-if analysis default is to changing each input cell by ± 10 percent.

Simulation Ready

The Monte Carlo simulation add-ins provide three main capabilities to Microsoft Excel and, in one case, to Lotus 1-2-3.

1. Sampling functions for popular and custom distribution shapes; and correlation.
2. Control of the simulation run process, storing selected output variables for each trial; monitoring convergence.
3. Analyzing the simulation results: presenting statistics and frequency distribution graphs.

Excel already has at least two sampling functions (#1) and data-analysis capabilities (#3). Persons familiar with Microsoft Visual Basic for Applications can write a procedure to handle the simulation looping (#2).

Monte Carlo Simulation

For spreadsheet models, there are the two strong choices.

Crystal Ball by
Decisioneering Corporation
1515 Arapahoe St., Ste. 1311
Denver CO 80202
Sales phone: (800) 289-2550
Sales direct: (303) 534-1515
Fax: (303) 534-4818
http://www.decisioneering.com

Crystal Ball Pro includes the OptQuest optimization program, which uses heuristics, tabu search, and neural networks. Fred Glover, my optimization professor at the University of Colorado, is the chief architect of OptQuest. He is world renowned, and therefore his association gave OptQuest instant credibility.

Figure B.2 shows an example Crystal Ball screen to define an input variable. The competing simulation tool is:

@RISK by
Palisade Corporation
30 Decker Rd.
Newfield NY 14867
Sales phones: (800) 432-7475 in the United States; otherwise: (607) 277-8000
Fax: (607) 277-8001
http://www.palisade.com

Figure B.3 shows an example outcome distribution with @RISK for Excel. Palisade offers @RISK versions for Lotus 1-2-3. @RISK for Microsoft Project allows most types of project plan numeric inputs to be a distribution.

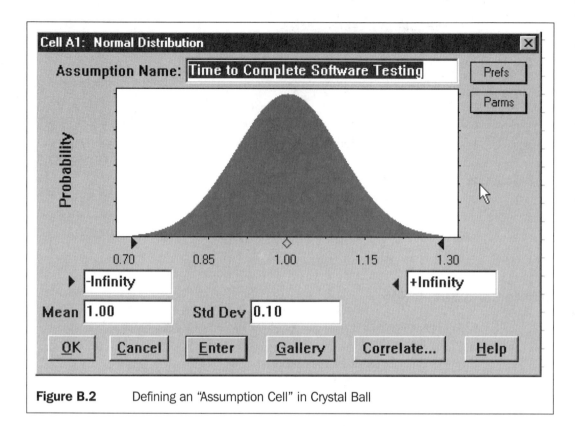

Figure B.2   Defining an "Assumption Cell" in Crystal Ball

❖ @RISK was initially developed for Lotus 1-2-3, which uses "@" to preface names for its functions, hence the name "@RISK" that provides additional @ functions for sampling distributions.

RISKOptimizer is Palisade's genetic algorithm optimization package built around @RISK. Although not an "intelligent" search strategy, I believe genetic algorithms will find a good solution to most any optimization problem.

In addition to @RISK for Project, here is one other product for adding simulation to Microsoft Project:

RISK+ by
C/S Solutions, Inc.
111 N. Sepulveda, Ste. 333
Manhattan Beach CA 90266
Phone: (310) 798-6396
Fax: (310) 798-4226
http://www.cs-solutions.com

If you are not a fan of spreadsheet modeling and like the influence diagramming technique, you might also consider:

Analytica by
Lumina Decision Systems
P.O. Box 320126

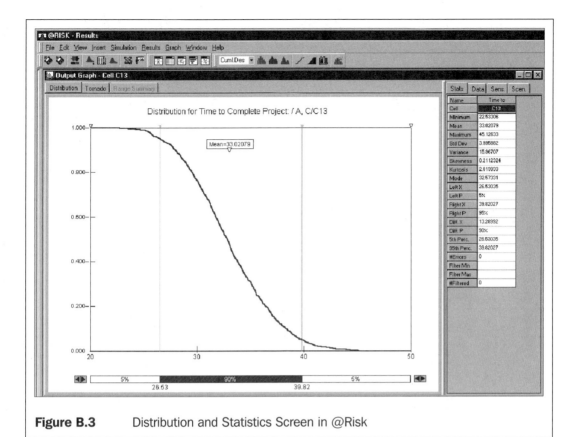

Figure B.3   Distribution and Statistics Screen in @Risk

Los Gatos CA 95032-0102

Phones: (877) 66-LUMINA (toll free) and (408) 354-1841

Fax: (408) 354-9562

http://www.lumina.com

Analytica also links to Excel models, though this product features an "intelligent arrays" approach for representing data.

Decision Tree Analysis

Perhaps the easiest-to-learn decision tree program is:

PrecisionTree by Palisade Corporation.

This program is the only one I know that builds the tree inside an Excel worksheet. If you are modeling in Excel, this makes linking easy, and all of the Excel formula functions are available.

PrecisionTree and @RISK are the pillars in Palisade's DecisionTools Suite. These are designed to work together, so that PrecisionTree is an especially good candidate for people who will be doing both decision tree and simulation analysis, and possibly linking both together. Figure B.4 is an example tree—a simple one—built with PrecisionTree.

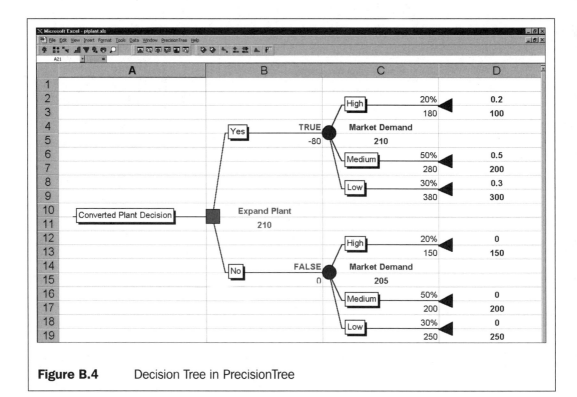

Figure B.4   Decision Tree in PrecisionTree

Another good program that I use is:

DATA by

TreeAge Software, Inc.

1075 Main St.

Williamstown MA 01267

Phone: (413) 458-0104 or 888-TREEAGE

Fax: (413) 458-0105

http://www.treeage.com

I perceive that DATA is more powerful than PrecisionTree, though more complex to learn and use for simple problems. DATA has been around longer and this one-product company focuses on excellence in its one tool. DATA has a particularly strong following in the medical industry, where its *Marcov chain* analysis features are widely used in modeling medical treatments. Figure B.5 shows an example sensitivity graph (modified slightly for clarity) for Daily Crane Cost in the Crane Size Decision from Chapter 3.

Yet another decision tree program worth a look is:

DPL by

Applied Decision Analysis, Inc.

2710 Sand Hill Rd.

Menlo Park CA 94025

Phone: (650) 854-7101

Fax: (650) 854-6233

http://www.adainc.com

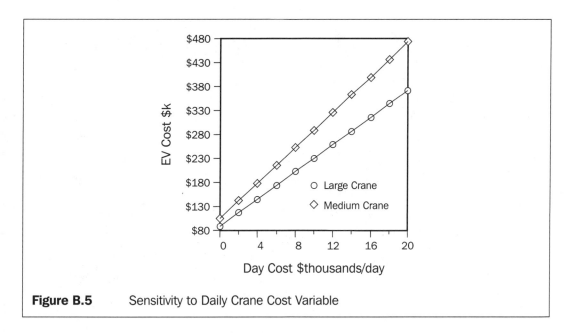

Figure B.5   Sensitivity to Daily Crane Cost Variable

All of the decision tree programs mentioned in this section are able to first develop the decision model as an influence diagram. With DATA and PrecisionTree, the conversion from influence diagram to decision tree is one way.

DPL is the only program where modifying the tree also updates the influence diagram. "DPL" stands for Decision Process Language, a scripting language, and the program interprets this to generate either a decision tree or an influence diagram.

Project Risk Management

Most people with a formal process for project risk management are doing it much the same. Chapter 8 embellishes the typical approach and adds emphasis on quantification in ways consistent with a decision analysis approach.

A colleague and friend, Jerry Gilland, worked in the aerospace industry for many years, and started doing this by hand. Jerry evolved into using spreadsheets and eventually wrote his system in Visual Basic.

PROAct by
Engineering Management Services, Inc.
4650 Shawnee Pl.
Boulder CO 80303-3816
Phone: (303) 494-8009
Fax: (303) 494-3515
PROAct demo: http://www.maxvalue.com/pa.htm

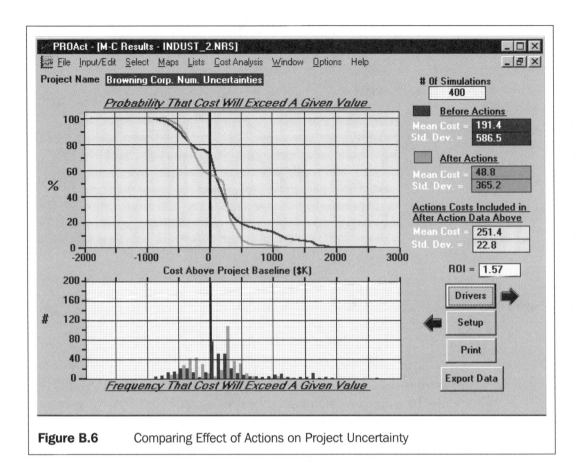

Figure B.6   Comparing Effect of Actions on Project Uncertainty

This is primarily a database for capturing and maintaining an inventory of risks and actions. What caught my eye was the overlay graph of distributions, shown in Figure B.6. PROAct uses a simple Monte Carlo simulation calculation for approximating project cost (or schedule) uncertainty, before and after implementing selected risk mitigation actions.

GLOSSARY

This glossary is organized into three sections:
- Abbreviations
- Symbols
- Terms (in one section, alphabetically)
  - Statistical and Probability
  - Project Management
  - Economic Analysis
  - Risk and Decision Analysis.

Abbreviations

AHP	analytic hierarchy process
AND	activity network diagram
CCPM	critical chain project management
c.d.f.	cumulative (probability) density function
CE	certainty (or certain) equivalent
CP	critical path
CPM	critical path method
DA	decision analysis
DCF	discounted cash flow (see *present value*)
DROI	discounted return on investment
E(x)	expectation or expected value of (some parameter)
EMV	expected monetary value
EU	expected utility
EV	expected value
MCDM	multi-criteria decision making
NCF	net cash flow
NPV	net present value (same as *PV*)
OR	operations research
OR/MS	operations research/management science

P(x) or p(x)	probability of event x
p.d.f.	probability density function
PDM	precedence diagramming method
PERT	program evaluation and review technique
PIR	post-implementation review
PRM	project risk management
PV	present value: PV.10 = PV @ 10%/year
R&DA	risk and decision analysis
ROI	return on investment
WBS	work breakdown structure

Symbols

μ	population mean
ρ	Pearson correlation coefficient
σ	population standard deviation
σ^2	population variance
$\sigma_{\bar{x}}$	standard error of the mean
σ_{ij}	covariance between i and j
$\displaystyle\sum_{n=1}^{N}(\text{expr.})$	summation series
	expression elements summed from $n = 1$ to N
i	annual interest rate or annual discount rate or annual inflation rate
P(A)	probability of (event) A
P(A + B)	probability of A or B (or both)
P(A · B) = P(AB)	probability of A and B (jointly)
P(A|B)	probability of A given B
r	risk tolerance coefficient (or risk aversion coefficient, inverse)
s	sample standard deviation
t	time, especially in PV formula
$\bar{x}$	sample mean
<	less-than
>	greater-than
< **= or** ≤	less-than or equal-to
> **= or** ≥	greater-than or equal-to
·	multiplication or "and" Boolean operator, e.g., "A·B"
+	addition or "or" Boolean operator
$\bar{A}$	not A

Terms

A

accuracy Jointly having both low *bias* **and** high *precision* characteristics; refers to the measurement's agreement with the true value.

accuracy ratio Ratio of (actual outcome)/(original estimate), used to gauge the objectivity of forecasts.

action In project risk management, this is an effort to affect a risk event or uncertainty. With threats, the desire is to reduce the likelihood of the chance event, its impact, or both. With opportunities, the desire is to increase the likelihood, its impact, or both.

activity An element of work as part of a project. An activity takes time and consumes resources.

addition theorem or rule Rule for calculating the "or" union of two events: $P(A + B) = P(A + P(B) - P(AB)$.

analytic hierarchy process (AHP) A system for multi-criteria decision making, where the task is to choose the best alternative with respect to value measured by a hierarchy of sub-objectives or attributes. Attributes are weighted by making pair-wise comparisons. Alternatives are also rated along each attribute by making pair-wise comparisons.

activity network diagram (AND) Any project activity diagram, typically either CPM/PERT-type diagram or precedence diagram method (PDM) type.

appraisal approach View that all three types of decision problems (ranking, valuing, and optimizing) can be solved calculating a numerical value measure.

artificial intelligence (AI) The broad area of computer science attempting to embody machines with human-like intelligence. Subsets of AI include *expert systems*, natural language systems, *neural networks*, robotics, and vision systems.

as-of date The effective date of an evaluation; the date to which cash flows are discounted.

assessor Expert; person responsible for providing judgments—assessments—about one or more uncertainty input(s) for an analysis.

asset Right to or ownership of something of value, such as property.

asset model A life-cycle model of a project, product, or other asset; concept feasibility analysis.

association See *correlation*.

assumption A condition, such as a relationship or a circumstance, that is presumed to hold for the purpose of the evaluation.

average Refers to any of the "central measures," most often to the mean. Generally, this term is ambiguous without clarification, because some people use this *average* when referring to the *mode, median*, or other central measure.

B

base case   A reference deterministic solution obtained by using the expected values of each continuous input distribution and (usually) the *mode* of each input discrete distribution. In project management, this is called the *base plan* or *baseline plan.*

Bayes' theorem   The formula used to revise probabilities based on new information. The concept used in *Bayesian analysis.*

beta distribution   A simple distribution that, depending upon two shape factors, can assume many shapes within two bounds. Used in the classic PERT project schedule calculations.

bias   A repeated or systematic distortion of a statistic or value, imbalanced about its mean.

binary risk event   A two-outcome chance event, usually "success" or "failure."

binomial distribution   A discrete distribution representing two-outcome chance events of independent trials.

Boolean algebra   Name for the common logic of AND, OR, and NOT operations. After James Boole.

buffer   In project management, refers to a planned interval to allow for one or more predecessors to finish before the next activity's planned start.

C

capital constraint   Any limit of funds. Literally, this would be a limit on capital investment (assets that will have a long-term life); however, in common use, this can be any budgetary restraint.

cash flow (noun)   Money entering or leaving the company treasury. Net cash flow equals cash receipts less cash disbursements. Often referring to the cash generated and available to reinvest in the enterprise or to distribute to creditors.

central limit theorem   The mean of the sum of a large number of independent distributions is approximately normal regardless of the shape of the component distributions. This requires that no component distribution contributes significantly to the sum.

central measure   In statistics, any of the measures of the "center" of a probability or frequency distribution, such as *mean, median,* and *mode.*

certainty equivalent or certain equivalent (*CE*)   The amount, known with certainty, a decision maker would be just willing to exchange for an uncertain gamble. The difference between *CE* and *EMV* is the *risk premium* or *risk penalty.* This difference is attributed solely to the decision maker's attitude toward risk.

certainty factor or confidence factor (*CF*)   See *confidence factor.*

chance event   An experiment, process, or measurement for which the outcome is not known beforehand. Represented in decision models as with (synonymous) *random variable, stochastic variable,* and *chance node.* These events cannot be controlled, as to *decision variable.*

complementary outcomes (events)   Two distinct and different outcomes that together represent all the possible outcomes of a chance event.

complement theorem or rule   Rule ensuring that the probabilities of complementary outcomes add (normalization requirement):
$P(A) + P(\overline{A}) = 1$.

conditional probability   The probability that an event will occur given that another event has already occurred. Sometimes called *contingent probability*.

confidence factor (*CF*)   A number, ranging from 0 to 1, that indicates the confidence in an assertion or inference. "0" means of no value, and "1" means with complete confidence. *CFs* are used in rule-based *expert systems*.

confidence interval   An interval range representing the degree of confidence in the estimate of a statistic. When involving two or more dimensions, the bounded surface is called a *confidence envelope*.

conservative (risk attitude)   See *risk aversion*.

contingency   1. A possible event that would change the project plan. 2. A reserve amount of project funding (or time) to accommodate risk elements that will likely occur.

contingency plan   An action or plan readied for execution in the event that a *contingency* occurs.

continuous event   A chance event having an infinite number of possible outcomes along a continuum.

continuous event simulation   A model solving for behavior of a system where time is advanced in small, uniform increments.

correlation   Relationship between variables such that changes in one (or more) variable(s) is generally associated with changes in another. Synonymous with *association*. Correlation is caused by one or more *dependency* relationships.

correlation coefficient   A measure of the linear correlation between two variables, ranging from –1 to +1.

crash (an activity)   Accelerate a project activity, usually by applying more time and money.

credible analysis   One that warrants the confidence of the decision maker as being suited to purpose.

credible model   One that is accepted and used by the decision maker.

critical chain project management (CCPM)   A philosophy of project management that places a buffer at the end of the project (to protect the client) and buffers at the end of activity chains feeding into the (presumed) critical path.

critical path (CP)   The sequence of activities that determines the completion time of a project.

critical path method (CPM)   A deterministic analysis of the *project activity network diagram* (AND) to determine which activities lie along the *critical path* and determine overall project completion time.

criticality index   The probability that an activity lies on the *critical path*, obtained from the fraction of times in a Monte Carlo project simulation where a specific activity was critical (i.e., contributed to lengthening the project completion time).

cumulative density function or distribution (c.d.f.)   Graph showing the probability that the parameter will exceed particular values (along the x-axis). Computed as the integral of the probability density curve. There are two forms: greater-than and less-than types, and both present equivalent information.

D

decision   A commitment of resources that is revocable only at some cost. See *good decision*.

decision analysis (DA)   A process for helping decision makers choose wisely under uncertainty. The subject involves concepts borrowed from probability theory, statistics, psychology, finance, and operations research. The formal discipline is called *decision science*, a subset of *operations research* (management science). Truly using decision analysis requires (1) capturing judgments about risks and uncertainty as probability distributions, (2) having a single value measure (usually *NPV, utility,* or an *objective function*), and (3) putting these together with *expected value* calculations.

decision criterion   Any parameter useful in making a decision.

decision rule   A procedural rule for decision making, intended to provide the optimal expectation of progress toward the entity's objective.

decision tree   A graphical representation of a decision problem and the expected value calculations, consisting of decision, chance, and terminal nodes connected by branches.

delta property   Feature of *expected value* such that a constant amount added to each outcome increases the *EV* by that amount.

density distribution (or function)   See *probability density function.*

dependence or dependency   When the outcome of one chance event influences, or is influenced by, the outcome of another chance event. Dependent relationships are often represented by formula relationships or with correlation coefficients. Opposite of *independence*. Partial or shared dependency is the cause of *correlation*.

deterministic   Said of a model where all parameters are fixed or "determinate." Single-point solution. Complementary term is *stochastic* (see).

discount rate   The "interest" rate used for *PV* discounting.

discounted cash flow (*DCF*)   The sum of individual yearly cashflow amounts that have been multiplied by the appropriate *PV* discount factors.

discounted cashflow analysis (DCF analysis)   Projecting a future cashflow stream and determining its present value.

discounted return on investment (*DROI*)   Ratio of PV/PV(investment), a popular criterion for ranking investments under a capital constraint.

discrete event or distribution   A chance event that has a finite number of outcomes, e.g., the number of "heads" from flipping ten coins. cf. *continuous event.*

discrete event simulation   Monte Carlo simulation where the emphasis is on state changes of objects within the system. cf. *continuous event simulation.*

discretizing   Converting a continuous probability distribution into an approximating n-level (often, three outcomes) discrete distribution.

distributive property   Feature of *expected value* such that when every outcome is multiplied by a factor, the *EV* changes by that factor.

distribution   See *probability distribution*.

dividend   Portion of corporate profits paid to investors. Usually, the corporate tax has been paid, and dividends are *taxed again* as ordinary income to the investors. The original investment capital is recovered when the stock is sold.

E

economic project   One judged to provide a positive value contribution. Most often, the test is whether *NPV* or *EMV* is positive.

elicit (judgment)   The process of interviewing an expert and drawing out that person's complete judgment about a chance event; similarly, drawing out a representation of the decision maker's preferences.

EMV decision rule   Decision policy to choose the alternative with the highest *EMV*. Suited when (1) enough money is available to do all *EMV*-positive projects, and (2) the company is risk-neutral.

evaluation   General term for any type of analysis used for asset appraisal, feasibility study, engineering evaluation, project assessment, and all other types of analyses related to decisions.

event   See *chance event*.

event tree   Tree diagram showing what failures could have caused particular events. Complement of *fault tree*.

expected monetary value (*EMV*)   Expected value of a measurement expressed in monetary terms. Usually refers to the expected value of present value, E(PV) or EV PV of net cash flow.

expected utility (*EU*)   Expected value utility, where utility is typically the risk-attitude-adjusted *NPV*, transformed with a *utility function*. Alternately, utility may be represented by an *objective function in multi-criteria decision making*.

expected value (*EV*)   Probability-weighted average of all possible outcomes. When the outcomes are measured in monetary units, the term is usually called *expected monetary value*.

expert system (ES)   A computer program (*knowledge system*) that contains expertise about a specific problem. Using the expert system allows a non-expert to perform the task at a proficiency level comparable to a real expert. The knowledge is usually represented by if-then rules.

exponential distribution   A distribution typically used for representing the time between arrivals of random events.

exponential utility function   Any of several equations, such as $U(x) = r(1 - e^{-x/r})$, translating objective value (such as *NPV*) into utility units.

F

feasible   The characteristic of a worthy project where the expectation is value-added (or cost-saved).

feedback   System concept where a portion of the output is fed back to the input, especially negative feedback used for stabilization or control.

float   The amount of time that an activity can be delayed from its earliest start and not delay the project. cf. *free float*.

forecast   A judged or predicted view of the event sequence or future state of the world. Usually calculation or estimation is involved. A *forecast* is the best *projection* (see).

> Futurists are careful to avoid the term "prediction" because it implies certainty. What they do, they say, is try to forecast what might happen, not what will happen.
>
> Eric Lekus, *The Baltimore Sun*

Prediction may imply a deterministic outcome. *Prediction, foretell,* and *prophesy* tend to be used when the outcome is specific (deterministic) and when special knowledge (e.g., divine communication or extraordinary ability) is involved.

free float   The amount of time that an activity can be delayed from its earliest start without delaying any successor activity starts. cf. *float*.

frequency distribution   A graph or other characterization of the observed values in a sample data set. Commonly graphed as a frequency histogram.

   Simulation trial results are often presented in the form of a frequency histogram (bar graph), whose shape approximates the true probability density function. It is called a *relative frequency diagram* when the frequencies are expressed as fractions.

full-cycle economics   Project analysis from the point of inception through asset abandonment.

event   The outcome of a chance event. Synonym: *outcome*.

framing   Putting the decision problem into context. This often involves limiting the scope of the analysis, relating to particular goals and objective(s), identifying a stakeholder or other value perspective, and recognizing various constraints. Framing bias is a psychological effect caused by perspective or context, such as wording a survey question in terms of people dying (or surviving) or in terms of project success (or failure).

frequency distribution   A graph of the probability density function; a histogram showing the frequency of occurrence of each value segment, approximating the probability density function.

fuzzy logic   Rules of logic based on the idea that events can be classified by degree of membership. For example, a qualitative assessment, such as "high cost," can be quantified and used in logical calculations.

G

Gantt chart   A chart with horizontal bars indicating the duration of project activities. The horizontal dimension is time.

Gaussian distribution   See *normal distribution*.

genetic algorithm   An optimization programming technique that uses an analogy of natural selection, including genes, cross-over, and mutation. No intelligence is involved. The system "evolves" to a good solution.

goal   A target or milestone, marking progress toward the organization's *objective*. A *goal* is usually measurable and has a stated time for achievement.

good decision   One that is logical and consistent with the values of the decision maker (or organization) and all of the data available at the time.

H

heuristic   Rule-of-thumb that provides rough guidance on actions and their consequences; technique that usually provides a good, although not optimal, solution.

histogram   Graph showing frequency of observations counted in segments of the value range, usually presented as a vertical bar chart. See *frequency distribution*.

hurdle rate   Minimum acceptable level of an investment selection criterion. Most often, this is the cost of capital; projects having an *IRR* less than the hurdle rate are automatically discarded.

I

impact   In project risk management, the effect that a risk or opportunity will have on cost, schedule, or performance.

independence   The characteristic where one event does not affect the occurrence of another, and vice versa.

indifference probability   That probability of success, in one lottery, at which you are indifferent between the reference and having this lottery. Similar to *certain equivalent* concept.

inflation   A rising general level of prices and wages in an economy, expressed as an annual percentage rate.

influence diagram   Network diagram of system variables with arcs indicating the direction of "influence" or time-sequenced relationships. Variables and formulas can be quantified and expected values solved by an iterative process as an alternative to decision tree calculations.

interest   1. Amount paid for the use of funds, e.g., interest earned by savings in a bank account. 2. Ownership in a project, asset, or entity.

internal rate of return (*IRR*)   A discount rate that yields a *PV* = 0. There may be multiple roots when the cumulative net cashflow curve changes sign more than once. Calculating *IRR* requires an iterative, trial-and-error procedure. Synonymous with *rate of return (ROR)* and *discounted cashflow rate of return (DCF-ROR)*.

intersection   A joint event comprised of two or more separate events. For example, the event (A and B) is a joint event.

intuition   The believed capacity for guessing accurately. Judgments based upon feelings and not logical thinking.

investment   An amount paid to acquire an asset.

J

joint probability   The probability of two or more events occurring together. Intersection of two sets, such as represented in a *Venn diagram*.

judgment   A probability distribution assessment performed, at least in part, by a human. *Subjective probability* assessment.

kurtosis   A measure of the peakedness of a probability density function. The *kurtosis* statistic is the fourth moment about the mean divided by σ^4. The benchmark for comparison is the normal distribution's kurtosis equals 3.

Latin hypercube sampling (LHS)   An improved sampling technique for Monte Carlo simulation that reduces the number of trials required to obtain acceptable convergence. The probability function to be sampled is stratified into equi-probable layers. For successive trials, each layer is sampled, without replacement.

law of large numbers   The sample mean can be made as close to μ as we desire by a sufficiently large sample size, i.e., $\lim_{n \to \infty} \overline{x} = \mu$.

likelihood   Usually synonymous with *probability*.

lognormal distribution   A frequently encountered positively skewed, continuous distribution. It arises when the value is the product of other distributions. The log values are normally distributed.

management science (MS)   See *operations research*.

marginal   Incremental difference. Said of cash flows, cost of capital, profit, and so on.

marginal probability   The unconditional or absolute probability, e.g., P(A). These are the probabilities that are in the "margins" of a probability table.

mean   The arithmetic average of equally likely outcomes or a set of observations. The probability-weighted average. This is usually the best estimator for a chance event. Synonymous with *expected value* when referring to the mean of a *probability distribution*. Symbols μ for populations (p.d.f.'s) and $\overline{x}$ for data.

median   The most central value of a population or sample set. Half of the other values lie above, and the other half below. With an even number of equally likely outcomes or observations, the median is the average of the two centermost values.

merge bias   The EV start time of a project activity is later than the maximum EV finish time of predecessor activities. This effect occurs at the joining or merging of arcs, moving left to right, in a project (activity) network diagram.

mitigate   To eliminate or lessen the risk or effect of; e.g., mitigate the impact of bad weather.

mode   The particular outcome that is most likely. This is the highest point on a probability density distribution curve. A curve with two localized maxima is called *bimodal*. With sample data having high resolution, there are seldom two identical values. Thus, with frequency *histogram* data, the mode is typically chosen as the midpoint of the bin having the most counts.

model   A simplified representation of a system of interest. Models for decision purposes usually represent a business enterprise, project, or transaction and consist of variables and mathematical formulas.

moment   First moment: the product of a point value times the distance to a reference axis. The second and higher moments have the distance squared, cubed, and so on. The *mean* is the first moment of x about the origin. The *variance* is the second moment of x about the *mean*.

monetary equivalent   The result of translating different facets of value into a single measure: money.

Monte Carlo simulation   See *simulation, Monte Carlo*.

multi-criteria decision making (MCDM)   Where an *objective function* is comprised of several criteria. Typically, the criteria are chosen to measure goodness along the dimension of each objective.

multiplication theorem or rule   Rule for calculating the "and" intersection of two events: $P(AB) = P(A) \cdot P(B \mid A)$.

multi-tasking   When a resource is concurrently performing multiple tasks. Considered less efficient than tasking sequentially.

mutually exclusive decision alternatives   A situation where no alternative contains another alternative. *Mutually exclusive* projects means only one project can be done.

mutually exclusive outcomes   A situation where outcomes are defined such that no one outcome contains values of another outcome.

N

nature's tree   Refers to the requirement that decision trees be constructed to recognize the natural sequence of events.

net cash flow (*NCF*)   Cash flow from operations, net of capital expenditures, overhead, and taxes.

net present value (*NPV*)   Same as *present value (PV*, see) or *present worth*. Usually, the "net" adjective is in reference to the principle that the cash flows should be net of the investment.

neural network (NN)   A computer circuit that attempts to replicate the operation of the human brain. The circuit consists of a simple arrangement of nodes, called neurons, and their interconnections. Successful applications include pattern matching, noise filtering, and vision recognition. Neural networks can be viewed as massive, multi-variable, non-linear regression.

node   Principally two types: decision point (decision node) or chance event (chance node), usually with reference to a *decision tree* or *influence diagram*. End nodes are *terminal nodes*. *Influence diagrams* additionally have objective variable (i.e., value measure) nodes and others.

normal distribution   The frequently encountered, bell-shaped distribution. Also called *Gaussian distribution*.

normalization requirement   The requirement that the sum of the probabilities of all possible outcomes equals one. *Normalizing* is a fundamental means of revising probabilities.

O

objective (noun)   The *purpose* of an organization. Often, less precisely used to mean a *goal*.

objective analysis   One that is free from bias, requiring bias-free assessment inputs, objective value measure, and calculation integrity.

objective function   A mathematical function to be optimized in decision making. This is typically *NPV*, which is converted to *expected utility* for the risk-averse decision maker. In *multi-criteria decision making* (MCDM), the objective function combines selected criteria into a composite value measure.

objective or neutral risk attitude   Describing a person, organization, or policy that is unwilling to pay (or require) a premium for uncertainty. With an objective risk attitude, the *certainty equivalent* is exactly the *expected monetary value*.

objective probability   A probability assessment that is determined from complete knowledge of the system or of the parent population. Not affected by personal beliefs.

objective value measure   A statistic that corresponds directly and logically to the objective(s) of the decision maker.

operations research (OR)   The science of applying systems analysis, statistics, and mathematics to problems of organizations. Synonymous with *management science* and often abbreviated together, i.e., *OR/MS*.

opportunity   Popularly, in project management, the potential for something to be better than expected; often used as an antonym of *threat*. *Risks* and *opportunities*, together, comprise risks.

optimal   Adjective meaning the variable is chosen to achieve the value *optimum* (noun).

option   1. Alternative. 2. An owned right to sell or buy at some future time.

outcome   A particular result of a chance event.

P

payoff table   A two-dimensional matrix used to calculate expected values, representing decision alternatives in one dimension and chance event outcomes in the other dimension.

population   The set of possible outcomes for a chance event. The entire set of values representing the event of interest. Synonymous with universe.

portfolio   A company or individual's holdings of projects, investments, or opportunities.

post-implementation review (PIR) or post audit   Analysis of a project after the general outcome has been determined. Also called *post analysis*, *post evaluation*, and *lookback analysis*. Typically based upon *full cycle economics*.

precedence diagramming method (PDM)   Building a project model of activities linked to show precedence constraint relationships (at least four types, e.g., Start$_j$ after Start$_i$).

precision   Ability to systematically repeat a measurement or obtain an evaluation result without regard to the true value.

prediction   See synonyms at *forecast*.

preference   A decision maker's attitude about a particular aspect of the decision process. Decision analysts classify preferences into three categories: objectives, time value of money, and risk attitude. These preferences are composites of the decision maker's beliefs and values.

present value (*PV*)   The sum of discounted cashflow values. The discount rate represents policy or attitude toward time preference of money.

probability P(*x*)   The likelihood of an event occurring, expressed as a number from 0 to 1 (or equivalent percentages). Synonyms: chance, likelihood, odds. The sum of the probabilities of all possible outcomes equals one. See *probability density function*, *objective probability*, and *subjective probability*.

probability density function (p.d.f.)   probability mass function (p.m.f.)
A mathematical or graphical representation that represents the likelihood of different outcomes from a chance event. The integral of a p.d.f. equals one. Also called *probability distribution* and *probability function*. "Mass" instead of "density" is often used when referring to a discrete distribution. Also called *probability distribution* and *probability function*. Common examples include binomial, normal, and triangle distributions.

probability distribution   See *probability density function*.

probability tree   A diagram of chance events, annotated with outcome probabilities, useful in calculating expected values and joint probabilities; a decision tree without any decision nodes, as is often the case in asset valuation.

program evaluation and review technique (PERT)   An analysis of a *project network diagram* to (1) determine which activities are on the deterministic critical path, and (2) to apply activity completion time distributions to determine a distribution for the overall project completion time. Flaw: neglects *merge bias*.

project network diagram (PND)   Any schematic showing the sequence of project activities. Also called a *precedence network diagram* because of the emphasis on precedence relationships between activities. Also called *activity network diagram*.

project risk management (PRM)   "Risk management is the systematic process of identifying, analyzing, and responding to project *risk*. It includes maximizing the probability and consequences of positive events and minimizing the probability and consequences of events adverse to project objectives. It includes the processes of *risk management planning, risk identification, qualitative risk analysis, quantitative risk analysis, risk response planning*, and *risk monitoring and control*" (Project Management Institute 2000, p. 206).

projection   A calculated future, usually involving production volumes, cash flow, and so on across time periods. A view of the sequence of events or future state of the world under an assumed set of assumptions. Synonyms: *scenario, case*; cf. *forecast*.

R

random error   A distortion in a statistic. Usually this is "noise" without bias.

random number   A number obtained from sampling (usually) a 0–1 uniform distribution and used for *sampling* in *Monte Carlo simulation*. A table of random digits serves the same purpose by placing a decimal point in front of the integers.

random variable   A symbol or measure of a chance event. Also called a *stochastic variable*.

rank correlation   The statistic used in popular Monte Carlo simulation software to express correlation. It is the Pearson rank correlation coefficient using the value *ranks* rather than the actual values.

rate of return (*ROR*)   Amount earned per unit of investment per time period. Typically, total return in one year divided by starting investment. Often used as if synonymous with *internal rate of return*.

regression   Determining coefficients of an equation that best fits to sample data. The names of regression analyses refer to the form of the dependent variable equation: linear, multiple linear, and polynomial (curve fitting). The coefficients are usually chosen so as to minimize the square of the errors (least-squares fit). See *neural network*.

reliability   Probability that a system or component will perform its intended function over a specified period of time.

reserve   In project management, an amount of money or time provided to mitigate risk.

return on investment (*ROI*)   Net benefits (cash flow before deducting investment) divided by the initial investment:

$$ROI = \frac{\text{net profit}}{\text{investment}}$$

Often, the numerator and, possibly, the denominator are averaged over the life of the asset. Also common are computing the return each year, then averaging.

risk   The quality of a system that relates to the possibility of different outcomes. There are unknowns about conditions of nature and about how systems operate. Risk is approximately synonymous with *uncertainty*.

Informally, "risk" is used when there is a large, usually *unfavorable* potential outcome (typically a *discrete event*). For example, risk of failure.

"Uncertainty" is used when there is a range of possible outcomes. For example, price uncertainty.

I prefer to use "risk" when there are dramatically different outcomes possible (e.g., success/failure) and use "uncertainty" when the outcomes are merely variable, such as when:

$$\frac{\text{high outcome}}{\text{low outcome}} < 2$$

Because there is no good antonym for *risk*, I'm okay with allowing risk to be the potential for either undesirable or desirable outcomes. In project management, especially, risk events are often classified as "threats" or "opportunities."

See *uncertainty*.

risk analysis   The process of assessing a probability or the shape of a probability distribution. The term is sometimes used in place of *decision analysis*. Some people combine into the inclusive R&DA, *risk and decision analysis*.

risk attitude   Preference about risk. One of: *risk averse* (risk avoiding), *risk neutral* (neutral about risk, e.g., an EMV decision maker), or *risk seeking*.

risk aversion   Dislike of risk; conservative risk attitude. The *risk aversion coefficient* is the reciprocal of *risk tolerance coefficient* (both used in *utility functions*).

risk penalty   See *risk premium*.

risk policy   Approved method for making tradeoffs between value and risk, often expressed as a *utility function*.

risk premium   The amount of expected monetary value forsaken by using a value derived from *risk policy*:

Risk Premium = EMV – Certainty Equivalent.

This difference is attributed solely to the decision maker's attitude toward risk. Sometimes called *risk penalty*. Risk premium is always non-negative.

risk tolerance coefficient   The parameter in an *exponential utility function* that represents the decision maker's risk attitude. This is typically one-fifth or one-sixth of the person's or entity's net worth. The reciprocal of *risk tolerance coefficient* is called the *risk aversion coefficient*.

robust model   A model whose formulas and structure are valid for all possible combinations of input variables.

robust solution   A solution obtained from a decision model that is insensitive to moderate changes in the value function and probability assessments.

S

sampling (with experimental data)   Obtaining representative examples from a parent population or from experiment.

sampling (for Monte Carlo simulation)   Obtaining a trial value of a probability distribution. With conventional Monte Carlo sampling, a random number between 0 and 1 is used to enter the y-axis on a cumulative probability distribution; the corresponding x-axis value is extracted and becomes that variable's value in the simulation trial. See *Latin hypercube sampling*.

sampling with and without replacement   When sampling from a finite population, sampling may or may not restore the original population set for the next sampling event; i.e., the sample is removed and not replaced in the population. This is sampling without replacement, and each sample alters the event probabilities for future sampling.

scenario   A possible sequence of events and a future state of the world. A *projection*.

scenario analysis   A planning technique that examines responses to plausible alternative futures.

scope   The problem definition that specifies what is and what is not included in the project deliverables.

sensitivity analysis   An analysis to determine how variations in input values affect the outcome value. Important to the evaluation team in understanding which variables are most important. Usually done by examining the effect of changing in one variable at a time from the base case assumptions. See *sensitivity chart*.

sensitivity chart   Chart showing prioritized importance of input variables based upon the *correlations* calculated between input variables and the outcome value measure. Variables can be ranked by *correlation coefficient*, rank correlation coefficient, or estimated contribution to total variance.

simulation   Representing artificially. In the context of business analysis, representing the essential features of a system in a model. The model is used to anticipate the behavior and performance of the system under assumed conditions.

simulation, Monte Carlo   A process for modeling the behavior of a stochastic (probabilistic) system. A sampling technique is used to obtain trial values for key uncertain model input variables. By repeating the process for many trials, a frequency distribution is built up, which approximates the true probability distribution for the system's output.

   This random sampling process, averaged over many trials, is effectively the same as integrating what is usually a very difficult or impossible equation.

skewness   A character of distributions when deviations about the mean are asymmetric. Positively skewed distributions appear to lean to the left and have a longer tail in the positive direction. The *skewness* statistic is the third moment about the mean divided by σ^3. A symmetric distribution has a skewness of zero.

spider diagram   A graph of the sensitivity of value to several input values.

standard deviation (SD, σ, or s)   Square root of the variance. The standard deviation is more meaningful because it has the same units as the distribution measured.

standard error of the mean (SEM or $\sigma_{\bar{x}}$)   A measure of the uncertainty of the sample mean, $\bar{x}$, in representing the true population mean, μ:

$$\sigma_{\bar{x}} \cong \frac{s}{\sqrt{n}}$$

   SEM is useful in determining whether a sufficient number of trials has been run in a Monte Carlo simulation. It overstates the error when Latin hypercube sampling is used.

statistic   A number that describes some attribute of a population or event space. The most common statistics are mean, median, mode, standard deviation, and variance. A statistic provides information about a distribution. To distinguish between statistics from populations and statistics from samples, different letters are used:

	Population	Sample
Mean	μ	$\bar{x}$
Standard Deviation	σ	s

stochastic (pronounced stow-kastic)   An adjective meaning *probabilistic, statistical, chaotic,* or *random.* (See *stochastic dominance* and *stochastic variable.*) The term is complementary to *deterministic* (see).

stochastic dominance   A situation when one alternative is better than all others at all levels of cumulative probability. This is observed with cumulative probability curves when the curves do not overlap. When (1) the curves do cross and (2) the best *EV* alternative is more risky, then risk attitude is important to the decision.

stochastic variable   Same as *random variable*.

stochastic variance   The difference between (1) the value obtained in a discrete model using expected value inputs (i.e., *base case*), and (2) the value obtained with a stochastic model that carries probability distributions through the calculations.

stopping rule   A test for halting a Monte Carlo simulation run after achieving sufficient convergence. This is often based upon the *standard error of the mean* statistic.

subjective probability   Probability assessment or judgment that is, at least in part, based on opinion, hunches, feelings, and/or intuition. A subjective probability is someone's belief about whether an outcome will occur.

substitution principle   Allows a chance node, in a decision or probability tree, to be equivalently replaced by its expected value.

sunk costs   Money that has already been spent. Prior costs (and benefits) should not be considered in making present and future decisions, except as to possible future tax or contract effects.

SWOT analysis   Abbreviation for a planning and brainstorming process, named after its elements, identifying: Strengths, Weaknesses, Opportunities, and Threats.

T

time value of money   The concept that a dollar today is worth more than a dollar tomorrow. The relationship is reflected in the *time preference* of the decision maker. The *present value* concept and formula are generally accepted to represent time value in the decision model's value function.

tornado diagram   A sensitivity graph showing the output value range produced by the range of each key uncertain input variable, arranged in decreasing magnitude of effect.

triangle distribution   A continuous distribution uniquely specified by its range (low and high) and its mode. This is the most popular distribution in *Monte Carlo simulation* because of its simplicity and ease of sampling.

U

uncertainty   Often used synonymously with *risk* (see). An informal distinction is that uncertainty is used when the outcome is variable, such as a future product price.

Some project management professionals are classifying *uncertainty* (i.e., a surprise or contingency) as the most general term. (I am not among them. I prefer and recommend the taxonomy described at *risk*.) This is divided into events with good outcomes called *opportunities* and those with bad outcomes called *risks* or *threats*. An event having both good and bad outcomes thus is classified as both a *risk* and an *uncertainty*.

uniform distribution   A continuous distribution with constant probability density between two bounds.

union   Composite event consisting of two or more events; e.g., (A or B), which includes the possibility of both A and B. Equivalent to the logical "or" operation.

unknown   1. *Stochastic variable*. 2. An event or variable not evaluated. 3. An event or variable not identified in the evaluation, perhaps because it was never thought of.

util (or utile)   Arbitrary unit of measurement expressing value on a utility scale. The origin location is also arbitrary.

utility   A scale of value reflecting a *preference* of the decision maker. Represents value versus an *objective* measure, such as money.

utility function   A graphic or mathematical function relating value of various outcomes to the intrinsic value to a particular decision maker. Also called *utility curve* and *risk preference curve*. Utility value is measured in arbitrary units called *utils* or *utiles*.

The x-axis (the utility function's argument) is calibrated in some directly measurable units, such as dollars. The y-axis origin and scale are arbitrary.

A popular (and recommended) utility function is the *exponential utility function*:

$$U(x) = r\,(1 - e^{-x/r})$$

where x is the outcome (usually in NPV), and r is the *risk tolerance coefficient*. This function is sufficient to completely and succinctly express a company's *risk policy*.

V

value   Monetary or material worth; worth in usefulness or importance to the possessor. *Utility* (see).

value engineering   Systematically designing a project or product constantly attending to life-cycle value improvement opportunities while still meeting the functional criteria. *Value analysis* is value engineering applied to something already designed or built.

value function   See *objective function*.

value of information   Value of being better able to assess the outcomes of chance events.

value of control   Value of being able to influence the outcomes of chance events.

values   Deeply-held beliefs about what is right and wrong. See *preference*.

variable   A symbol in a model that has a value or can be evaluated. Synonyms: parameter, input value.

variance (σ^2 statistic)   1. A popular measure of uncertainty. The expected value of the sum of the squared deviations from mean. Variance is the *standard deviation* squared (see). 2. Difference between the forecast and actual outcome. Normally calculated so that an unfavorable variance is negative.

variance analysis   A post-evaluation for the purpose of reconciling (explaining) the difference between the forecast and actual outcome, usually detailed by components. *Variance* in this context is the difference between forecast and actual.

Venn diagram   A diagram showing relationships between all possible outcomes of chance events.

W

work breakdown structure (WBS)   An outline of a project that details, in hierarchical levels, the work to be performed.

Y

yield   The amount earned during one year on an investment divided by the investment value at year start. Often used as synonymous with *return on investment*. For multi-year situations, *internal rate of return (IRR)* is the most common yield measure, although there is much confusion and debate about its usefulness.

BIBLIOGRAPHY

Capen, E. C. 1976. The Difficulty of Assessing Uncertainty. *Journal of Petroleum Technology* (August): 843–50.

Center for Business Practices. 2001. Killing the Project in Time. *Project Management Best Practices Report* (January).

Collins, James C., and Jerry I. Porras. 1997. *Built to Last: Successful Habits of Visionary Companies*. HarperBusiness.

Elton, Jeffrey, and Justin Roe. 1998. Bringing Discipline to Project Management. *Harvard Business Review* (March–April): 153–59.

Goldratt, Eliyahu. 1984. *The Goal: A Process for Ongoing Improvement*. Great Barrington, MA: North River Press.

———. 1997. *Critical Chain*. Great Barrington, MA: North River Press.

Keeney, Ralph L. 1992. *Value-Focused Thinking: A Path to Creative Decisionmaking*. Cambridge, MA: Harvard UP.

Kotkin, Joel. 2000. The Future Is Here! But Is It Shocking? (Interview with Alvin and Heidi Toffler.) *Inc.* (December): 112.

Leach, Larry P. 1999. Critical Chain Project Management Improves Project Performance. *Project Management Journal* (June): 39–51.

McKim, Robert A. 1993. Neural Network Applications for Project Management: Three Case Studies. *Project Management Journal* (December): 28–33.

Moravec, Hans. 1999a. Rise of the Robots. *Scientific American* (December): 125–35.

———. 1999b. *Robot: Mere Machine to Transcendent Mind*. Oxford UP.

Newbold, Robert C. 1998. *Project Management in the Fast Lane: Applying the Theory of Constraints*. St. Lucie Press.

Pitagorsky, George. 2000. Lessons Learned Through Process Thinking and Review. *PM Network* (March): 35–39.

Project Management Institute. 2000. *A Guide to the Project Management Body of Knowledge (PMBOK® Guide) – 2000 Edition*. Newtown Square, PA: Project Management Institute.

Saaty, Thomas L. 1994. How to Make a Decision: The Analytic Hierarchy Process. *Interfaces* 24 (November-December): 19–43.

Santell, M. P., J. R. Jung Jr., and J. C. Warner. 1992. Optimization in Project Coordination Scheduling Through Application of Taguchi Methods. *Project Management Journal* 23 (September): 5–15.

Schuyler, John R. 1995. Rational Is Practical: Better Evaluations through the Logic of Shareholder Value. *Proceedings*, 1995 Society of Petroleum Engineers' Hydrocarbon Economics and Evaluation Symposium, Dallas, March 27–28, Paper No. 030066.

Zehedi, Fatemeh. 1989. The Analytic Hierarchy Process—A Journey of the Method and Its Applications. *Interfaces* 16 (July-August): 96–108.

INDEX